FREE

Free Study Tips Videos/DVD

In addition to this guide, we have created a FREE set of videos with helpful study tips. **These FREE videos provide you with top-notch tips to conquer your exam and reach your goals.**

Our simple request is that you give us feedback about the book in exchange for these strategy-packed videos. We would love to hear what you thought about the book, whether positive, negative, or neutral. It is our #1 goal to provide you with quality products and customer service.

To receive your **FREE Study Tips Videos**, scan the QR code or email freevideos@apexprep.com. Please put "FREE Videos" in the subject line and include the following in the email:

    a. The title of the book

    b. Your rating of the book on a scale of 1-5, with 5 being the highest score

    c. Any thoughts or feedback about the book

Thank you!

SIE Exam Prep

2023 - 2024

3 Practice Tests and Securities Industry Essentials
Study Guide Book for the FINRA Assessment
[4th Edition]

J. M. Lefort

Written and edited by APEX Publishing.

ISBN 13: 9781637750872
ISBN 10: 1637750870

APEX Publishing is not connected with or endorsed by any official testing organization. APEX Publishing creates and publishes unofficial educational products. All test and organization names are trademarks of their respective owners.

The material in this publication is included for utilitarian purposes only and does not constitute an endorsement by APEX Publishing of any particular point of view.

For additional information or for bulk orders, contact info@apexprep.com.

Table of Contents

Test-Taking Strategies

1. Reading the Whole Question

A popular assumption in Western culture is the idea that we don't have enough time for anything. We speed while driving to work, we want to read an assignment for class as quickly as possible, or we want the line in the supermarket to dwindle faster. However, speeding through such events robs us from being able to thoroughly appreciate and understand what's happening around us. While taking a timed test, the feeling one might have while reading a question is to find the correct answer as quickly as possible. Although pace is important, don't let it deter you from reading the whole question. Test writers know how to subtly change a test question toward the end in various ways, such as adding a negative or changing focus. If the question has a passage, carefully read the whole passage as well before moving on to the questions. This will help you process the information in the passage rather than worrying about the questions you've just read and where to find them. A thorough understanding of the passage or question is an important way for test takers to be able to succeed on an exam.

2. Examining Every Answer Choice

Let's say we're at the market buying apples. The first apple we see on top of the heap may *look* like the best apple, but if we turn it over we can see bruising on the skin. We must examine several apples before deciding which apple is the best. Finding the correct answer choice is like finding the best apple. Some exams ask for the *best* answer choice, which means that there are several choices that could be correct, but one choice is always better than the rest. Although it's tempting to choose an answer that seems correct at first without reading the others, it's important to read each answer choice thoroughly before making a final decision on the answer. The aim of a test writer might be to get as close as possible to the correct answer, so watch out for subtle words that may indicate an answer is incorrect. Once the correct answer choice is selected, read the question again and the answer in response to make sure all your bases are covered.

3. Eliminating Wrong Answer Choices

Sometimes we become paralyzed when we are confronted with too many choices. Which frozen yogurt flavor is the tastiest? Which pair of shoes look the best with this outfit? What type of car will fill my needs as a consumer? If you are unsure of which answer would be the best to choose, it may help to use process of elimination. We use "filtering" all the time on sites such as eBay® or Craigslist® to eliminate the ads that are not right for us. We can do the same thing on an exam. Process of elimination is crossing out the answer choices we know for sure are wrong and leaving the ones that might be correct. It may help to cover up the incorrect answer choices with a piece of paper, although if the exam is computer-based, you may have to use your hand or mentally cross out the incorrect answer choices. Covering incorrect choices is a psychological act that alleviates stress due to the brain being exposed to a smaller amount of information. Choosing between two answer choices is much easier than choosing between four or five, and you have a better chance of selecting the correct answer if you have less to focus on.

4. Sticking to the World of the Question

When we are attempting to answer questions, our minds will often wander away from the question and what it is asking. We begin to see answer choices that are true in the real world instead of true in the world of the question. It may be helpful to think of each test question as its own little world. This world

1

may be different from ours. This world may know as a truth that the chicken came before the egg or may assert that two plus two equals five. Remember that, no matter what hypothetical nonsense may be in the question, assume it to be true. If the question states that the chicken came before the egg, then choose your answer based on that truth. Sticking to the world of the question means placing all of our biases and assumptions aside and relying on the question to guide us to the correct answer. If we are simply looking for answers that are correct based on our own judgment, then we may choose incorrectly. Remember an answer that is true does not necessarily answer the question.

5. Key Words

If you come across a complex test question that you have to read over and over again, try pulling out some key words from the question in order to understand what exactly it is asking. Key words may be words that surround the question, such as *main idea, analogous, parallel, resembles, structured,* or *defines*. The question may be asking for the main idea, or it may be asking you to define something. Deconstructing the sentence may also be helpful in making the question simpler before trying to answer it. This means taking the sentence apart and obtaining meaning in pieces, or separating the question from the foundation of the question. For example, let's look at this question:

> Given the author's description of the content of paleontology in the first paragraph, which of the following is most parallel to what it taught?

The question asks which one of the answers most *parallels* the following information: The *description* of paleontology in the first paragraph. The first step would be to see *how* paleontology is described in the first paragraph. Then, we would find an answer choice that parallels that description. The question seems complex at first, but after we deconstruct it, the answer becomes much more attainable.

6. Subtle Negatives

Negative words in question stems will be words such as *not, but, neither,* or *except*. Test writers often use these words in order to trick unsuspecting test takers into selecting the wrong answer—or, at least, to test their reading comprehension of the question. Many exams will feature the negative words in all caps (*which of the following is NOT an example*), but some questions will add the negative word seamlessly into the sentence. The following is an example of a subtle negative used in a question stem:

> According to the passage, which of the following is *not* considered to be an example of paleontology?

If we rush through the exam, we might skip that tiny word, *not*, inside the question, and choose an answer that is opposite of the correct choice. Again, it's important to read the question fully, and double check for any words that may negate the statement in any way.

7. Spotting the Hedges

The word "hedging" refers to language that remains vague or avoids absolute terminology. Absolute terminology consists of words like *always, never, all, every, just, only, none,* and *must*. Hedging refers to words like *seem, tend, might, most, some, sometimes, perhaps, possibly, probability,* and *often*. In some cases, we want to choose answer choices that use hedging and avoid answer choices that use absolute terminology. Of course, this always depends on what subject you are being tested on. Humanities subjects like history and literature will contain hedging, because those subjects often do not have absolute answers. However, science and math may contain absolutes that are necessary for the question to be answered. It's important to pay attention to what subject you are on and adjust your response accordingly.

8. Restating to Understand

Every now and then we come across questions that we don't understand. The language may be too complex, or the question is structured in a way that is meant to confuse the test taker. When you come across a question like this, it may be worth your time to rewrite or restate the question in your own words in order to understand it better. For example, let's look at the following complicated question:

> Which of the following words, if substituted for the word *parochial* in the first paragraph, would LEAST change the meaning of the sentence?

Let's restate the question in order to understand it better. We know that they want the word *parochial* replaced. We also know that this new word would "least" or "not" change the meaning of the sentence. Now let's try the sentence again:

> Which word could we replace with *parochial,* and it would not change the meaning?

Restating it this way, we see that the question is asking for a synonym. Now, let's restate the question so we can answer it better:

> Which word is a synonym for the word *parochial?*

Before we even look at the answer choices, we have a simpler, restated version of a complicated question. Remember that, if you have paper, you can always rewrite the simpler version of the question so as not to forget it.

9. Guessing

When is it okay to guess on an exam? This question depends on the test format of the particular exam you're taking. On some tests, answer choices that are answered incorrectly are penalized. If you know that you are penalized for wrong answer choices, avoid guessing on the test question. If you can narrow the question down to fifty percent by process of elimination, then perhaps it may be worth it to guess between two answer choices. But if you are unsure of the correct answer choice among three or four answers, it may help to leave the question unanswered. Likewise, if the exam you are taking does *not* penalize for wrong answer choices, answer the questions first you know to be true, then go back through and mark an answer choice, even if you do not know the correct answer. This way, you will at least have a one in four chance of getting the answer correct. It may also be helpful to do some research on the exam you plan to take in order to understand how the questions are graded.

10. Avoiding Patterns

One popular myth in grade school relating to standardized testing is that test writers will often put multiple-choice answers in patterns. A runoff example of this kind of thinking is that the most common answer choice is "C," with "B" following close behind. Or, some will advocate certain made-up word patterns that simply do not exist. Test writers do not arrange their correct answer choices in any kind of pattern; their choices are randomized. There may even be times where the correct answer choice will be the same letter for two or three questions in a row, but we have no way of knowing when or if this might happen. Instead of trying to figure out what choice the test writer probably set as being correct, focus on what the *best answer choice* would be out of the answers you are presented with. Use the tips above, general knowledge, and reading comprehension skills in order to best answer the question, rather than looking for patterns that do not exist.

FREE Videos/DVD OFFER

Achieving a high score on your exam depends on both understanding the content and applying your knowledge. **Because your success is our primary goal, we offer FREE Study Tips Videos, which provide top-notch test taking strategies to help optimize your testing experience.**

Our simple request is that you email us feedback about our book in exchange for the strategy-packed videos.

To receive your **FREE Study Tips Videos**, scan the QR code or email freevideos@apexprep.com. Please put "FREE Videos" in the subject line and include the following in the email:

a. The title of the book

b. Your rating of the book on a scale of 1-5, with 5 being the highest score

c. Any thoughts or feedback about the book

Thank you!

Introduction to the SIE Exam

Function of the Test

The Securities Industry Essentials (SIE) exam was created to determine the depth and understanding of basic financial knowledge and terminology of potential securities professionals. The test covers a variety of topics including types of securities, markets, regulatory agencies, and rules and regulations used in the financial industry. Anyone over the age of eighteen is eligible to take the test, and it can be used by professionals to demonstrate their competency to prospective employers. Test takers are not required to be associated with a firm to be able to take the exam. An additional qualification exam specific to a sector of the financial industry, such as the Series 7 or the Series 82, must be passed along with the SIE to allow an individual to register with a Financial Industry Regulatory Authority (FINRA) member firm.

Test Administration

The SIE exam is administered on the computer at Prometric testing centers, and the cost of the exam is $60. Before the exam begins, a tutorial is offered with tips on how to complete the exam. There are no reference materials allowed in the testing area. Calculators, scratch paper, and pens are provided at the testing center.

Testing sessions are both video- and audio-monitored to prohibit cheating on the exam. Cheating has severe consequences which range from invalidation of test results to preventing candidates from registering with a FINRA member firm. If candidates do not pass the test, retesting is allowed thirty days after the prior exam was taken. If a candidate fails the exam three or more times in a row, the waiting period for retesting is 180 days.

For accommodations due to disabilities and/or learning impairments, candidates must submit the FINRA Special Accommodations Eligibility Questionnaire and Special Accommodations Verification Request Form. FINRA will make appropriate accommodations in accordance with the Americans with Disabilities Act (ADA) and based on the documentation provided.

Test Format

The exam contains 75 scored multiple choice questions, and the candidate has one hour and 45 minutes to complete the exam. The exam also contains 10 pretest items that are unscored and randomly distributed. The content of the exam covers both general industry knowledge and concepts as well as specific rules and regulations. The exam is divided into the following content areas:

Sections	Percentage of Exam	Number of Questions
Knowledge of Capital Markets	16%	12
Understanding Products and Their Risks	44%	33
Understanding Trading, Customer Accounts, and Prohibited Activities	31%	23
Overview of the Regulatory Framework	9%	7
Total	**100%**	**75**

Scoring

The passing score for the SIE exam is 70, and guessing is not penalized on the exam. The pass/fail test results can be viewed on the computer screen at the end of the testing session. The candidate will also receive a printed copy of the results. Score reports for those who passed will not contain any additional scoring details. For candidates who do not pass, the actual exam score is provided along with a score breakdown by topic. This is intended to assist candidates who wish to retest in improving test scores.

Scores are calculated using a method called equating. This process places scores on a common scale to adjust for small variations in the difficulty levels of different exam items.

Recent Developments

FINRA announced on July 13, 2020 that a remote exam option would be available in a limited capacity to potential test takers. Online testing appointments will depend on availability as well as certain technical and remote environment requirements. This option was intended to address the need for remote testing during the COVID-19 pandemic, and it has not been announced how long the remote exam option will be available.

Study Prep Plan for the Series SIE Exam

 **Breathe**
Reducing stress is key when preparing for your test.

 Build
Create a study plan to help you stay on track.

 **Begin**
Stick with your study plan. You've got this!

1 Week Study Plan

Day 1	Day 2	Day 3	Day 4	Day 5	Day 6	Day 7
Knowledge of Capital Markets	Understanding Products and Their Risks	Understanding Trading, Customer Accounts and Prohibited Activities	Overview of the Regulatory Framework	Practice Test #1 & #2	Practice Test #3	Take Your Exam!

2 Week Study Plan

Day 1	Day 2	Day 3	Day 4	Day 5	Day 6	Day 7
Knowledge of Capital Markets	Market Structure	Understanding Products and Their Risks	Packaged Products	Hedge Funds	Exchange-Traded Products (ETPs)	Understanding Trading, Customer Accounts and Prohibited Activities

Day 8	Day 9	Day 10	Day 11	Day 12	Day 13	Day 14
Customer Accounts and Compliance Considerations	Prohibited Activities	Overview of the Regulatory Framework	Practice Test #1	Practice Test #2	Practice Test #3	Take Your Exam!

30 Day Study Plan

Day 1	Day 2	Day 3	Day 4	Day 5	Day 6	Day 7
Regulatory Entities, Agencies, and Market Participants	Market Structure	Economic Factors	Offerings	Products	Debt Instruments	Options

Day 8	Day 9	Day 10	Day 11	Day 12	Day 13	Day 14
Municipal Fund Securities	Hedge Funds	Accredited Investors	Exchange-Traded Products (ETPs)	Investment Risks	Strategies for Mitigation of Risk	Trading, Settlement and Corporate Actions

Day 15	Day 16	Day 17	Day 18	Day 19	Day 20	Day 21
Investment Returns	Trade Settlement	Customer Accounts and Compliance Considerations	Anti-Money Laundering (AML)	Business Continuity Plans (BCP)	Prohibited Activities	Use of Manipulative, Deceptive, or Other Fraudulent Devices

Day 22	Day 23	Day 24	Day 25	Day 26	Day 27	Day 28
Overview of the Regulatory Framework	Reportable Events	Practice Test #1	Answer Explanations #1	Practice Test #2	Answer Explanations #2	Practice Test #3

Day 29	Day 30
Answer Explanations #3	Take Your Exam!

Knowledge of Capital Markets

Regulatory Entities, Agencies, and Market Participants

Securities and Exchange Commission (SEC)

Purpose and Mission of Securities Regulation
During the 1920s, business expansion was accompanied by an increasing level of speculation in the stock market. After the stock market crash of 1929, the 1933 Securities Act was enacted to bring stability to the capital market, requiring fair disclosure of new stock issues through registration.

Definition, Jurisdiction, and Authority of the SEC
Section 4 of the Securities Exchange Act of 1934 established the SEC. The **Securities and Exchange Commission (SEC)** seeks to encourage investors to provide equity and debt capital by enforcing federal securities laws made by Congress and developing and enforcing regulations for the securities markets in a way that informs and protects investors.

The SEC enforces the following laws, among others:

- Securities Act of 1933
- Securities Exchange Act of 1934, which created the SEC
- Trust Indenture Act of 1939
- Investment Company Act of 1940
- Investment Advisers Act of 1940
- Sarbanes–Oxley Act of 2002

Self-Regulatory Organizations (SROs)

Purpose and Mission of a Self-Regulatory Organization
In addition to the congressionally established SEC, some **self-regulatory organizations (SROs)** are allowed to develop and enforce industry standards of behavior.

The following are some SROs outside the capital market industry:

- American Bar Association
- Institute of Nuclear Power Operations (INPO)
- Financial Planning Association (FPA)
- American Council of Life Insurers (ACLI)
- American Institute of Certified Public Accountants (AICPA)

The SEC invites public comments regarding rules proposed by these and other SROs.

Jurisdiction and Authority of SROs
The jurisdiction of the Chicago Board Options Exchange (CBOE) for trading includes the following countries:

- British Virgin Islands
- Cayman Islands

- Croatia
- Czech Republic
- Gibraltar
- Hong Kong
- Indonesia
- Ireland
- Israel
- Isle of Jersey
- Korea
- Luxemburg
- Mauritius
- Poland
- The Netherlands
- United Arab Emirates
- United Kingdom
- United States

Depending on the SRO and industry or profession involved, the SRO will have a certain amount of jurisdiction instead of the government oversight.

The ***Financial Industry Regulatory Authority's (FINRA's)*** jurisdiction generally includes its member broker-dealer firms and registered investment adviser firms and associated persons of those member firms, especially registered representatives and investment adviser representatives. Persons and firms that were former members may be subject to FINRA's jurisdiction related to complaints filed while the firm was a member, or a person was associated with a member firm.

The jurisdiction of the Municipal Securities Rulemaking Board (MSRB) was originally defined by Congress to include banks and broker-dealers that handled transactions involving municipal securities. In 2010, Congress added the oversight of municipal advisors, which are firms and their qualified individuals who advise governmental and other municipal organizations about offering municipal securities.

Other Regulators and Agencies

Department of the Treasury/Internal Revenue Service
The Department of the Treasury administers federal finances by the following:

- Receiving taxes through its bureau, the Internal Revenue Service (IRS)
- Paying bills
- Managing currency, government accounts, and public debt
- Enforcing finance laws and, through the IRS, tax laws

State Regulators
The ***North American Securities Administrators Association (NASAA)*** consists of securities administrators in the fifty states, the District of Columbia, Puerto Rico, the U.S. Virgin Islands, Canada, and Mexico. NASAA works to assist companies in obtaining capital by requiring disclosure of appropriate

information to those who invest in securities or purchase investment advice. They exercise jurisdiction over a large number of issuers and brokers who sell securities, by the following actions:

- Licensing companies and their representatives who meet and maintain the necessary requirements
- Looking into possible violations of laws
- Initiating penalty actions as needed
- Providing information to potential investors about possible fraud

NASAA members coordinate the following:

- Incidents that involve more than one state or territory
- Information sharing
- Annual training and education seminars for securities agency staff

The table below provides a view of how federal and state regulation of securities overlaps in some cases and not in others. This list only relates to whether offerings qualifying for the Securities Act exemptions listed here are otherwise subject to state registration. Some securities are only subject to federal regulation, some are only subject to state regulation, and some are subject to both federal and state regulations.

Securities Act Exemption	Subject to State Registration or Qualification
Section 4(a)(2)	Yes
Rule 506(b)	No
Rule 506(c)	No
Rule 504	Yes
Regulation Crowdfunding	No
Regulation A, Tier 1	Yes
Regulation A, Tier 2	No
Rules 147 and 147A	Yes
Rule 701	Yes

The Federal Reserve

Congress established the *Federal Reserve System* in 1913 as the central banking system in the United States. It exists to promote a predictable and healthy financial culture by seeking to eliminate volatility in the costs of everyday purchases and eliminate unemployment. The Board of Governors, also known as the Federal Reserve Board, oversees the system, which includes twelve regional Federal Reserve Banks, each with its own board of directors and president. The system also includes twenty-four branch banks. The system supervises private banks through bank examinations.

Securities Investor Protection Corporation (SIPC)

After a number of broker-dealers' bankruptcies occurred as a result of the unfavorable economic conditions in 1969 and 1970, Congress passed the ***Securities Investor Protection Act (SIPA)*** of 1970 to promote stability of the capital market through the following actions:

- Increasing the financial strength of brokers and dealers
- Reestablishing the willingness of investors to purchase securities by guaranteeing, up to certain limits, investors' funds and securities held by a member broker-dealer in the case of bankruptcy of the broker-dealer (not guaranteeing against loss of market values)

FINRA Rule 2266 (Securities Investor Protection Corporation [SIPC] Information) provides that, except for members, who are specifically excluded, and those whose financial products are excluded from SIPC coverage, when opening an account and at least one time each year thereafter, all FINRA members are required to inform, in writing, each of their new investors of the following:

- The investor's ability to learn about the SIPC, and obtain the SIPC brochure, by contacting SIPC
- The SIPC website address and telephone number

When a client is using both an introducing firm and clearing firm, only one firm needs to provide these notices.

Federal Deposit Insurance Corporation

The ***Federal Deposit Insurance Corporation (FDIC)*** was established in 1933 to insure individuals' deposits and encourage prudent banking management. Fractional reserve banking refers to banks not holding all of their customers' deposits on hand but using part of those deposits to make loans that earn interest. Banks had not always been required to maintain cash but could loan as much of their depositors' funds as they chose. By 1820, some New England banks agreed to hold adequate gold to back up their bank-issued paper money, but many states had no such requirement until the Civil War. When the public chose to withdraw their funds during times of economic uncertainty in the late nineteenth century and after the stock market crash of 1929, the banks were not able to provide liquid assets.

When the Federal Reserve was established in 1913, one role was to be the "lender of last resort." Meeting depositors' withdrawals was not the only goal. The amount of deposits a bank needed to maintain began to be adjusted as a tool of monetary policy, either encouraging or discouraging credit through increasing or decreasing the ability of banks to make loans and increase the money supply.

The FDIC has helped ensure depositors that they may always withdraw their funds up to the amount of the insurable limit per bank, which in 2022 is $250,000 per depositor. From time to time, as mutual funds continued to provide returns significantly greater than interest rates on certificates of deposit (CDs), bank customers increasingly chose to invest in mutual funds rather than CDs. Therefore, some banks arranged for brokerage firms to set up business in their offices. Strict measures were implemented to make sure those investing in mutual funds in a bank's office understood that the mutual funds were not insured by FDIC and that the investor could lose part of all of the investment.

Market Participants and Their Roles

Investors

Regulators have made a distinction among various types of investors. ***Retail investors*** are those who do not buy and sell stocks, bonds, or similar investments with enough frequency and volume to obtain discounted fees. The Securities Act of 1933 intended to require issuers of securities to retail investors to register with the SEC. Part of that registration includes information that the SEC requires to be shared with retail investors.

Persons with more experience investing, or with a higher net worth and therefore able to withstand a loss of their investment, are allowed to invest with fewer requirements for the issuer to disclose information to them. For example, the SEC only allows a hedge fund to have thirty-five investors who do not qualify as "accredited" investors.

Even less information may be required to be provided by an issuer to institutional investors. An institutional investor is an organization that has invested assets from a number of other persons or institutions and invests those funds on behalf of the original investors. This would include many banks, insurance companies, and mutual funds.

Broker-Dealers

In general, ***brokers*** are persons or organizations that have demonstrated a sufficient level of knowledge and amount of invested capital that they are allowed to purchase investments on behalf of the investor. Brokers typically do not buy or sell on their own behalf, or they would also be called dealers. ***Dealers*** are persons or organizations that have demonstrated a similar level of knowledge as brokers, with higher capital available, and who purchase investments for their own purposes. Some individuals or firms that do both are known as ***broker-dealers***.

Some brokers, like ***introducing brokers***, take orders from a client and pass the order to an entity, like ***clearing brokers***, that is qualified to match the buy order with a sell order from another person. The capital requirements for a clearing broker are higher than for an introducing broker. Prime brokers bundle services for the convenience of institutional investors, such as mutual funds, or individuals, generally with a high net worth, who have a frequent and high-volume pattern of investment transactions. These services may include consolidated reporting of transactions from a number of other broker-dealers patronized by the high-volume institutional or individual investor.

Investment Advisers

Investment advisers are defined in the Investment Advisers Act of 1940. After the stock market crash of 1929, followed by the Securities Act of 1933 and the Securities Exchange Act of 1934, Congress responded to a concern from the SEC about persons providing guidance regarding the buying and selling of investments. The definition of an investment adviser was based on whether a person causes an investor to think they are an investment adviser, or otherwise, depending on the following:

- The type of guidance provided
- The method of compensation for the guidance
- The proportion of the adviser's earnings related to providing that guidance

However, if the provision of guidance is relatively insignificant as a part of their professional services, the definition may not apply to them.

Municipal Advisors

Municipal advisors provide guidance to entities offering municipal securities. The following are some rules established by the MSRB regarding issuance of municipal securities:

- **MSRB Rule G-1**: Primary Offering Practices specifies coordination between the lead underwriter and the group of underwriters (syndicate) that is purchasing the issue and reselling to the public. Orders for municipal bonds must be fulfilled in the sequence specified by the issuing municipality unless that municipality has authorized the issuer exceptions.

- **MSRB Rule G-32**: Disclosures in Connection with Primary Offerings requires reporting if the municipality issuing the bonds chooses to give preference to retail investors.

- **MSRB Rule G-34**: Committee on Uniform Securities Identification Procedures [CUSIP] Numbers, New Issue, and Market Information Requirements provides for municipal advisors, when serving as a financial advisor on a competitive municipal security sale, to apply to the CUSIP for CUSIP numbers for the securities to be issued. CUSIP numbers are used to specify all American and Canadian registered stocks as well as American government bonds and municipal bonds.

Issuers and Underwriters

Companies issuing securities typically obtain investment banking services to advise on registration requirements, pricing of the stock, or coupon interest rates on bonds, etc. The investment bank may also agree to be the lead underwriter and thereby agree to assist with the offering in a variety of agreement types, including the following:

- **Best efforts**: The lead underwriter agrees to make a good faith effort to sell as many of the securities as possible. This is often used for initial public offerings (IPOs). It may be used when market conditions are difficult.

- **Mini-maxi**: This form of best efforts underwriting has a minimum threshold that must be sold in order for the agreement to be effective. Once the underwriter sells the minimum, the underwriter can sell up to the maximum quantity in the agreement.

- **All or none**: The lead underwriter assumes responsibility to attempt to sell all of the issue, understanding that if that is not successful, the issuer will not allow the completion of any sale.

- **Part or none**: A threshold is determined for how many of the securities the lead underwriter must sell.

- **Firm commitment**: The lead underwriter purchases all the securities of the issue and must resell the securities in order to realize a profit.

- **Standby underwriting**: An entity, usually an investment bank, agrees to purchase a certain quantity of a rights offering. This may be used if the market price is volatile.

- **Backstop underwriting**: The investment bank agrees to purchase all unsold rights on this type of standby underwriting. Due to the risk taken by the purchaser, this may involve significant fees.

Traders and Market Makers

Dealers purchase investments for their own purposes. They may occasionally sell an investment to a customer or purchase an investment from a customer.

Traders are dealers who buy and sell investments for their own purposes, looking for short-term profits based on the movement of the market. A trader does not necessarily stand ready to continuously offer both a bid and a sell price.

A ***market maker***, typically a large financial institution, stands ready continuously to buy at a "bid" price or sell at a "sell" price one or more securities. This provides a level of certainty that a holder of that specific security can readily find a purchaser willing to pay a reasonable price, and an investor desiring to purchase the security can readily find a seller willing to sell for a reasonable price. The market maker's profit is the difference between the bid and ask prices. A given security may have multiple market makers. Market makers' actions provide liquidity in the market.

Custodians and Trustees

A ***custodian*** is a firm, often a bank, that maintains possession of assets, such as investments, for the beneficiary named in a founding document, such as the following:

- A will
- An investment account in the name of a minor or person without the capacity to make legal decisions
- A trust deed

The ***Uniform Gift to Minors Act (UGMA)*** allows a person, such as a parent, to give assets to a minor person, such as a child. A bank account or securities account may be opened in the name of the trust, with the minor as the beneficiary, and no attorney may be required.

A custodian is chosen by the trustee, who is named in the founding document. The trustee may be a business firm, a natural person, or a public organization. The trustee has a fiduciary responsibility to make decisions in the best interest of the beneficiary. Having assets held by an entity other than the trustee helps avoid conflicts of interest, but in some cases, the trustee may act as the custodian.

Transfer Agents

An entity issuing securities retains a bank, trust company, or other capable firm as a ***transfer agent*** to manage the records of the investors' ownership of securities issued by the firm. When the transfer agent receives documentary authorization regarding a transaction, the evidence of ownership is transferred or received, and records are updated to reflect the transaction. The SEC rules set standards of correctness and speed for handling transactions by transfer agents.

Depositories and Clearing Corporations

A ***depository*** is a firm that holds electronic evidence of investment ownership. The electronic records reflect "dematerialization" of shares of ownership in accounts known as DEMAT accounts. A stock exchange works with a clearing corporation, also known as clearing firms or clearing houses, to confirm, settle, and deliver investment transactions. When a buyer and a seller agree to a transaction, the clearing corporation serves as the "go-between," helping accomplish the agreed-upon transaction, whether it involves stocks, bonds, futures, or derivatives, such as options. The clearing corporation conveys the evidence of ownership from the seller to the buyer and provides transaction reports to the stock exchange and other interested parties.

16

An example of a firm that fulfills both roles is the ***Depository Trust & Clearing Corporation (DTCC)***. The DTCC was formed in 1999 by the joining of a depository (the Depository Trust Company [DTC]) and a clearing corporation (National Securities Clearing Corporation [NSCC]). It settles by far the most securities transactions of any firm in the United States.

The ***Options Clearing Corporation (OCC)***, founded in 1973, is the world's largest clearing corporation for options. OCC guarantees all listed stock options contracts in the United States. The SEC supervises the OCC.

Market Structure

Types of Markets

Primary Market

The ***primary market*** refers to the initial issuance of securities by the original issuer. The 1933 Securities Act was enacted to bring stability to the capital market. Following are some parts of that act specifically related to the primary market for securities.

Section 7: Information Required in a Registration Statement

One key part of the 1933 act was to require a company issuing a security to provide accurate and complete information that a retail investor would need to make a rational decision regarding purchasing the security. Categories include the following:

- The issuer's assets, products, and services
- The security being issued
- Managers of the firm
- Audited financial statements

Section 8: Taking Effect of Registration Statements and Amendments Thereto

The registration statement typically is effective twenty days after the date it is filed, or earlier if the SEC approves. If an amendment is made to the filing, the twenty days may start over as of the date the amendment is filed unless the SEC deems the amendment to be integral to the original filing.

Section 10: Information Required in Prospectus

A final prospectus must contain the following:

- The issued security's main characteristics
- The company's past activities
- Leadership persons
- Offering price
- Offering date
- Any price reduction with conditions
- What the company will purchase with the sale proceeds
- The type of underwriting agreement
- Balance sheet and income statement information
- Possible reasons that investors may lose part or all of their investment

- Attorney's statement about the issuer's beginning
- Acknowledgement that the SEC takes no position on the accuracy of the information in the prospectus

Section 23: Unlawful Representations

The issuer is forbidden from suggesting that the SEC's acceptance of registration or silence regarding the registration is evidence that the SEC approves of the content of the registration as being true or in any way approves of the offering.

SEC Rule 215: Accredited Investor

SEC Rule 501(a) of Regulation D defines an accredited investor, which may be a firm, a natural person, or two natural persons, as possessing enough knowledge to make reasonable investment decisions and financially able to sustain more risk than a firm or person who does not meet the stated standards. Therefore, issuers who market only to accredited investors are not required to disclose as much information regarding an issue as issuers who are marketing to non-accredited investors.

SEC Rule 431: Summary Prospectuses

As the name indicates, a summary prospectus provides summary information. This allows issuers of qualifying securities to provide simplified documents to prospective investors. At the beginning or end, the document must include the following statement: "Copies of a more complete prospectus may be obtained from …" (insert name(s), address(es) and telephone number(s)).

Schedule A: Schedule of Information Required in Registration Statement

Unless subject to an exception if the SEC so chooses, Schedule A is required for registration of any security not issued by a foreign government or a political subdivision of a foreign government. Schedule A includes the issuer's name, location, principal office, directors and managers, underwriters, owners of more than 10 percent of stock, type of business, capitalization, options, debt, commissions, proceeds and their use, security price, vendors, contracts, patents, balance sheets, income statements, underwriting agreements, legal opinions, founding documents, and underlying agreements.

Schedule B: Schedule of Information Required in Registration

Unless subject to an exception if the SEC so chooses, Schedule B is required for registration of any security issued by a foreign government or a political subdivision of a foreign government. Schedule B includes the government entity's name, authorized agent in the United States, underwriters' contact information, debt, defaults, three years of history of receipts and expenditures, proceeds and their use, proceeds in the United States, price in the United States, commissions, expenses other than commissions, counsel, agreement to furnish opinion of counsel, and underwriting agreements regarding sale in the United States.

The Secondary Market

The **secondary market** refers to the sale of securities to and by investors. This occurs after the issuance of securities by the issuer. The vast majority of these transactions occur on various exchanges, which started out as physical locations. Now the exchanges perform most of their trading electronically. An over-the-counter (OTC) market is conducted electronically, without the parties meeting in person. Under certain circumstances, an issuer may repurchase its own security in the secondary market.

18

The Securities Exchange Act of 1934 was intended to ensure the secondary market operated with the following conditions:

- Investors knowing enough accurate information about the securities traded to make reasonable decisions
- Issuers and investors not unfairly manipulating prices
- Fraud kept to a minimum

The following are included in the 1934 act:

Section 3(a): Definitions and Application of Title defines the terms exchange, facility, and member.

Section 12: Registration Requirements for Securities in general specifies the following:

- Maximum value of assets ($10 million) of an issuer that does not need to be registered
- The maximum number of persons who are not accredited investors (500) who may own a security that does not need to be registered
- The maximum number of persons (2000) who may own a security that does not need to be registered

Section 15: Registration and Regulation of Brokers and Dealers in general requires natural persons and firms engaged in the securities business outside of a single state to be registered and become a member of an SRO, such as FINRA.

Section 15A: Registered Securities Associations provides for registration of an association of brokers and dealers as either a national securities association or an affiliated securities association, subject to rules the SEC is authorized to establish.

Regulation D: Rules Governing the Limited Offer and Sale of Securities Without Registration Under the Securities Act of 1933 allows securities to be sold by the issuer without SEC registration (private placements) to certain purchasers, typically firms or individuals with significant net worth, who therefore are expected to be able to judge the possibility of losing part or all of their investment, wait for an extended period of time to sell their investment, and understand the investment strategies set by managers.

FINRA Rule 2269: Disclosure of Participation or Interest in Primary or Secondary Distribution requires a member broker-dealer to notify a customer from whom the broker-dealer expects to receive compensation if the broker-dealer is involved in an issuer's distribution of the same security as the broker-dealer is assisting the customer in buying or selling.

FINRA Rule 5250: Payments for Market Making prohibits a market maker from receiving payment from the issuer of the security for which the market maker provides a constant offer to buy (at a bid price) or sell (at an offer price), called a two-sided quote.

The Securities Act of 1933 included the following:

Rule 144: Persons Deemed Not to be Engaged in a Distribution and Therefore Not Underwriters identifies persons who purchase securities from an issuer "with a view to distribution." An underwriter is a person who acts as a step in providing a newly issued security to the public. The intention of the person is interpreted based on future actions. If the person is determined to have purchased securities, not "with a view to distribution," the person is not involved with a distribution and cannot be considered an underwriter.

Rule 144A: Private Resales of Securities to Institutions provides conditions under which securities issued in private placements may be sold with shorter waiting periods (six or twelve months) than otherwise would be allowed (twenty-four months) to firms who are considered to be institutional buyers.

Rule 145: Reclassification of Securities, Mergers, Consolidations, and Acquisitions of Assets provides that, when an issuer submits to the owners of its securities an opportunity to vote on whether they will surrender their securities and receive in their place new securities, restricted securities surrendered subsequent to that approval begin a new holding period.

Such votes typically relate to corporate capital restructuring in conjunction with an event such as the following:

- A reclassification of securities, in which a set of securities is turned in to the issuer and the issuer provides a replacement set of securities

- A transaction with another entity, in which the issuer receives a set of securities and provides, in their place, a security of the other entity (merger, consolidation, acquisition, etc.)

- A sale of assets in exchange for securities of the purchasing entity that are distributed to the seller's security owners

Rule 147: "Part of an Issue," "Person Resident," and "Doing Business Within" for Purposes of Section 3(a)(11)

Rule 147 excludes from SEC registration requirements those securities that are sold only within the state in which the issuer resides as long as the issuer does not sell the securities through the means of communication used in interstate commerce (see comment on Rule 147A) and at least one of the following applies:

- 80 percent or more of its revenues come from activities on property in the state or territory.

- 80 percent or more of its revenues come from services provided to residents of its state or territory.

- 80 percent or more of its assets are in the state or territory.

- 80 percent or more of the funds from the securities issued, less expenses, will be used for activities in the state or territory.

- 80 percent or more of the funds from the securities issued, less expenses, will be used for buying real estate in the state or territory.

- 80 percent or more of the funds from the securities issued, less expenses, will be used to provide services in the state or territory.

- More than 50 percent of the issuer's employees work in the state or territory.

Some additional requirements include the following:

- The issuer must fulfill the registration requirements of its state or territory.

- The issuer must obtain a document from any business buying the securities stating its principal place of business is in the state or territory.

- After a person or entity in the state buys the securities, that buyer must wait six months before selling the security to someone outside of the state or territory.

Congress updated the rule with Rule 147A, allowing the use of technology such as the Internet, which incidentally offers the securities to persons living outside of the state as long as only persons living in the state are allowed to buy the securities.

Rule 164: Post-Filing Free Writing Prospectuses in Connection with Certain Registered Offerings

Rather than using a statutory prospectus, issuers who meet certain eligibility requirements may attempt to sell a security using other information, called a Free Writing Prospectus (FWP), which includes emails, press releases, and promotional brochures.

However, a Well-Known Seasoned Issuer (WKSI) may use an FWP before or after the registration effective date if also providing references to how a potential investor may obtain a statutory prospectus. A WKSI is qualified to use the short form registration (S-3 or F-3; see "seasoned issuer" below) and has the following additional characteristics:

- Within sixty days of a decision about eligibility, ownership worldwide by persons other than the issuer itself, or its affiliates, must amount to one of the following:
  - $700 million or more of the issuer's registered common stock
  - $1 billion or more of the issuer's registered non-convertible bonds and other securities (other than common stock) that was issued by the issuer as primary offerings, for which the issuer received cash
- The WKSI is not an "ineligible issuer" regarding FWPs, under SEC regulations

A seasoned issuer may issue an FWP after the registration filing if also providing reference to how a potential investor may obtain a statutory prospectus. A seasoned issuer is qualified to use the short form registration (S-3 or F-3 for some foreign issuers), which requires the following:

- At least $75 million of publicly held common stock
- Consistently paid preferred dividends
- Meeting all bond coupon payments
- Up-to-date SEC filings

An unseasoned issuer or a non-reporting issuer may issue an FWP after the registration filing if also providing a statutory prospectus. An unseasoned issuer is required to file reports with the SEC according to the 1934 act, Section 13 or 15(d) but does not meet the requirements for using the short form registration (S-3 or F-3) for a primary offering. A non-reporting issuer is not required to file reports with the SEC according to the 1934 act, Section 13 or 15(d), whether or not the issuer actually files such reports.

The Third Market

The **third market** refers to the buying and selling of securities listed on a national exchange, which does not occur on an exchange. These transactions occur in the OTC market. Large companies use this market, working with broker-dealers who are not members of an exchange, in some cases to obtain one or more of the following:

- Lower security prices
- Lower brokerage fees
- Faster settlement
- Privacy regarding some elements of the transactions

The Fourth Market

The **fourth market**, sometimes called dark pools, involves companies buying and selling securities in an OTC market, with trades sometimes having one or more of the following characteristics:

- Companies dealing directly with each other
- Low transaction costs, without broker commissions or exchange costs
- A wide range of securities, including creatively designed derivatives, such as swap options, customized for the parties involved
- Greater privacy than the third market
- Exchange volume and prices being unaffected by fourth market activity, which is not publicly reported

Economic Factors

The Federal Reserve Board's Impact

Monetary vs. Fiscal Policy

Congress controls fiscal policy, which stimulates the economy by deficit spending. Made up of elected officials, Congress generally takes action based on political ideology and broad and complex political goals rather than consensus economic analysis and specific, quantifiable goals.

The **Federal Reserve Board**, an appointed body and somewhat independent of the electorate, impacts business activity and market stability through monetary policy, both directly and indirectly, to promote steady economic growth without an unhealthy level of inflation. Direct actions (open market activities) and indirect actions (changing interest rates) are described below. In a separate category are facilities allowing firms to borrow money anonymously.

The graphic below shows the two different policies and how they affect the economy.

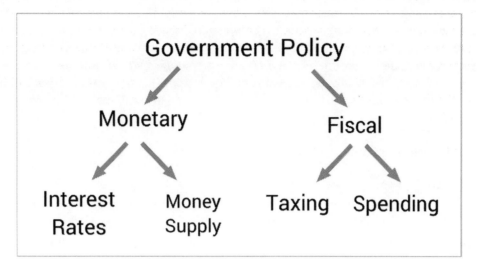

Term Auction Facilities and Term Securities Lending Facilities

When the prevailing interest rates charged for loans increased in 2007 and 2008 due to higher business and private defaults, the Federal Reserve added a tool to its monetary policy activities. The Federal Reserve developed term auction facilities and term securities lending facilities. ***Term auction facilities*** allowed firms to anonymously offer to borrow funds for a short-term time frame at a given interest rate. This stimulated extension of credit by financial firms because the firms making the loans were not publicly known the way borrowing from the discount window at the federal funds rate would be. Therefore, depositors were less likely to withdraw their deposits. ***Term securities lending*** facilities allowed firms to exchange troubled collateralized debt obligations backed by mortgages, with declining worth, for Treasury securities, with more stable worth. Otherwise, financial firms could have become insolvent.

Public Comment by the Federal Reserve

The Federal Reserve has the ability to affect the economy directly or indirectly (monetary policy). When the financial climate is expanding too fast, the price of everyday purchases may increase. The Federal Reserve may release a public statement mentioning the increase. The Federal Reserve can also use its available monetary policy tools to increase interest and offset the characteristics that prompted the warning. As a result, the investing public may change their investment behavior in anticipation of the Federal Reserve's possible action.

Open Market Activities

The Federal Reserve's indirect method involves selling and purchasing government securities on the open market, known as ***open market activities***. Selling securities results in money flowing out of the open market. This results in less money in the economy to purchase available goods. It is intended to slow down the economy in general and restrain inflation in particular. This helps retain the purchasing power of workers' earnings. Purchasing securities results in money flowing into the open market. This results in more money in the economy to purchase available goods and is intended to stimulate the economy. Purchasing too many securities can cause an increase in inflation.

Different Rates

Whereas buying and selling government securities is an indirect method of influencing the level of economic activity, a direct method is to influence banks' loan interest rates. This may be done by adjusting the federal funds rate, the rate the Federal Reserve charges banks for overnight loans, as they adjust their cash to meet their discount requirement. Another way is by adjusting the discount rate, which increases or decreases the cash banks need to maintain overnight. This tightens or loosens banks' ability to issue loans to individuals and businesses. This change in available credit results in a change in overall economic activity.

Business Economic Factors

Purpose of Financial Statements

The purpose of *financial statements* depends on the audience to which they are presented. Statements may be presented to internal personnel for the purpose of informing them of their own performance as triggers for bonuses. Statements may be presented to the owners, or the board of directors, in order to measure the performance of the executive officer and their staff. In the context of public companies, the purpose is to indicate to the investing public whether the company's stock should be held, sold, or purchased, and to current and potential creditors, whether loans should be called or extended.

Statements may be presented to governmental taxing authorities, for example, to calculate income taxes. Financial statements may be shown with different sets of accounting principles. American publicly held companies most often use Generally Accepted Accounting Principles, reflecting valuations based on the going-concern assumption. American insurance companies use Statutory Accounting Principles, based on a liquidation valuation. The domiciliary state Insurance Commissioner's office will review the statements with a view to ensuring the company's ability to pay claims and that the company is charging adequate, but not excessive, premiums.

Business Cycle

Historically, the U.S. economy has periods of expansion followed by contractions, which are graphically represented, using quantified measures of economic activity. The parts of the graph below are used to describe the phases of the business cycle:

- **Expansion** refers to the rising portion.
- **Peak** refers to the highest quantity.
- **Contraction** refers to the time frame of diminishing values.
- **Trough** refers to the time period during which the lowest quantity is displayed.

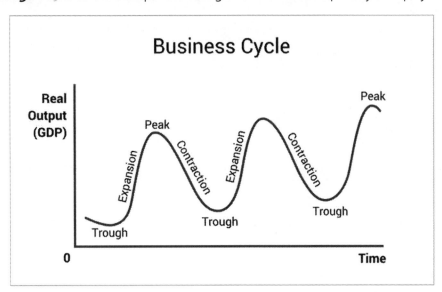

Indicators

Leading indicators reflect how the economy will change in the near future. **Coincident indicators** reflect the current state of the economy. **Lagging indicators** change only after the economy in general has changed. Some indicators may be considered as coincident by some and as lagging by others (see below). **Individual indicators** have fluctuations that require expert interpretation and comparison with other indicators to determine whether the specific change in a specific indicator is an exception or a true sample of how the economy in general is doing.

Leading indicators include the following:

- Manufacturing activity/industrial production, if it reflects retail orders for individuals' purchases and likely future wage and salary increases; otherwise it may increase inventory levels

- Inventory levels which, when high, reflect optimism on the part of the business leaders or possibly a lack of demand

- Retail sales (a component when calculating gross domestic product [GDP]) depending on the degree to which these are driven by earnings rather than credit

- Building permits suggesting future construction activity and real estate sales but may be overly optimistic

- Housing market, both prices and quantity of sales transactions

- Level of new business start-ups, leading to additional jobs and innovation

- Broad stock market (although some stocks may be counter-cyclical), based on expectations of profitability, which may be erroneous; may be manipulated by non-economic factors such as governmental quantitative easing, increased deficit spending, and other politically motivated intervention

Coincident indicators include the following:

- (Real) GDP, generally used as the measure of the economy, when measured over a two-quarter period, yet can be manipulated, as the stock market can be, by government intervention; categorized by some as a lagging indicator

- Real earnings/personal income (earnings discounted for inflation), which may vary for groups of people with different demographics; categorized by some as a lagging indicator

- Increased (real) salary/wage rates, adjusted for inflation

- Average weekly hours worked in manufacturing

- Unemployment rate, number of persons looking for employment (may miss persons who would work but are not currently looking), as a proportion of all workers; categorized by some as a lagging indicator

Lagging indicators include the following:

- Real GDP (see above); categorized by some as a coincident indicator

- Real earnings/personal income (see above); categorized by some as a coincident indicator

- Unemployment rate; categorized by some as a coincident indicator

- Consumer Price Index (CPI), intended to reflect the cost of living by summarizing the costs of essential needs which, when increased, results in inflation

- Currency strength, the comparison of a country's ability to buy or sell goods or services with other countries; may be a benefit to a strong dollar for purchasing or to a weak dollar for selling

- Interest rates, which are affected not only by the general level of economic activity but also by the government's actions

- Corporate profits, which may match the change in GDP but may at least partly reflect cost cutting by outsourcing and layoffs

- Balance of trade, difference between funds going out of the country and funds coming in; favorable, if a reasonable surplus

- Gold, silver, and other commodities as substitutes for the U.S. dollar, which reflect the strength or weakness of the dollar

Effects on Bond and Equity Markets

Bond values typically decline as interest rates increase. Interest rates typically increase during periods of high inflation, which generally precede or accompany the expansion phase. The broad stock market is considered to be a leading indicator for the business cycle. Cyclical stocks, such as equipment and vehicles, tend to follow the business cycle. However, defensive stocks of companies providing necessities, such as food, beverages, and utilities, typically maintain profitability through all phases of the cycle. Growth stocks often do well during the optimism prevailing at the beginning of the expansion phase when the economy's recovery is speeding up.

Principal Economic Theories

Keynesian theory, created by John Maynard Keynes, promotes government intervention to encourage economic health of a country through taxation policies and deficit spending. Monetary theory encompasses the use of various methods to adjust the money supply and available credit to the desired level of economic activity.

International Economic Factors

U.S. Balance of Payments

The ***balance of payment (BOP)*** of a country lists all transactions made between citizens and businesses of that country with countries in the rest of the world, as shown in the following table:

Trade Deficit	Trade Surplus
A country spends more in other countries than they spend in their own country.	A country receives more in payments than it spends in other countries.
A country goes into debt to finance its foreign purchases.	The country is able to fund all its economic production.
Over time, this could result in excessive debt owed to other countries for necessities.	Over time, a country could become dependent on foreign capital.

GDP and Gross National Product

The ***gross domestic product (GDP)*** reflects the total of a country's goods and services produced and used or consumed during a period of time. The ***gross national product (GNP)*** reflects the total of a country's goods and services produced during a period of time.

Exchange Rates

Exchange rates are the proportion of one country's money that can be exchanged for another country's money. It represents a country's ability to buy or sell goods or services with other countries on a favorable basis. It is typically affected by a country's prevailing interest rates.

Offerings

Roles of Participants

In a securities offering, a lead investment banker is typically engaged in assisting the company in gathering the information necessary, choosing the pricing, and completing the regulatory requirements, including, in the case of stocks, a registration filing with the SEC. The underwriting syndicate is a collection of investment bankers who assist in the securing of offers for, and eventually selling of, the stock to the investing public appropriate for that offering. Municipal advisors perform a role for municipalities issuing bonds, similar to the investment bankers' role with for-profit

Public vs. Private Securities Offering companies.

Types of Offerings

When an issuer sells securities intended for the public (public securities offering) through an intermediary, the SEC registration and disclosure requirements are more stringent than if the issuer chooses to offer securities only to accredited investors (private securities offering).

IPO, Secondary Offering, and Follow-On Public Offering

One type of public securities offering occurs when a company first issues securities to the public (IPO). Another type of public securities offering occurs when the company later issues additional new securities to the public and/or shares held by the owner or a few stockholders owning more than 50 percent of the shares offer shares to the public (secondary offering/follow-on public offering [FPO]).

Methods of Distribution

A "firm commitment" underwriting agreement involves the syndicate accepting responsibility for selling all the stock, removing the risk of undersubscription from the issuing company. This is preferred by some issuing companies as the way to ensure maximum effort by the underwriting syndicate. A "best efforts" underwriting agreement requires the syndicate to make a good faith effort to sell the stock, but the risk of undersubscription remains with the issuing company. An "all or none" agreement conditions the actual placement of any stock upon a complete subscription to all the stock. A "standby" agreement provides for unsold stock to be purchased by the investment bank(s) signing the agreement.

Shelf Registrations and Distributions

SEC Rule 415 allows an issuer to register an issue of securities but not immediately sell them (shelf registration). Rather, the issuer may sell them over the next two years. This allows the issuer to complete the registration process (if desired, for multiple future issues of securities with one registration process and reduced registration costs) and thereby preserve the ability to select the timing for the offerings to obtain a more favorable sales price than is available at the time of the registration. The public's awareness of the shelf registration may affect the sales price. During the two-year period, the company files required reports with the SEC.

Types and Purpose of Offering Documents and Delivery Requirements

To promote stability of capital markets, various acts of Congress and rules of SROs directly or indirectly require issuers of securities to distribute a document describing pertinent details about the issuer and the security being offered (offering document) so the potential investor is aware of the benefits and risks involved.

The issuer of a municipal security publishes a document to describe the security (official statement). The document will provide potential purchasers of the security with information regarding the financial strength of the issuer and the coupon rate, maturity date, and other characteristics, such as call provisions, of the security.

A municipality establishing a 529 college savings program prepares a document (Program Disclosure Document/Program Disclosure Statement/Plan Disclosure Document) for review by persons interested in opening a 529 account. The document describes the program, including the fact that the program is specifically to be used to put away funds for future educational purposes. The document is available to the public through the Electronic Municipal Market Access (EMMA) website, operated by the MSRB.

Persons promoting an issue of an SEC-registered security provide a document that has been filed with the SEC (prospectus), which has information about the history, management, and financial strength of the issuer as well as characteristics and risks of the security. The person considering purchasing the security receives the prospectus before buying the security or no later than the time the security is bought.

For non-U.S. investors who are not subject to U.S. taxes, hedge funds domiciled outside of the United States provide an offering document that describes the way the fund buys and sells assets.

Regulatory Filing Requirements and Exemptions

An issuer issuing a security follows federal SEC disclosure rules and/or state Blue Sky disclosure laws in providing the regulator and potential investors with information about the issuer and the security. The SEC has exemptions for certain firms or securities, depending on conditions such as the total dollar value of the issue and whether the issue will only be sold in a certain state.

See our SIE Resource Page for links to current rules and regulations.

You can visit by going to https://www.apexprep.com/sie or by scanning the QR code.

Understanding Products and Their Risks

Products

Equity Securities

To conduct business, a company sometimes obtains money to start, continue, or expand its activities. It may sell partial ownership, or equity, in the firm. A corporation provides stock in exchange for money to operate. After that initial issuance, the stockholder may sell the stock to another party. Due to the stock market crash of 1929, the 1933 Securities Act, also known as the "truth in securities law," and the 1934 Securities Exchange Act were passed. The 1933 act regulates the disclosure of new stock issue through registration with the Securities Exchange Commission (SEC). The 1934 act regulates the subsequent trading of stock after its initial issuance. An example of a way in which the 1934 act attempts to protect the investing public is through limiting a company's ability to manipulate the public value of its stock by limiting the purchases of its own stock. Under Section 10b-18, such purchases must meet four conditions:

- One broker or dealer used each day
- Time of purchases
- Price of purchases
- Volume of purchases

To promote fairness, in Rule 144, the SEC requires transactions with certain transactional histories to be registered with the SEC prior to being sold, unless they satisfy exemption requirements.

A security expresses a monetary value that is transferable from one person to another for payment due or can be exchanged for another item of equal monetary value. The following is the Securities Exchange Act of 1934 Section 240.3a11-1 definition of the term equity security, as amended:

- ***Equity security*** encompasses any stock or similar security, certificate of interest or participation in any profit sharing agreement, preorganization certificate or subscription, transferable share, voting trust certificate or certificate of deposit for an equity security, limited partnership interest, interest in a joint venture, or certificate of interest in a business trust; any security future on any such security; or any security convertible, possessing or withholding consideration into such a security, or possessing any warrant or justification to subscribe to or purchase such a security; or any such warrant or right; or any put, call, straddle, or other option or leverage of buying such a security from or selling such a security to another without being bound to do so.

- The definition of equity security was updated to include a security future by the Commodity Futures Modernization Act of 2000.

Broker firms facilitate transactions for customers in equity and debt securities. These firms are required to be members of the Financial Industry Regulatory Authority (FINRA), an independent regulator of member broker firms operating in the United States. To protect persons who may purchase or own securities, FINRA licenses broker firms and establishes and enforces rules by which those firms operate. Some of these rules require member firms to make disclosures, either when requested by a customer or voluntarily, to enable the recipient to make an informed decision regarding selection of a firm or security.

For example, ***FINRA Rule 2261*** – Disclosure of Financial Condition requires a member broker firm, when requested by a customer, to provide its financial condition from the most recent balance sheet, either

30

printed or electronic. ***FINRA Rule 2262*** – Disclosure of Control Relationship with Issuer requires a brokerage firm that is an affiliate of the issuer of any security to report this relationship to any customer before beginning to arrange a transaction for the issuer's security. If this report is not made in writing, it must be provided in printed or electronic form by the time a transaction is executed in the issuer's security for a customer. FINRA maintains a website (finra.org) to assist the investing public, such as by offering a place to file a complaint against a member firm or a representative. FINRA's website (brokercheck.finra.org) allows the public to acquire background information about individual representatives.

An equity security represents ownership of a portion of the amount of money available to shareholders if a company was liquidated, that is, if all assets of the company were sold and all debts were paid. Market value of equity securities may fluctuate according to the expectations of the investor public regarding the company's future profits and therefore the anticipated future liquidation value of the company. An advantage of equity securities such as common stock and preferred stock of a corporation is limited liability, which means the stockholder has no personal liability for any of the corporation's liabilities during its existence or for its liabilities being greater than its assets at liquidation.

Types of Equities

Equity securities include stock, which may be common or preferred; rights; warrants; and American depositary receipts (ADRs).

Common Stock

Common stock represents ownership that would be last in line to receive monetary value in the case of a company liquidation.

Owners of common stock receive dividends if declared by the board of directors, typically from current earnings. In some cases, the board of directors declares and pays common stock dividends annually after the annual operating results are known. However, the board may declare common stock dividends quarterly. If the board declares and pays common stock dividends, it must also declare and pay preferred stock dividends. Investors desiring immediate income should find common stock with a history of paying dividends that matches their investment objective. If the board declares dividends equal to most or all current profits, the growth of the company's value and possible increase in market value of the common stock may be limited.

Common stock has voting rights—typically one vote per share—regarding election of members to the board of directors, mergers, and other major issues of the company. The method of voting to elect members to the board of directors is stated in the stock issue and is typically either cumulative or standard voting. With cumulative voting, each shareholder is allowed to cast a number of votes equal to the quantity of shares owned multiplied by the number of seats being filled. The stockholder may distribute the total number of votes among the seats as desired, even to cast them all for a single candidate. For example, if the stockholder owns five hundred shares and three positions are being filled, the stockholder may cast 1500 votes. With standard voting, a stockholder may only vote the number of shares held for each seat to be filled. In the above example, the stockholder could vote five hundred shares for each of three candidates. Cumulative voting may help minority stockholders elect a member to the board of directors.

In addition to dividends, common stock's attraction to investors includes the possibility of an increase in its market value. If the company chooses to reinvest most or all of its profits into growing its operations internally rather than paying dividends, the holders may gain value in the future due to the compounding

31

effect of the company's internal value increase. If potential investors anticipate the growth in the company will continue, the market value may increase. Investors with little or no need for immediate income may prefer the possibility of receiving greater value over several years through this reinvestment than would be received through current dividends declared and paid over the same number of years. Due to various risks perceived by the investing public, however, the market value may decline from time to time.

Preferred Stock

Preferred stock represents ownership that would receive monetary value after all debtors are paid but before holders of common stock are paid.

Depending on the structure of the preferred stock issue, the board of directors may declare and pay preferred dividends. The board must do this before it declares and pays common stock dividends. However, in some cases, the preferred stock issue mandates payment of dividends as fixed obligations of the company, and preferred dividends may be paid quarterly or even monthly. The preferred stock issue may state a rate of dividends, usually a percentage of par value, in its title, for example, "5 percent preferred." On cumulative preferred stock, the board must declare and pay dividends that are in arrears before declaring and paying dividends to holders of common stock. Holders of preferred stock have no voting rights.

Preferred stock has characteristics of equity, which allows for potential increase in its market value. It also has characteristics of debt because of its dividends and its claim to payment prior to common stock in the event of company liquidation. This combination of equity and debt characteristics may be attractive to some investors. The market value of preferred stock may not fluctuate as much as common stock due to its expected dividends.

Preferred stock may be convertible, in which case it can be exchanged for common stock according to the terms stated when it was issued. In this case, its market value will likely track with the market value of the common stock in proportion to the number of preferred shares that can be converted to a common share.

Rights

As an incentive for persons to purchase shares in a new company, the company may issue common stock with a specified right of first refusal. This provides the purchaser the opportunity, but not an obligation, to buy additional shares of any future common stock issue prior to the shares being available to the public, based on the quantity of shares held (rights issue ratio) by the shareholder. This allows shareholders to maintain their percentage of voting rights in perpetuity as the rights are exercised. This will require an additional purchase of common stock of the company at the time of each future common stock issue. This opportunity is usually only offered to majority shareholders or investors who invested in the company's early years. It is usually offered for a limited time frame, often from sixteen to thirty days.

As an example, if a company issued 1 million shares and an investor purchased 500,000, that investor has a 50 percent stake in the company. If the company later issues 100,000 additional shares, that investor would have the opportunity to purchase 50 percent of the new offering, or 50,000 shares, to maintain 50 percent ownership. If the investor does not exercise that opportunity during the specified time, the company could sell those shares to another investor. The first investor's ownership percentage would then be diluted, that is, less than the original percentage, which in this example was 50 percent.

This typically occurs when the company chooses to raise additional capital funds to pay off some debt or to invest in a new project by offering stock to current shareholders at a discounted subscription share

32

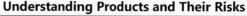

price for a limited time. A right may be issued for each share of stock, but multiple rights may be required to purchase a newly issued share.

For example, a company that has 1 million shares of stock outstanding chooses to issue an additional 250,000 shares through a stock offering. The company issues one right to each outstanding share, which could purchase one-fourth of a share of the new stock issue. The outstanding shares trade immediately with the rights attached, or "rights on." Unless the rights issue specifies non-renounceable rights, each right would afterward trade on its own, or "rights off," until the right expires. The rights offering may provide those receiving it the opportunity to obtain shares at a lower price than they might have paid for shares issued earlier. More shares (in this case, 25 percent more) will be outstanding, and therefore the market value may decline after a rights offering because future dividends will be distributed among a greater number of shares, unless the company uses the capital received to increase future dividends proportionate to the increased number of outstanding shares.

In an insured, or standby, rights offering, a backstop purchaser agrees to purchase unexercised rights. In a direct rights offering with no backstop purchaser, unexercised rights may result in the issuer receiving less than the full amount of the issue.

Using rights to sell stock to current shareholders avoids the cost of retaining an investment banker to prepare registration for a new issue to the public. This can help a company in need of cash. If not exercised, stock rights would receive no monetary value at liquidation, receive no dividends, and have no voting rights.

Warrants

When a company chooses to raise funds, it may provide an incentive for current holders to purchase a bond or preferred stock by offering a stock call warrant in combination with the bond or preferred stock. This provides the owner of the call warrant an opportunity, but not a requirement, to purchase a single share of stock directly from the issuing company at a specific exercise price during a specified time in the future—sometimes six months or one year from the issue date—and ending at a later date. The exercise price would be higher than the current market price but hopefully lower than the market price would eventually be at the time of exercise. Instead of being exercised, the call warrant could generally be sold on the open market, especially after the market value of the underlying security has risen above the exercise price on the call warrant. The right to sell shares of stock back to the issuer in the future at a certain price is a put warrant.

If not exercised, stock warrants would receive no monetary value at liquidation, receive no dividends, and have no voting rights.

American Depositary Receipts (ADRs)

Americans can invest through American markets with American dollars in foreign companies through **American Depositary Receipts (ADRs)**, a form of equity security issued by an American broker or bank on behalf of a foreign company. American investors receive dividends in American dollars but do not have preemptive rights. If a foreign company pays a depositary bank to issue ADR shares of its stock in the United States, it has sponsored ADRs and the company may raise capital in the United States and have its ADRs listed on either the New York Stock Exchange (NYSE) or Nasdaq. If the foreign company does not pay those costs, the unsponsored ADR shares trade in the over-the-counter (OTC) market.

Depending on the level of compliance, unsponsored ADRs may trade OTC (Level I) and sponsored ADRs may be listed on a major exchange such as the NYSE (Level II). Some sponsored ADRs may raise capital by issuing shares in the United States (Level III). ADRs have additional risks compared to stock of American companies.

Type of Equity	Ownership?	Order of Liquidation	Voting Rights?	Convertible?	Factors Affecting Market Value
Common stock	Yes	Last	Yes	NA	Anticipated growth in earnings; dividend policy
Preferred stock	Yes	After debt and before common stock	No	Some but not all	Due to dividends, may fluctuate less than common stock unless convertible, in which case it may track closer to common stock
Stock rights	Only after exercise	None before exercise	Only after exercise	Yes, with exercise payment	Intrinsic value/ conversion ratio plus time value, which may include discount for dilution
Stock call warrants	Only after exercise	None before exercise	Only after exercise	Yes, with exercise payment	Intrinsic value/ conversion ratio plus time value, which may include discount for dilution
ADRs	Yes, like common stock	Last, like common stock	Yes, like common stock	NA	Like common stock, anticipated growth in earnings; dividend policy

Debt Instruments

Treasury Securities

The U.S. government issues **Treasury securities**. The government may issue or repurchase treasuries for the purpose of implementing fiscal policy (financing deficit spending) or monetary policy (increasing or decreasing the money supply to encourage economic growth while controlling inflation). The U.S. government guarantees treasuries with the full faith and credit of the government, and therefore investors consider them to have no risk of default. Investors pay federal income tax on interest received on treasuries but no state and local income tax on that (state and local exempt) interest. Brokerage firms develop **Treasury receipts** with U.S. government securities as collateral.

Treasury bills (T-bills) mature in one year or less. They may have maturities of just a few days but generally four, eight, thirteen, twenty-six, or fifty-two weeks. The government issues Treasury notes (T-notes) with maturities of two, three, five, seven, or ten years and Treasury bonds (T-bonds) with maturities of more than ten years.

T-bills and Treasury receipts make no interest payments before maturity. Investors purchase them at a discount and receive the face value at maturity. Like corporate bonds, T-notes and T-bonds pay a fixed interest rate in semiannual payments, and the bondholder receives the face value at maturity.

The U.S. Treasury issues T-bills with face values of $100 or greater in multiples of $100, but usually $1000, with a maximum of $5 million. The Treasury issues T-bonds with face values of $1000 or more than $1000 in $100 increments if bought directly from the U.S. Treasury.

The level of inflation affects the earning power of period interest payments. The Treasury adjusts the effective interest rate, based on the change in the Consumer Price Index (CPI), by changing the principal amount on which it calculates the interest payments. The principal will not decrease below the issued value ($1000 for Treasury Inflation-Protected Securities [TIPS] with an issued maturity principal value of $1000.)

Treasury auctions are held on a regular basis:

- 13-week and 26-week bills weekly (Mondays)
- 2-year notes monthly
- 5-year notes monthly
- 10-year notes February, March, May, June, August, September, November, December

Buying treasuries correlates to investors' perceptions of the expected performance and strength of the U.S. economy. Low purchase activity would indicate that the U.S. economy is growing slowly or that the government would default.

The interest rate, or yield, of treasuries impacts other interest rates in the economy, such as home mortgages. High demand results in decreased yields, whereas low demand results in higher yields.

Agency

Agencies of the federal government, including the Government National Mortgage Association (GNMA, or Ginnie Mae), and government-sponsored enterprises (GSEs), including the Federal Farm Credit Banks (FFCBs) and Federal Home Loan Banks (FHLBs), borrow money by issuing securities. Even though the U.S. Treasury does not issue agency securities, investors expect them to pay without default. Agency securities pay a higher interest rate than Treasury securities. The Securities Act of 1933 exempted from registration any securities issued by the U.S. government or its agencies.

Debt instruments that are based on pools of home mortgages (mortgage-backed securities) include securities issued by the GNMA, the Federal National Mortgage Association (FNMA, or Fannie Mae), and the Federal Home Loan Mortgage Corporation (FHLMC, or Freddie Mac). An investor may purchase a mortgage-backed pass-through certificate, the most common of those issued by federal agencies. The certificate entitles the investor to share in the monthly cash flow of principal and interest payments (less administrative costs) made by homeowners represented in the pool of mortgages.

Corporate Bonds

A corporation can raise money to expand its operations through borrowing money by selling **corporate bonds**. The company makes regular interest payments on the bonds and pays the principal upon maturity. In the case of the company's liquidation, bondholders receive any earned but unpaid interest plus the principal before stockholders receive anything. Selling bonds does not share ownership or profits.

Although the market value of a bond may increase if interest rates decline, the owner of a bond does not typically expect any significant growth in the market value of the bond over its term.

A company offering a debt issue typically engages an investment bank as a lead underwriter to advise on the interest rate and other characteristics of the issue. The lead underwriter may form a syndicate by inviting other investment banks to assist in the selling of the issue in exchange for commission on the sales. The lead underwriter may advise the issue on questions such as increasing its marketability by offering convertible bonds. The bondholder would be able to convert the bonds to common stock with certain conditions in certain time frames. The issuer may include a provision to call or redeem the bonds earlier than the stated maturity date(s), especially if interest rates decline.

If specific assets of the company secure the bonds (secured bonds), in the event of liquidation those bondholders would have claim on the assets used to secure the bonds. Those assets could be mortgages on real estate (mortgage bonds), particular equipment used by the company in its operations (equipment trust certificates), or another business's securities or government securities placed in escrow by the firm offering the bonds (collateral trust bonds).

The general financial strength of the issuer, not specific assets, provides backing for unsecured bonds, or debentures. In the case of liquidation, they would have a later claim on the assets of the company than secured bonds but an earlier claim than stockholders. They usually have a higher interest rate than secured bonds.

Municipal Securities
Municipal bonds may be issued by governments other than the federal government and by authorities and commissions established by governments other than the federal government. These issuing governmental entities include states, territories, and possessions of the United States, counties, cities, school districts, and organizations they establish.

Interest received from municipal bonds is usually exempt from federal income tax. This makes the tax-effective rate higher than the coupon rate, and these are more attractive to persons and businesses as their marginal federal income tax rate increases. Federal capital gains income tax is paid on profits from the sale of municipal bonds. Although the interest paid on municipal bonds may be otherwise exempt from federal income tax, for certain taxpayers the interest may be subject to the alternative minimum tax.

The Municipal Securities Rulemaking Board (MSRB) seeks to issue rules that protect those involved and promote an equitable and well-organized market for municipal securities. Two fundamental rules include the following:

- MSRB Rule G-17 requires those who guide municipalities in issuing securities to honestly serve the municipalities and those who purchase their securities.

- MSRB Rule G-30 requires a dealer to use prices that are fair and reasonable when entering into transactions regarding municipal securities to buy from, or sell to, customers. It also requires a dealer to make a reasonable effort to find fair and reasonable prices for customers when arranging transactions with another party.

General Obligation (GO) Bonds
Rating agencies review the creditworthiness of the issuing authority and the terms of the issue because investors consider municipal bonds to be riskier than treasuries. The terms of the issue identify the basis

of the bond's guarantee. The full faith and credit of the issuing authority guarantees a general obligation (GO) bond. Only taxing authorities issue this kind of bond and only by voter approval.

General Obligation (GO) bonds enable the governmental unit to provide non–income-producing services for the entire community. Sources to provide debt service on GO bonds include state-collected taxes, such as income and sales tax for state GO bonds, and property taxes for local GO bonds. The revenue from selling GO bonds pays for operating expenses of the issuing government entity and for such things as construction and maintenance of government buildings, schools, roads without tolls, bridges, and parks.

Revenue Bonds

A source of revenue other than the full faith and credit of the issuing authority guarantees a **revenue bond**, so it does not require voter approval. The revenue generated by the project or facility for which the revenue bond was issued funds the interest payments and pays the principal at maturity.

For a municipality to sell an issue of bonds, the details of the issue may be advertised (competitive sale) or a specific underwriter selected (negotiated sale) who will purchase the bond issue and resell to its customers. The selected underwriter would ask potential purchasers for their interest (presale) before the issue is finally priced. A competitive sale would typically be most advantageous to the municipality. Several factors could lead to the municipality using a negotiated sale, including weak credit rating, high amount of issue, the municipality being newly established, creative characteristics of the issue, and a season of uncertainty in financial markets.

Revenue bonds generally support services that only benefit the persons paying for the services. Some funding for municipal projects comes from the interest on endowments. The commitment from the project to debt service may be prior to operating or other expenses (gross pledge) or after payment of operating expenses (net pledge). Because a source other than the full faith and credit of the issuing municipality will provide a revenue bond's debt service, potential purchasers of the bonds should carefully review the credit rating of the issue. Both the issue and the issuer are reviewed initially and periodically going forward to determine whether to change the rating. The following are the three most prominent agencies that rate bonds and the approximate market share of each:

- Standard & Poor's (S&P's) Global Ratings, 40 percent
- Moody's Investors Service, 40 percent
- Fitch Ratings, 15 percent

For a special tax bond, the credit rating could be affected by what is being taxed and whether its tax base or usage is expected to remain steady or change. For an education bond, the credit rating could be affected by the following:

- The perception of the school's reputation and expected ability to maintain stable enrollment
- The expectation that dependence on student aid or grants may be affected by government budget adjustments
- A rating firm's expectation that public universities will have more financial challenges than private ones if public tuition is not increasing as much as previously and labor costs are rising

A transportation bond's credit rating for a transit system may be affected by whether the municipality is highly dependent on public transportation and therefore might readily raise rates to ensure debt service. Rating firms may look carefully at healthcare/hospital bond issues because a noticeable portion of

municipal bonds in default are in this sector. Rating firms and therefore potential bond purchasers should consider the extent to which the revenue projects are essential and legal protections are in place for bondholders. Lower-rated bonds will usually need to pay higher interest rates. Careful investors will scrutinize lease rental bonds, which require legislative action for each budget cycle's payment to the trustee of monies for debt service as well as operating and other expenses. Revenue bonds typically pay a higher interest rate due to the higher perceived risk. Revenue bonds also usually involve a feasibility study to justify the issue.

When used to build facilities for the public, interest payments on revenue bonds are typically exempt from federal income tax and sometimes state income tax if the investor resides in the state where the bonds are issued. Examples include hospitals, bridges, toll roads, and airports. When used to build facilities not used by the public, they may not be exempt from federal income tax. GO bonds account for a little less than one-third of all sales of municipal bonds. Revenue bonds account for approximately two-thirds of those sales, with other types of bonds making up the remaining sales.

The following are major types of revenue bonds in approximate descending order of usage: transportation, utility/water and sewer/electric, special tax, hospital, education/dormitory, lease/rental, and other revenue bonds. Government entities use private activity bonds to improve the economic climate by allowing companies to lower their borrowing costs and provide some public benefit. The interest paid on these bonds is subject to federal income tax unless the bonds qualify for a federal exemption based on the use of the bond proceeds. For certain taxpayers, the interest on a qualified bond may be subject to the alternative minimum tax.

Revenue bonds are typically sold with a $5,000 principal value. Maturities typically range between twenty and thirty years. If the municipality does not want the entire issue to mature on the same date, it issues serial bonds, with some maturing on one date and others a later year.

Special tax bonds obtain revenues from taxing a specific item or activity, for example, hotel/motel room visits, gasoline, tobacco, alcohol, and excise taxes on gasoline used by vehicles on public roads.

If a state legislature approves a revenue bond issued by a municipality to be a moral obligation bond, the state is morally, but not legally, obligated to pay any shortfall in interest and principal if project revenues are inadequate. Defaulting on the pledge would affect the issuing government's credit rating because investors regard the moral obligation as credible as if it were legally binding.

These hybrid bonds are backed by the project's revenue as well as the full faith and credit of the municipality. They may be used with a wide variety of projects.

A private insurance company writes an insurance policy on the bond issue, which covers any default of the municipality due to inadequate funds or project revenue to provide debt service. An insured bond issue will have a higher credit rating than a noninsured issue, and therefore a lower interest rate could be paid. This lower interest rate helps offset the cost of insurance.

Type of Revenue Bond	Subtype	Project	Normal Revenue Source for Debt Service
Transportation	Airport	Airports	Landing/fuel fees, lease payments
	Highway/toll road	Toll roads	Tolls
	Highway/Bridges	Bridges	Gasoline tax
	Other	Tunnels and transit systems	User fees/government subsidies
Utility	Electric	Power plants	Sale of electricity
	Other	Gas, water, and sanitation	User rates and fees
Healthcare/ hospital	NA	Nonprofit hospitals/healthcare facilities	Hospital revenues
Education/college and university	Dormitory	Higher education housing/facilities	Students
	Student loan	College student loans	Loan repayments
Housing	NA	Single/multifamily housing	Mortgage payments
Special assessment	NA	Water/sanitation, sidewalks, streets	Paid by those who benefit
Private activity	All	Private entity	Private entity
	Industrial development revenue (IDR)	Private company's facility: factories, industrial parks, and stadiums	Fees, concessions, lease payments
Taxable municipal	NA	Significant benefit to only a small fraction of the general public	Paid by those who benefit

Debt with a term of less than one year (short-term) matches a company or individual having a short-term excess of needed cash with a counterpart having a short-term need for cash. The primary concern is the stability of the principal value and certainty of repayment when requested. The level of interest is typically of secondary concern.

Other Debt Instruments

Money Market Instruments

The **money market** refers to short-term investments for companies that have excess cash at the present time but will need it in a few days. Similarly, other companies may need cash for a few days but expect to have cash by then to repay the short-term debt. Similar instruments are in mutual funds, which individuals may use for cash positions requiring a stable value and a relatively low interest rate.

Certificate of Deposit (CD)

Certificates of deposit (CDs) are issued by a bank, usually with a higher rate of interest than a demand savings account, in exchange for keeping the cash for a known amount of time.

Bankers' Acceptance

A **bankers' acceptance** is a bank draft committing the bank to pay the bearer of the instrument a stated amount on a certain date, from 1 to 180 days from the date of issue but generally 90 days.

Commercial Paper

Commercial paper is an unsecured, short-term loan bought and sold at a discount from face value by corporations used for payroll, immediate expenses, inventory purchases, and other short-term liabilities. Commercial paper may last for only a few days and generally not longer than 270 days. Because it is unsecured, it is mainly used by large firms with high credit ratings in denominations of at least $100,000. Other companies, financial intermediaries, individuals with large amounts of cash, and investment companies are usually the purchasers of commercial paper.

Options

Options are derivative trading products that track the value of an underlying asset. Unlike stock rights and warrants, which are only issued by the issuer of the associated security, traders may develop options on an issuer's securities. Options trade with much more volume than rights or warrants. **FINRA Rule 2360** "Options" lists definitions and requirements regarding the use of options. Chicago Board Options Exchange (CBOE), the largest option exchange in the United States, published definitions in its Rule 1.1. CBOE rules were most recently updated May 11, 2020.

Options allow the buyer (holder) to possibly gain from market fluctuations in financial assets with less initial cash outlay than required to purchase them. The holder's amount at risk is the premium paid. The seller (writer) receives a premium and therefore profits if the option expires unused.

The holder of an option maintains the prerogative, but not necessity, to purchase or sell a stated quantity of an associated asset for a specific (exercise) price on or before a particular day and time (American style) or on a particular day (European style). All listed American stock options use American style. Listed stock index and foreign currency options predominantly use European style. Holders or writers of European-style options may trade during the time before expiration. Options expire on the third Friday of the expiration month.

If an investor purchases an option or sells an option based on an asset owned (covered, or long, position), the investor has a limited maximum possible loss. However, if an investor sells an option based on their obligation to purchase an asset or to sell an asset that the investor does not own (uncovered/naked, or short, position) at a specific price, the investor's maximum possible loss is unlimited. Largely due to this possibly devastating loss, before buying or selling an option, a person must receive a copy of the option disclosure document (ODD), formally named "Characteristics and Risks of Standardized Options."

It explains how options work and highlights risks an inexperienced investor considering using options should understand. The document is issued by the Options Clearing Corporation (OCC), a registered clearing agency that guarantees all options traded on registered American exchanges, known as listed options. As stated on OCC's website (theocc.com), the firm's purpose is to promote stability and financial integrity in the marketplaces by focusing on sound risk management principles. In this role of guarantor, the OCC oversees that the terms of contracts they clear are upheld and satisfied. The listed options have standardized terms regarding strike prices, expiration dates, settlements, and clearing.

Exchange-traded options have a larger number of transactions, making it easier to find a counterparty and reducing the cost for clearing compared with the OTC options market.

Options contracts purchased in the OTC market may have privately negotiated terms to serve the purpose of the investors involved. Because OTC options are not guaranteed by the OCC, the risk of nonperformance by either the buyer or seller is higher.

Types of Options
Puts and Calls
A **call option** is a contract to buy. A **put option** is a contract to sell. Either contract specifies the quantity of the associated asset, the (strike) price, and the month and year. The holder must provide notification of an intention to exercise the contract by 5:30 p.m. on the third Friday of the expiration month.

Equity vs. Index
Listed (exchange-traded) options deal with equity securities, stock indexes, government debt securities, or foreign currencies with standardized terms. Other options, including those with negotiated terms, trade OTC.

The exercise of an option begins when the holder notifies the broker-dealer of the intention to exercise the contract. The broker-dealer then notifies OCC. OCC issues the exercise notice to a broker-dealer who is randomly selected from all broker-dealers with a matching short option position. The broker-dealer who receives the exercise notice uses one of three methods to select a client and assign the notice to that writer. The assignment methods are random selection; first-in, first-out (FIFO); or any other method considered as fair and equitable. Each broker-dealer must notify their clients as to how assignments will be made.

Derivatives
Derivatives (including rights, call warrants, and call options) derive their value from the underlying security. Rights, call warrants, and call options provide no voting rights but do give the owner the opportunity to purchase a stock or perhaps a different type of security. A derivative's market value equals the sum of its intrinsic value plus its time value. Its intrinsic value equals the current market value of the underlying security minus the exercise price of the derivative. If positive, an immediate profit could be made by exercising the derivative and selling the underlying security at the current market price. If the derivative's market value exceeds its intrinsic value, the excess of the market value of the derivative over its intrinsic value is called the *time value*. The time value represents the investing public's perception of the opportunity for the intrinsic value to increase further before expiration.

The time value may be discounted for the dilution of future dividends over a greater quantity of shares outstanding. Theoretically, this discount could be lessened if the capital infusion provides hope for a proportionate increase in future dividends. A derivative is said to be "in the money" when the market price of the underlying security exceeds the strike price of the derivative, "out of the money" when the market price of the underlying security is less than the strike price of the derivative, and "at the money" when the market price of the underlying security is equal to the strike price of the derivative.

Packaged Products

Investors who seek the benefits of diversification without spending time to personally research and perform transactions in multiple investments may obtain investment advice, asset diversification, professional investment management, and reporting services through investment company products authorized in the Investment Company Act of 1940 ('40 Act) and variable contracts (annuities). The '40 Act mentions investment companies (closed-end and open-end), unit investment trusts (UITs), and face-amount certificate companies.

Types of Investment Companies
Closed-End Investment Companies
A ***closed-end investment company*** conducts itself like a company issuing common stock in several ways:

- It usually issues common shares when organized, such as an initial public offering (IPO) of common stock.
- Its shares are typically publicly traded throughout the trading day with no requirement to provide a prospectus after the initial issue.
- The shareholder cannot typically ask the closed-end investment company to redeem shares for cash.
- An investor purchasing shares of a closed-end investment company pays a commission.
- A closed-end investment company may also issue preferred stock or bonds.

Typically, one or more underwriters purchase the shares when initially issued. The purchasing underwriters then offer them on an exchange.

Open-End Investment Companies (Mutual Funds)
The most well-known category of investment companies are ***open-end investment companies***, which are called ***mutual funds***. For a mutual fund, transactions are not handled throughout the trading day. A mutual funds shareholder may place orders during the day, but the mutual fund company will only execute buy or sell orders for its mutual fund shares based on the net asset value (NAV) after trading ends for a given day. A front-end sales load may be added to purchases. A mutual fund company commits to purchasing back shares at the NAV calculated after closing, adjusted for the contingent deferred sales charge (CDSC), if any.

After trading has closed, the NAV is calculated by adding all the closing market values for the securities held in the portfolio and dividing that sum by the number of outstanding shares.

After purchasing shares in a mutual fund that is part of a fund family, the shareholder may typically exchange shares in the fund held for shares with an equivalent NAV as net transactions without any fees. When purchasing the shares, however, the investor may pay not only the NAV but also an initial sales charge ("front-end sales load"), some of which the investment management company uses to compensate representatives for soliciting the investor, advising the investor on the selection of fund(s) to purchase, and providing service to the investor after the sale. The sales load may be charged to the investor at the time of purchase (front-end sales load), at the time of sale as an exit fee or CDSC, or on a level basis during the time the investor owns the shares with a 12b-1 fee, which is defined in the corresponding section of the '40 Act.

FINRA allows 12b-1 fees with up to 0.75 percent of a fund's net assets per year for marketing and distribution purposes and up to 0.25 percent of a fund's net assets per year for shareholder service. These are deducted from the NAV daily.

Management companies may sell no-load funds directly to investors without a commissioned sales representative being involved. No-loads have no front-end load and no CDSC. FINRA allows a 12b-1 fee of up to 0.25 percent per year to be charged on a fund represented as a "no-load" fund.

The SEC's website (sec.gov) describes the contents of the primary disclosure document, or "prospectus," which may be one of two kinds. The more familiar is the long-form statutory prospectus. Some mutual funds provide the much shorter summary prospectus. Both provide the following information about the fund:

- Investment objectives
- Strategies for accomplishing those objectives
- Principal risks accepted by investing in the fund
- Fees and expenses
- Past performance

The longer prospectus has more information, such as the fund's investment managers and details of how to initiate purchase and sales transactions. Although mutual funds are required to provide a fund prospectus to an investor after purchasing shares, the investor has the prerogative to request a prospectus beforehand. If following the SEC's recommendation, the investor should read the prospectus before investing.

Because mutual funds sell shares as a primary issuance, the representative is expected to provide a prospectus prior to, or at the time of, every purchase without changing or marking on the prospectus. The representative is obligated to recommend a suitable class of shares of a suitable fund for the investor. The prospectus is intended to provide information to allow the investor to understand significant characteristics about the fund in order to make an informed choice rather than relying only on the representative's recommendation.

Upon request, the representative is required to provide a Statement of Additional Information (SAI), which must be included as Part B of the fund's registration statement to the SEC. This SAI is consistently revised and information is added to include not only the fund's financial statements, but also key information concerning management of said fund's activity, especially as surrounding its investments.

In addition to sales charges and/or 12b-1 fees, shareholders are charged an ongoing investment management fee and an ongoing service fee. The investment management fee may be minimized by the economies of scale because the management team executes transactions of a much greater size than an individual investor could. The investment management company provides services, such as handling account questions from the investor. The company also provides recordkeeping, which can help the investor when filing taxes as well as when reviewing performance of the investor's shares. The total of the ongoing investment management fee, service fee, and 12b-1 fee equals the expense ratio.

Investment management companies issue different types of share classes, which offer various combinations of sales charges and 12b-1 fees, so investors can select a sales charge appropriate to their investment horizon.

Long-term investors may benefit from Class A shares, paying a front-end sales charge, with little or no 12b-1 fees and no CDSC. If the cumulative purchases in a fund family reach certain amounts (breakpoints), the investor may obtain reduced up-front sales charges. ***FINRA Rule 2342*** requires mutual funds to let investors know the reductions available and forbids the sale of any amount that is close to, but less than, a breakpoint. If the investor signs a letter of intent to purchase shares up to a given breakpoint, the investor has thirteen months to invest the amount qualifying for a breakpoint.

For purchases during that thirteen-month period, the reduced sales charge for the breakpoint will be allowed for all purchases. If cumulative purchases do not reach the breakpoint by the end of the thirteen-month period, the investment company will charge back the amount of the sales charge discount that was not earned. Rights of accumulation (ROAs) allow an investor to receive a discount on the front-end sales charge when purchasing additional shares by adding the purchase amount to the market value of shares in the same class already held in the fund family.

Some investors may consider a short-term or medium-term investment to get acquainted with mutual funds. These investors may be open to eventually changing to a long-term investment. Such persons could benefit from Class B shares, paying no up-front sales charge but incurring 12b-1 fees and a CDSC when liquidating the shares if held less than five or six years. If the investor ends up holding the shares for longer than originally intended (usually at least seven or eight years), Class B shares may convert to Class A shares, ending the ongoing 12b-1 fees and having no CDSC.

Investors who are just starting to get acquainted with investment companies and are uncertain as to their investment horizon may prefer Class C shares. Class C shares may or may not have a front-end load (if so, sometimes 1 percent). Class C shares will typically have permanent 12b-1 fees, which are higher than the 12b-1 fees on Class A shares and equal to the 12b-1 fees on Class B shares. A Class C shareholder will typically incur a 1 percent CDSC if selling shares within one year of their purchase. Class C shares typically do not convert to Class A shares. Class C shares may have less sales costs early in the holding period, but if held for the long term they may have significantly more sales charges (through unending 12b-1 fees) than either Class A or Class B shares.

Regulators have scrutinized the behavior of representatives who sell management company shares without regard to the suitability of the sales charge to the investor's time horizon. In response, some mutual fund companies developed Class T shares, which have lower maximum sales charges. The maximum front-end sales charge is typically 2.5 percent, with a 0.25 percent 12b-1 fee.

Investors owning a variable annuity, which is typically a long-term investment, who want the choice of treating it as a short-term investment may prefer Class L shares. Class L shares allow payment to begin earlier than other shares but with higher associated costs.

Some mutual fund companies issue "clean shares," which have no sales load or 12b-1 fees. Advisers may charge for their advice when recommending these shares. In that case, the investor can more clearly see the fees.

Unit Investment Trusts (UITs)

In contrast with closed-end and open-end investment companies, **Unit Investment Trusts (UITs)** are not governed by boards of directors. They have no ongoing management fees because they are not actively managed investment portfolios. Instead, the sponsor writes a trust indenture to form a UIT. The indenture typically specifies either a trustee, custodian, or agency but most often a trustee, so reference in this explanation will be made to a trustee. The indenture also specifies an evaluator which, under U.S. law, cannot be the same entity as the trustee. Per the terms of the indenture, the sponsor selects a set of income-producing investments and provides to the trustee either the investments or legal documents obligating the sponsor to provide the investments.

In return, the sponsor receives unit certificates that document ownership. The evaluator appraises the investments to help determine the unit offering price. The UIT and the ownership units are registered so the units may be sold to the public through one or more underwriters. The trustee then holds the investments, maintains investor records, and handles financial and tax reporting requirements. The UIT is formed with a stated termination date, although it may not be for decades after establishment. On that date, all invested assets are sold, with the proceeds going to the investors. UITs do not use investment managers after the initial selection. UITs issue shares of beneficial interest (SBIs), usually in amounts of at least $1,000, each representing an undivided interest in the UIT's set of securities in proportion to the amount of money invested. Investors buy and sell SBIs on exchanges.

A UIT is different from an open-end fund (mutual fund) in that a UIT is a trust, as its name indicates, administered by a trustee and with no board of directors. A mutual fund is typically a corporation with a board of directors. When established, a UIT's investments are selected and held, whereas a mutual fund is actively managed throughout its existence. A UIT has costs of setting up the trust, conducting the IPO, executing the purchase of the investments, up-front sales charges, CDSCs, and lower ongoing fees for the simplified management of the trust. A mutual fund may have an up-front sales charge and a CDSC but usually does not incur as many expenses to begin operation.

Partly due to an active management and distribution process, a mutual fund typically has higher ongoing fees, including but not limited to administrative, investment management, custody, and 12b-1 fees. A UIT's assets are typically fully invested, whereas a mutual fund's assets are usually not. A UIT issues an IPO and may continue to issue additional units. Without the focus of an initial offering, mutual funds deliberately pursue a process of continually issuing shares. A UIT's unit's value is determined daily, and the units of many UITs trade throughout the trading day on an exchange. A mutual fund's share value is also determined daily, but its shares do not trade on an exchange. A UIT has a stated termination date, whereas a mutual fund does not.

Face-Amount Certificate Company

A **face-amount certificate company** issues debt certificates that pay a set interest rate. Investments occur in a lump sum or installments, receiving fixed interest payments if held until maturity. Redemptions prior to maturity receive a discounted surrender value.

Variable Contracts/Annuities

Investors may also obtain investment advice, asset diversification, professional investment management, and reporting services by purchasing a variable contract (variable annuity) with an insurance company. Equity-indexed contracts (EICs) have some features of variable annuities.

Benefits of a variable annuity (or an EIC) can include the following:

- Income tax deferral, even if not within a qualified retirement account
- Investments in excess of the limits for qualified retirement accounts
- Selection of investments/subaccounts that resemble mutual funds
- (EIC) selection of index investments that track stock market activity, along with a selection of limited or no downside exposure
- Converting the investment value into a series of guaranteed regular payments (annuitization)
- (EIC) "bonus" additions in excess of the cash amount invested as the basis for calculating death benefits and annuitization, subject to certain conditions
- Death benefits for one or more beneficiaries

In the past, annuitization required the abandonment of ownership of the accumulated investment balance. However, variable annuities now offer an increasing selection of payment choices as a combination of death benefit and annuitization options, including the following:

- Payments for the life of the annuitant, usually the contract owner
- Payments for the combined life of the annuitant and another person
- Payments for the life of the contract owner or for a certain amount of time, with payments made to a beneficiary for the remainder of the specified time if the contract owner dies before the end of that time
- Payments for the life of the contract owner, with remaining value at death passing to a beneficiary, either in a lump sum or in periodic payments

Variable annuities are typically purchased for an extended number of years, with surrender charges if liquidated during the surrender period. The surrender period is a set number of years, as specified in the contract, but is typically between six and ten years. As mentioned above, investors owning a variable annuity may prefer Class L shares, allowing the option to treat it as a short-term investment but with additional costs. Variable contracts typically have more guarantees than mutual funds, UITs, or SBIs, so internal fees are higher.

Representatives are typically paid commissions for selling variable annuities that are proportionally greater than for selling other investment products. Therefore, *FINRA Rule 2330* requires the company issuing the variable annuity and the representative soliciting and recommending the variable annuity to ensure the suitability of the contract as a whole and the selection of specific investment choices (subaccounts) for the investor.

If the representative is recommending that the investor replace another annuity or life insurance product in order to fund the purchase of a variable annuity or EIC, the comparison of the benefits of the new contract with the previous product should be provided to the investor. A variable contract application to replace a product issued less than thirty-six months earlier requires justification, especially if the replaced product incurs a surrender charge. The representative is expected to know enough about the investor's overall financial objectives, liquidity, and net worth to determine the suitability for recommending a variable annuity. For example, the representative may be expected to document that the investor owns liquid assets equal to living expenses for a certain amount of time, such as one year.

Equity Indexed Contracts (EICs)
An *equity indexed contract (EIC)* provides the contract holder with a minimum guaranteed rate of return along with a limited upside potential that is linked to the increase in an equity index. For example,

one choice may be the greater of a minimum interest rate of 4 percent or 80 percent of the increase in the S&P Index, up to a maximum of 8 percent.

For example, if the S&P Index increases by 12 percent, 80 percent of 12 percent equals 9.6 percent. The contract would be credited with 8 percent, which is the maximum upside potential but greater than the guaranteed minimum 4 percent.

If the S&P 500 Index increases 7 percent, 80 percent of 7 percent is 5.6 percent, which is greater than the guaranteed minimum return of 4 percent. The contract would be credited with 5.6 percent.

On the other hand, if the S&P Index decreases by 5 percent, the contract would be credited with the minimum 4 percent return. Thus, the contract is protected on the downside. EICs may have a surrender charge for up to fifteen years, so the representative must know enough about the contract holder's finances to reasonably expect the funds will not be needed during the surrender period.

Municipal Fund Securities

The term ***municipal fund security***, per MSRB Rule D-12, refers to a municipal security issued by an issuer that is similar to an investment company except that it is not primarily involved in holding or trading securities, like a governmental unit—generally a state or municipality. In other words, a municipal fund is like a mutual fund except it is managed by a municipal (or state) government instead of a private investment company. So, a municipal fund security may be backed by some of the same types of securities owned by mutual funds.

The selection of securities is determined by the purpose of the fund. Therefore, municipal fund securities may not resemble traditional municipal securities, many of which are municipal bonds. The value of a municipal fund security will vary with the sum of the market values of all securities held rather than having values determined by a single issuer, such as principal values, coupon rates, and maturity dates. Three forms of municipal fund securities are local government investment pools (LGIPs), 529 college savings plans, and 529A plans. MSRB Rule G-45 requires reporting by those administering 529 savings plans or Achieving a Better Life Experience (ABLE) Act programs, including the following:

- Semiannually: program description, assets, asset allocation description for each allocation choice, contributions, withdrawals, fees, and costs
- Annually: performance data

529 Plans

Section 529 of the Internal Revenue Service (IRS) Code, as amended in 1996, provides for states to sponsor two types of tax-deferred plans to assist in advanced planning for college costs; prepaid tuition plans (PTPs), which are not considered to be municipal fund securities; and college savings plans, which are considered to be municipal fund securities.

Prepaid Tuition Plans (PTPs)
Prepaid tuition plans (PTPs) are designed to prepay tuition costs at public colleges and universities, perhaps only in the state in which the person prepaying tuition resides. Donors can choose to pay tuition amounts at one time in a lump-sum payment or in a series of installments. The price of the specific contract is set before it is purchased, typically depending on the characteristics of the contract, the current and projected cost of tuition, and the current grade of the beneficiary.

Some PTPs freeze the college cost for future students at current levels, guaranteeing to cover future increases. They may cover one to five years of tuition, book, and lab fees and sometimes dormitory rent or meals. Other plans may be applied to graduate school. The PTP donor has no choice of investments. Some PTP plans allow for the beneficiary to be changed to a sibling, depending on the sibling's age. If an exchange is not allowed and the donor cancels the plan, any earnings on the plan may be lost and only the original contribution will be returned. Some PTP contracts may deduct an exit fee from withdrawals.

College Savings Plans

College savings plans are made with after-tax dollars and offer a sometimes-limited selection of investments in a tax-deferred account. Investment choices may include age-based selections adjusted as the beneficiary ages by reallocating assets from equities to debt instruments as college approaches. Dividends, interest, and capital gains are generally tax-exempt at the federal level. Depending on the characteristics of the plan, they may or may not be tax-exempt at the state level. Eligible college costs may include tuition and fees, room and board, books, supplies, and equipment.

Since 2018, up to $10,000 may be distributed annually from the funds of 529 college savings plans for expenses related to grades kindergarten through grade 12 at public, private, or religious institutions.

With the 529 plan, the annual $15,000 limit for any person to give a tax-free gift to any other person may be multiplied by five and given in one year rather than over a five-year time span. So, a donor may initially contribute $75,000 each to 529 plans for several beneficiaries. However, each state determines the total amount that may be contributed to a 529 plan. Usually, the limit is what is adequate for an undergraduate degree.

Some plans allow an unlimited time frame for the plan, with the donor able to maintain control of funds no longer in the donor's estate. The donor may transfer the assets in the plan to another 529 plan twice each year without incurring current income tax as long as the beneficiary is not changed. This may be done to take advantage of lower fees, a better return, or a more generous state tax treatment. Some plans allow a change of beneficiary once a year, which can be helpful for the following reasons:

- If a family wishes to begin a plan for an unborn child, a spouse may be named beneficiary until the baby is born.

- If investment changes are desired more frequently than twice per year, an investment change can be made when the beneficiary is changed.

- If a family is using one plan to provide for multiple children (a separate plan for each child allows each plan's investment horizon to match each child's age).

- If funds are left over after the original beneficiary finishes the desired education, a transfer may be made to a qualifying relative with the exemption from federal income tax remaining intact.

Some states offer direct-sold 529 plans through a website or by mail only to their residents. Direct-sold investors may pay lower fees, and they receive no personalized professional investment advice. Some states offer adviser-sold 529 plans through broker-dealers who have met the state requirements. Adviser-sold plans may have higher fees and offer investment advice from a professional adviser.

Local Government Investment Pools (LGIPs)

To support efficient management of government entities' cash reserves, one or more state or local governments set up a *Local Government Investment Pool (LGIP)* trust. Multiple state agencies or municipalities then pool their cash reserves into the trust. The trust is established according to the state's law. The investment objectives may include minimal principal risk, daily availability without penalty, and a favorable rate of return. As more government moneys (not private moneys) are placed in LGIPs, all participants gain from diversification, professional asset management, and the spread of management costs over a larger investment base.

Section 529A Plans (529 ABLE)

A disabled person otherwise eligible for Supplemental Security Income (SSI) benefits from the Social Security Administration will be disqualified from receiving SSI if the person owns assets worth more than $2,000 or earns more than the income limit, also known technically as the federal benefit rate (FBR). The FBR is $841 per month in 2022. The ABLE Act allows families to make after-tax contributions (for federal income tax purposes) to a state-managed savings account and use that account to supplement future private insurance and government benefits. Medicare or Social Security payments and state benefits will not be reduced because of the ABLE savings account as long as it equals $100,000 or less. If the ABLE savings account value is temporarily above $100,000, federal and state aid will be suspended but restarted when the ABLE value is again below $100,000. Contributions up to $15,000 annually and totaling no more than $500,000 may be deposited in an ABLE account. Depending on the state, contributions may be nontaxable for state income tax purposes.

Earnings withdrawn for qualified expenses are income-tax free. Earnings withdrawn for nonqualified expenses are taxable at ordinary rates, and a 10 percent tax penalty applies. The ABLE Act authorized the rollover of up to $15,000 per year without penalty from a 529 college savings plan into an ABLE account of the 529 plan's beneficiary or a qualifying relative. When a person dies or is no longer disabled, the remaining contents of the ABLE plan repay the state Medicaid payments that were made after setting up the ABLE account. The investments may be eligible for a tax-free transfer to a brother or sister. The MSRB maintains the online repository, the Electronic Municipal Market Access (EMMA) system (emma.msrb.org). EMMA contains information regarding 529 plans and 529A (ABLE) plans.

Direct Participation Programs (DPPs)

Some investors choose nontraditional investments, which, broadly speaking, are investments other than cash, stocks, and bonds. These nontraditional investments will often be "unlisted," that is, not traded on national exchanges. Investing in these assets can have benefits, including diversification into asset classes whose values will likely not correlate with the fluctuations of the markets for stock and bonds. However, investors who are interested in direct participation programs (DPPs), as well as broker-dealers and representatives who consider offering DPP-related services to investors, should understand their characteristics and the associated SEC and FINRA regulations. For example, the ability to sell ownership units of DPP products is not like selling a stock on a registered exchange. The units are generally illiquid because they are usually not redeemed by the issuer during the time frame of the undertaking, which could be lengthy. Also, they are not traded on a national exchange. However, in some cases, another purchaser may be found.

One classification of nontraditional investments is the DPP, also known as *direct participation plan*, which is described in the Securities Act of 1933. A DPP is defined by *FINRA Rule 2310* as follows:

Direct participation program (program)—a program which provides for flow-through tax consequences regardless of the structure of the legal entity or vehicle for distribution including, but not limited to, oil and gas programs, real estate programs, agricultural programs, cattle programs, condominium securities, Subchapter S corporate offerings and all other programs of a similar nature, regardless of the industry represented by the program, or any combination thereof .... Excluded from this definition are real estate investment trusts, tax qualified pension and profit sharing plans pursuant to Sections 401 and 403(a) of the Internal Revenue Code and individual retirement plans under Section 408 of that Code, tax sheltered annuities pursuant to the provisions of Section 403(b) of the Internal Revenue Code, and any company including separate accounts, registered pursuant to the Investment Company Act.

Investors in a DPP join directly with others in a business undertaking's finances and are taxed only once on profits ("pass-through tax treatment") reported as passive on their personal income tax returns. The tax returns of the DPP owners reflect their proportionate part of the DPP's financial results, including operating losses. The DPP is not an income tax–paying entity. This avoids double taxation, as happens when a tax-paying entity, such as a corporation, distributes after-tax profit to the owners, such as through dividends, which are taxable to the stockholder.

Types of DPPs
A DPP's legal entity may be structured as a general partnership, a joint venture, or a subchapter S corporation. Many are formed as limited partnerships (LPs) or limited liability corporations (LLCs), investing in real estate. The DPP real estate project's anticipated duration is usually over an extended time frame of many months or even years. So, the DPP is not structured for public trading and the associated liquidity, unlike listed equities, debt securities, and options, which are traded daily on national exchanges. The below explanation will expand on DPPs that are real estate LPs and then compare and contrast that business model with tenant in common (TIC) real estate transactions, which also allow the participant to share directly in the finances of the undertaking but in a different way.

Limited Partnerships
The partnership must have one general partner (GP) who invests at least 1 percent of the partnership's capital, manages the program, and retains unlimited liability. The limited partnership (LP) entity owns all assets and is party to all mortgage loans. Only the GP can provide a guarantee on a loan. The GP has a fiduciary relationship to limited partners by receiving capital contributions, directing the program, and maintaining accounting records. The GP receives compensation for these services. Not reporting to a board of directors, the GP may operate with limited oversight.

The partnership must also have at least one (passive investor) limited partner with limited liability who generally has no voice in the program's management. If a limited partner participates in management decisions, the limited partner incurs the risk of being identified as a GP, thereby taking on unlimited liability.

Depending on the terms of the capital call agreement in the partnership agreement, the limited partner(s) may make a commitment to contribute a total amount of capital, to be provided as installments, upon identification of investment opportunities; for example, properties to purchase. At that time, the GP will make a capital call, or "draw down," giving the limited partner(s) a specific amount of time in which to transfer the funds to the GP. A limited partner's failure to meet the capital call may or may not result in a reduction or loss of the limited partner's (or LLC member's) interest, depending on state law and state court decisions.

A limited partner's year-end tax planning and filing may need to consider changes in related tax laws or IRS rulings that could impact future profitability.

Tenants in Common (TIC)

Tenants in common (TIC) transactions typically involve real estate. Section 1031 of the IRS code allows an owner of real estate to postpone tax on realized capital gains if the proceeds of a sale are invested in another similar property, or "like-kind" property. TICs are helpful for investors who need to complete a Section 1031 tax-deferred exchange, which has strict time frames. Section 1031 allows a forty-five-day time frame for locating up to three potential replacement real estate investments. Section 1031 limits the time to complete the replacement transaction to no more than 180 days after the replaced property was sold or the latest date for filing income tax for the year of the transaction, whichever is earlier. For real estate investors who recognize changes in the real estate market, the Section 1031 exchange can be valuable if the qualifications for the tax-free exchange are fulfilled.

All participants are borrowers who individually sign the mortgage. The loan is generally nonrecourse, so the participants would have no personal liability to the mortgage company from personal assets. Because each loan could be unique, a lender could require TIC investors to sign personal guarantees in case certain actions are taken or not taken regarding the loan, such as embezzlement, voluntary bankruptcy, refusal of property inspections, and delinquency on real estate taxes.

LPs Compared with TICs

Real estate LPs and TICs have some similarities. Both provide investors the opportunity to join with others in real estate investment to obtain the "pass-through" tax benefit. Both are structured as securities for securities law purposes and partnerships or LLCs for tax purposes. Here are some other comparisons:

Formation
- LP: A GP files a Certificate of LP with the state. Each LP receives a certificate with its units and the percentage of ownership it represents.
- TIC: A TIC generally exists only for a transaction or a set of transactions. In many cases, no legal entity is formed. An LLC may be formed, with no tax significance. A participant receives a deed as evidence of ownership.

Transfer of Ownership/Participation
- LP: The certificate can be assigned to the next owner with GP approval.
- TIC: The lender must approve the investor candidate as a new borrower on the mortgage.

Capital Call
- LP: An LP may have no personal liability and no obligation to fulfill any capital call above the original commitment, as specified in the partnership agreement.
- TICs: Investors would be responsible for their proportionate part of the needed funds.

Major Decisions
- LP: The LP entity's decisions can generally be made either by the GP alone or a majority of the limited partner interests. The minority may have no effective voice.
- TIC: Significant actions about the property, such as sales, refinancing, leases, or renewal of a management contract, require unanimous concurrence of all TICs. Otherwise, the action would wait until all TICs agree. TIC agreements typically include a way to buy out a resistant TIC.

Quantity of Investors Involved

- LP: Securities law may limit the sponsor to fewer than 500 investors. The IRS code has no limit.
- TIC: The IRS code limits the number of investors in any one transaction to 35.

Investment Amount

- LP: The minimum capital commitment by an LP could be as low as $5,000 but is generally approximately $25,000.
- TIC: One published report of the average cash investment in TICs was approximately $400,000.

Secondary Markets

- LP: Because some broker-dealers maintain contact information about unlisted DPPs and receive commissions for their help, investors interested in learning about opportunities to invest in DPPs such as LPs may more easily find assistance than if trying to learn about some other nontraditional investments.
- TIC: A TIC investor may need to search carefully for a buyer of ownership in a TIC.

Real Estate Investment Trusts (REITs)

One nontraditional investment category excluded from the FINRA Rule 2310 definition of DPPs is ***real estate investment trusts (REITs)***. The Securities Act of 1933 sets requirements for REITs, including the sending of prospectuses to public purchasers. Although REITs have some features in common with mutual funds, REITs were not addressed by the '40 Act. An REIT investment typically contains several properties.

The Internal Revenue Code allows an REIT to avoid double taxation on dividends if 90 percent of the ordinary income generated from assets is distributed to investors. In addition, 20 percent of the income distributed by an REIT is nontaxable if the REIT passes the following income tests:

- At least 95 percent of its gross income must be derived from dividends, interest, and rents from real property.
- At least 75 percent of its gross income must be derived from real property income.
- No more than 30 percent of its gross income may be derived from the sale or disposition of stock or securities that have been held for less than twelve months.

REITs generally provide regular dividends, which is partly what attracts investors to them. These dividends are fully taxable to their shareholders as ordinary income, and REITs do not pass operating losses to their shareholders.

Types of REITs

REITs may be categorized by the way they are invested:

- ***Mortgage REITs:*** Like banks, these earn cash flow from the difference in interest rates between money borrowed from investors and mortgages made to purchasers of real estate.

- ***Equity REITs:*** Equity REITs take ownership in income-producing properties and manage them. Rents in excess of expenses represents profit with a cash flow. Appreciation in property values would provide capital gains.

- *Hybrid REITs:* These use mortgage interest rate spreads (like mortgage REITs do) and rent and capital gains on commercial buildings (as equity REITs do) to provide cash flows from both types of sources.

Like REITs, DPPs often invest in real estate. The following real estate organizations offer education and/or networking for persons interested in alternative investments in real estate:

- Because of the influence of the 1986 tax act on the real estate industry, the Real Estate Investment Association (www.reia.org) was formed by real estate business people to "... identify new business opportunities, share information that could benefit their survival and future growth, and promote networking that would not only provide introductions but lead to collaboration on new business ventures between members."

- The Institute for Portfolio Alternatives (www.ipa.com) is an advocacy group for investments such as REITs, business development companies (BDCs), interval and close-end funds, energy and equipment leasing programs, and private-equity funds, among others, which can include DPPs.

Hedge Funds

Another alternate investment to cash, stocks, and bonds is a *hedge fund*. Although it shares the second word of mutual fund, it has many differences from most mutual funds, and there are vast differences among hedge funds. Hedge funds must be treated as an entirely new and broad category of pooled alternate investment. In some cases, mutual funds are adding hedging processes to their fund management practices, especially to reduce risk to the overall portfolio.

Hedging
Hedge fund refers to a fund whose goal is typically to attain "absolute return," that is, favorable returns in both good markets, and bad by "hedging" the market. Hedging typically involves balancing the risk of purchasing one investment by purchasing another investment that will do well when the other investment does poorly. Examples of hedging strategies include the use of short selling, derivatives, inverse exchange-traded funds (ETFs), and assets whose values do not correlate with stocks or bonds.

However, the term hedge fund encompasses a large variety of funds, some of which pursue goals in addition to mere hedging. Many hedge funds also pursue a goal to obtain returns superior to the market when the market does well. This may be attempted using leverage, that is, borrowing to purchase more investments than the capital invested in the fund. It could also involve long-term investments, such as real estate, that may provide a better return over an extended amount of time.

Additional Costs
When a hedge fund manager pursues investment policies that will do well in a down market and better than an up market, additional costs may be incurred, including the following:

- Ongoing research of opportunities that are "outside the box," including investments and strategies that many mutual fund investment managers are forbidden to pursue, or at least many mutual fund managers would not choose to explore as an additional cost.

- Purchasing derivatives, such as puts or calls, in addition to the underlying securities when exercised, may be costs that the typical mutual fund manager would not incur.

- Significant compensation to the hedge fund manager tasked with accomplishing the unique goals of the hedge fund may be included.

Offshore and Onshore Hedge Funds

The fund manager may choose to set up two funds so that both non-U.S. and U.S. investors can benefit from the manager's strategy.

For non-U.S. investors who are not subject to U.S. taxes, **offshore hedge funds** are usually established as offshore corporations with articles of incorporation and are domiciled outside the United States (e.g., Bermuda, Cayman Islands). The legal document, or offering document, describes the investment activity of the fund.

For U.S. investors who are subject to U.S. taxes, **onshore hedge funds** are usually established as LLCs or LPs using a legal document called a partnership agreement.

Another document, the subscription agreement, which states the number of shares purchased, price per share, why the securities are exempt from registration with the SEC, and an evaluation of risk, is typically required for each investor. The fund's GP as well as the investor must sign it. The subscription agreement typically includes documentation that the deal is appropriate for the subscriber. One reason hedge fund investors need significant financial resources is that the minimum investment for a hedge fund is typically no less than $100,000, and in many funds, it is $1 million.

Transparency

The **private placement memorandum (PPM)**, or offering document, serves a function like a prospectus for public issues, informing a prospective investor of the following, along with other details regarding the fund:

- Its mode of operations
- The people on the team
- How the fund manager intends to pursue the stated goals
- Reasons for possible delays or failures to meet the goals
- Fees
- Restrictions

Comparison with Mutual Funds

Because mutual funds are so relatively well known, reviewing the similarities and differences between them and hedge funds may aid in learning how different most hedge funds are from most mutual funds. This could provide a person who has knowledge and experience with mutual funds some protection from overconfidence that one's mutual funds knowledge and experience automatically transfers to dealing with hedge funds.

As the chart below shows, both mutual funds and hedge funds pool investors' money to make a positive return. Both are subject to prohibitions against fraud and owe a fiduciary duty to the investors. However, those few similarities are not enough to allow a person experienced with mutual funds to assume other similarities that do not exist. For example, hedge funds generally have fewer constraints on their approaches to investment and may significantly change their approaches without notice or approval of the investors. Hedge funds generally use more leverage, short selling, and derivatives than most mutual funds. Mutual funds that use derivatives may use them for hedging, whereas many hedge funds may use derivatives to increase returns in rising markets as well as hedging against declining markets. Hedge funds

54

may focus on a specific company or industry in a way that most mutual funds would not. Hedge funds may engage in arbitrage, which is taking advantage of inefficiencies in the markets by purchasing an investment and then immediately liquidating the same, or a similar investment. Most mutual funds would do little or no arbitrage.

Mutual funds register with the SEC as registered investment advisers (RIAs) with a high level of disclosure and representations are relatively easy to verify, which provides significant protections to their investors. To become an RIA, a person passes either the Series 65 Exam (Uniform Investment Adviser Law Exam) or both the Series 7 Exam (General Securities Representative Exam) and the Series 66 Exam (Uniform Combined State Law Exam). Many hedge fund companies are not set up as RIAs, so they may not advertise freely. Hedge funds may disseminate information on the internet, and the SEC reviews that information.

A wealthy individual may make up one's mind based on a hedge fund's history and the manager's explanation, without reference to others' opinions. A philanthropic institution with a large amount to invest may be interested in the benefits of a hedge fund, partly because one or more major donors have invested in a hedge fund. However, the organization's decision may take longer because it is done by a board that wants more information before finalizing the decision. Such an organization may retain an investment professional to assist in guiding the decision-making process.

Hedge fund investors are typically institutions or high net-worth investors. These organizations and individuals likely have experience and expertise or can afford to hire persons with experience and expertise, which allows the hedge fund the opportunity to be analyzed with an awareness of the special risks involved, including general illiquidity, use of leverage, and long-term investment horizons.

Accredited Investors

If the hedge fund does not plan to charge performance-based fees, the SEC defines a category of accredited investors who may invest in the fund. Over the life of a hedge fund, the SEC allows it to have no more than thirty-five investors who do not qualify as accredited investors. For example, these may be relatives or close acquaintances of the hedge fund management team. The SEC's Rule 501(a) of Regulation D defines an accredited investor as one of the following:

- A financial institution, such as a bank or pension plan
- A director, executive officer, or a GP of the issuer
- An individual with a net worth of at least $1 million (not including the individual's primary home)
- An individual who has two years of income greater than $200,000 annually and reasonably expects the same level of income to continue
- A couple who have two years of income greater than $300,000 annually and reasonably expects that same level of income to continue

Qualified Clients

A hedge fund may only charge performance-based fees to **qualified clients**, which includes those in one of the following categories:

- Net worth of at least $2.1 million, not counting the first home
- Executive officer, trustee, GP, director, or employee of the adviser
- At least $1 million in assets under management (AUM), with the adviser immediately after the investment advisory contract begins

- "Qualified purchaser," which is made up of persons or firms in one of the following categories:
  - An individual, who is then also known as a ***super-accredited investor*** because of the requirement for greater financial assets, which is at least $5 million in invested assets
  - A trust, if not set up mainly to invest in the fund
  - A professional investment manager or corporation controlling investments of $25 million or more

The potential number of investors in a typical mutual fund is unlimited, and most members of the general public can benefit from investing in one or more mutual funds. Daily liquidity provides mutual fund investors with the ability to redeem or exchange shares at will. Therefore, they may hold more of their unneeded assets in mutual funds and less in cash equivalents.

In contrast, the maximum number of investors for a hedge fund is generally one hundred or five hundred, and those are limited to institutions and individuals with a certain level of income or net worth. The '40 Act provides two ways in which a private investment company may be exempt from some SEC rules and reporting. Section 3(c)(1) allows this exemption if no more than one hundred persons invest and the company is not currently making a public offering (PO) and is not planning to make a PO.

Section 3(c)(7) allows this exemption if the company has up to 499 "qualified clients" and is not currently making a PO and is not planning to make a PO. One significant difference is the long-term nature of hedge funds, indicated by typical lock-in periods of at least one year, surrender fees for as many as seven years, and opportunities to withdraw funds only once a month, once a quarter, or once each year.

Description	Mutual Funds	Hedge Funds
Pools investors' money	Yes	Yes
Invests to make positive return	Yes	Yes
Subject to prohibitions against fraud	Yes	Yes
Managers owe fiduciary duty	Yes	Yes
Flexibility	Expected to follow stated strategy; considerable constraints	Fewer constraints; can also change strategy significantly
Use leverage (borrowing)	Generally not	May use
Short selling	Not often	More often
Derivatives	Limited	May use significantly
Subject to regulations to protect investors	More	Less
Registered with the SEC	Yes	Depending on amount of assets but most are not
Level of disclosure	High	Low
Representations	Easier to verify	May be difficult to verify

Description	Mutual Funds	Hedge Funds
Protections common to most mutual funds	Yes	Investors do not receive the same
Potential number of investors	Unlimited	Under 3(c)(1), not more than 100 investors. Under 3(c)(7), fewer than 500 investors who must all be "qualified clients"
Generally must be an accredited investor to invest	No	Yes
May advertise freely	Yes	No
Marketing paperwork	Prospectus	PPM
Suitable investors	Most of general public	Only carefully defined, sophisticated investors
Liquidity	Generally daily	Long-term; may have one-year lock-in, withdrawal fees, and monthly, quarterly, or annual withdrawals

As larger institutions attempt to accomplish their goals of favorable ("absolute") returns by investing in hedge funds, those funds are asked to disclose what they contain as well as their characteristics.

Because the hedge fund manager's ability to choose investments is proprietary, the institutions' appetite for information may be satisfied through summary reporting of risk factors inherent in investments that are being held, without detailed listings of specific investments currently held.

Hedge funds are sometimes connected with investors by using a third-party marketer, an outside person/firm who contacts potential clients for the funds. Various websites provide information on potential third-party marketers. Brokers, banks, and insurance agents may have clients they refer to hedge funds. Hedge fund consultants and hedge "fund of funds" (FOF) managers may also aid in finding investors. An (FOF) is a fund that purchases shares of other funds. This attempts a greater degree of numerical diversification through an increase in the sheer number of underlying securities held by all the funds combined. An investor may also use an FOF as a tool for asset allocation by choosing different types of funds according to the desired proportions of various asset classes.

Compensation

Another difference between mutual funds and hedge funds is how the investment manager is compensated for managing the fund. Although the SEC does not limit the sales charge of mutual funds, FINRA does limit the charge to 8.5 percent of the fund's PO price, that is, the sum of the NAV plus the sales charge. However, hedge funds expect a greater return and are more complex to manage, and so they typically charge fees that are higher and different in nature. One typical fee structure is a two-and-twenty fee, in which the hedge fund manager receives an annual management fee equal to 2 percent of the net value of the AUM, charged quarterly (instead of daily for mutual funds), and in addition to that, a performance fee of 20 percent of all profits.

A smaller hedge fund may determine the annual management fee percentage based on the operating costs of managing the fund. A larger fund may offer a higher management fee percentage to attract and retain expert fund management personnel.

Some large investment management firms charge as much as 40 percent of the profits. Hedge fund managers are typically not penalized for losses. So, to attract investors, some hedge funds restrict performance fees in a way called high water mark that requires losses to be recouped before paying performance fees on growth. For example, if a fund sustains a loss, the fund pays no performance fee until a new all-time high value for the fund is reached. Some investors would not invest in a hedge fund without the high water mark arrangement. Other investors feel the high water mark results in the manager taking on more risk.

Another guideline for performance fees is a minimum acceptable rate of return, or hurdle rate, which is an external benchmark the fund must match for a performance fee to be paid. The rate may be a preset percentage or another rate from the financial industry. This assures investors that no performance fee will be paid if the profit is not greater than profit on certain other investments.

Because hedge fund managers undertake long-term strategies, in addition to a management fee and a performance fee, a hedge fund may charge a withdrawal fee to discourage an investor from removing their money unnecessarily. This is a penalty for money withdrawn by an investor earlier than a set time or in excess of a certain amount or percentage of the amount owned. Some funds may use lock-up periods, not allowing withdrawals for a certain amount of time after the original investment.

Considerations Before Investing

An individual considering an investment in a hedge fund may review the items mentioned above as well as the any of following items:

- Review the offering document or PPM before making a decision.

- Consider obtaining advice from an investment professional, paying attention to any disclosed conflicts of interest, such as the professional receiving a higher compensation for recommending the hedge fund than another investment.

- Match the fund's investment strategies and associated risks with one's personal investment goals, time horizons, and risk tolerance.

- Understand the use of leverage, short-selling, and derivatives.

- Identify conflicts of interest.

- Understand the fund's valuation method or methods, including any discretion allowed for valuing illiquid securities, use of external authorities for valuation, and whether fees are deducted during the calculation.

- Understand how the fund's management fee and performance fee are calculated.

- Understand schedules for withdrawing part of the investment as well as restrictions, such as a lock-up period, withdrawal fees, or the prerogative to suspend redemptions during down markets or when investments cannot be readily sold for a reasonable price.

- Understand the experience, qualifications, and any disciplinary history of the fund managers by doing the following, if possible:

    o Viewing the firm's Form ADV (a required disclosure on file with the SEC, which describes its managers, investment practices, and the amount of investments being managed) by using the SEC's Investment Adviser Public Disclosure (IAPD) website or contacting the state securities regulator where the adviser's principal place of business is located

    o Searching FINRA's BrokerCheck database

- Understand reviews of the fund manager's handling of the assets and whether an annual financial audit is conducted by an independent auditor.

- Understand where evidence of the fund's investment assets' ownership is kept and whether an outside person or firm certifies the ownership.

- Consider contacting external persons and firms retained by the fund to confirm accuracy of information provided by the fund, such as the prime broker, certified public accountant (CPA), and evaluation agent.

Questions or concerns about a hedge fund investment, including suspected fraud, can be directed to the SEC, FINRA, or the North American Securities Administrators Association (NASAA) for assistance. The NASAA consists of sixty-seven state, provincial, and territorial securities administrators in the fifty states, the District of Columbia, Puerto Rico, the U.S. Virgin Islands, Canada, and Mexico. The same questions or concerns may be directed to the state securities regulator.

Exchange-Traded Products (ETPs)

Types of Exchange-Traded Products
Exchange-traded products (ETPs) include two categories: **Exchange-traded funds (ETFs)** and **exchange-traded notes (ETNs)**. Whereas ETNs are quite different from mutual funds and will be described later in this section, ETFs can be compared and contrasted with mutual funds, having significant similarities.

ETFs
Although mutual funds are by far the most common type of investment company, ETFs are developing momentum to become more attractive than mutual funds to an increasing number of investors who want the following characteristics of mutual funds:

- Diversification
- Professional management
- Conventional investment strategies
- A goal of matching an appropriate benchmark over a relatively intermediate term or long term period

ETFs also offer potential improvements over mutual funds, including the following:

- Lower internal fees than a mutual fund pursuing the same goal
- Exchange trading, providing liquidity throughout the trading day

- Improved tax efficiency from fewer taxable events, using basket trades (see below), and no realized capital gains until the ETF is sold
- Full investment
- Lower cost to sell
- Elimination of render share classes

Some ETFs, which, like mutual funds, are registered investment companies, may better match the goals of investors seeking lower fees and intraday liquidity. In general, ETFs issue shares that represent an interest in a portfolio of securities, and the shares trade on a national exchange. Many ETFs using low-cost passive investment strategies are designed to match the return of a specific index, such as the S&P 500, either by purchasing all the securities in the index or by purchasing derivatives that will accomplish a similar result.

Some of the target indexes may relate to the equities market in a particular country or industry. In addition to providing their share's NAV at the end of a trading day, they distribute an estimate of its value, which may be called an intraday indicative value, usually every 15 seconds throughout the trading day. ETFs using active investment management would have higher fees. During 2019, two SEC rule changes, SEC Rule 6c-11 (called the ETF Rule) and approval of the Precidian ActiveShares ETF model, made the legal environment significantly more conducive to establishing ETFs and operating actively managed ETFs by discontinuing the requirement to daily divulge evidence of their investment strategy.

The ETF Rule reduces the time for some ETFs to begin operation by as much as six months. It addresses the following exemptions that ETFs need (under the '40 Act, which regulates open-end investment companies) to begin operations:

- **Redeemable Securities**: The '40 Act defined an open-end investment company as issuing redeemable securities, meaning each security was redeemable. The ETF business model can only operate with a redemption exemption because it does not allow for an investor (generally referred to as an authorized participant) to redeem less than a minimum number of shares.

- **NAV Trading**: The '40 Act specifies that transactions in redeemable securities be executed at the next calculated NAV. The ETF can only operate with a pricing exemption because a significant feature of an ETF is to trade on an exchange where the market value of the ETF shares will not necessarily be equal to the NAV of the investment portfolio.

- **Transactions With Affiliated Persons**: The '40 Act generally requires the open-end investment management company to only enter transactions with a person who is an employee or is categorized as closely affiliated with the fund (which an authorized participant would be), using securities issued by the fund. ETF issuers typically prefer to issue and redeem funds using a basket of securities that is equal in value but not issued by the fund. A basket has multiple securities of a similar nature. In many cases, the basket is a creation unit, which an ETF manager structures to nearly match the proportionate distribution of fund assets. Processing basket orders avoids the necessity of processing the transactions individually. Also, it allows simultaneous execution of a pairs trade, which is buying a stock and selling another stock short, or a covered call, which is buying a stock and selling a call. It would also allow all stocks whose prices change significantly with virtually no trading in between to be traded in a basket.

   A typical example is the opening price being higher or lower than the previous day's closing price, called gapping up or gapping down. Institutional ("program") trading uses the term basket on the NYSE to refer to fifteen or more stocks traded as a basket, with an aggregate value of more than

$1 million. To manage multiple securities involving large monetary values, a program can make such trades quickly at the same time. Manual processing would be unwieldy. SEC approval of the Precidian ActiveShares ETF model allows ETFs, like mutual funds, to disclosure portfolio investments in detail only quarterly, rather than daily, which would make their investment decision public for anyone to mimic. Actively managed ETFs are expected to become more common.

Another set of investors may want features that are somewhat removed from those typical of mutual funds, such as borrowing to increase leverage and using derivatives to offset adverse changes in asset values or to attempt to gain from anticipating market changes. These leveraged and inverse ETFs are designed to accomplish their goal over a day, and most reset their investment allocation daily to reach their goal. Generally, they are only appropriate for short-term strategies.

A *leveraged ETF* may purchase securities on margin to increase return on capital if the market value increases or purchase derivatives, such as options, futures, and swaps, that would accomplish a similar goal.

An *inverse ETF* is intended to provide a return that is opposite of the target index's return. This may be done by selling short the investments in the index, which could require a significant outlay of funds, or using futures or derivatives that provide the opportunity without such an outlay. However, the costs for the derivatives and futures may be in addition to the eventual cash outlay to execute the derivatives.

A *leveraged inverse ETF* pursues a return that is a multiple of the opposite return of the target index. More and more investors prefer ETFs to mutual funds because of their lower internal fees, the opportunity to borrow ETFs and sell them without owning them, and the provision to borrow funds to purchase more ETFs than could be purchased for cash.

Market ETFs, the vast majority of ETFs, each track a broad market index. Understanding the most popular indexes provides a context for grasping the increasing popularity of market ETFs.

- The *S&P 500*, or simply the S&P, tracks the large-cap market. The S&P Index committee chooses five hundred securities to provide a picture of the U.S. large-cap market. They typically choose most, but not all, of the five hundred largest companies by market cap. The performance of the ten largest companies accounts for more than 20 percent of the performance. The S&P is respected, in that the Conference Board, a nongovernmental organization, determines the value of the Conference Board Leading Economic Index from the values of ten factors, of which the S&P is one.

- The *Russell 2000* tracks the small-cap part of the U.S. stock market. It follows the performance of approximately 2000 of the smallest-cap American companies in the Russell 3000 Index, which is made up of 3000 of the largest U.S. stocks, or approximately 98 percent of all publicly traded U.S. stocks. In other words, the Russell 2000 has the lower two-thirds of the Russell 3000.

- The *Dow Jones Industrial Average (DJIA)*, or simply the Dow, is a price-weighted index of thirty large cap U.S. stocks selected by the editors of the *Wall Street Journal*. It is possibly the most well-known market index. For various reasons, including the fact that it only has thirty large-cap companies and is not weighted by market capitalization, some do not consider the Dow as representative of the stock market as the S&P or the Russell 2000. In the past, industrial companies were heavily used in the index, but many of the thirty companies now selected are not significantly related to the industrial sector.

61

- The ***Nasdaq 100***, a large-cap index with a heavy technology element, tracks slightly more than one hundred equity securities issued by the one hundred largest international and U.S companies by capitalization traded on Nasdaq. Heavily represented industries include technology, health care, industrial, consumer discretionary, and telecommunications. Being weighted by market capitalizations with some limits to the weighting of the largest companies, its performance is greatly affected by companies such as Apple, Amazon, Google, and Facebook. It does not have any financial companies, which were put in a separate index, the Nasdaq Financial-100.

The following are examples of market ETFs:

- ***SPY***, or "SPDR® S&P 500® ETF Trust": Tracking the S&P, SPY is the ticker symbol for the most well-known, oldest, and largest ETF. As a UIT, it owns the stocks of the index, does not lend securities, and cannot reinvest portfolio dividends between distributions. It has reached a daily trading volume of more than 250 million unit shares, which makes it attractive to investors seeking liquidity.

- ***IWM***, or "iShares Russell 2000 ETF": Tracking the Russell 2000 Index, IWM is the ticker symbol for an index ETF that usually holds at least 90 percent of its assets in securities or depositary receipts of the index elements. The other 10 percent of its assets may include securities outside of the underlying index, futures, options, swap contracts, cash, and cash equivalents. IWM is the heaviest traded Russell 2000 ETF but still has only one-quarter of the volume of SPY. Russell 2000 ETFs may lead S&P 500 ETFs in an economic recovery and the following expansion but with more volatility.

- ***DIA***, or "SPDR DJIA ETF": Tracking the DJIA, DIA is the ticker symbol for an index ETF that holds stocks of the thirty companies that are in the DJIA in approximately the same proportions as the securities in the index. It has reached a daily trading volume of more than seven million shares.

- ***QQQ***, or "Invesco QQQ Trust": Tracking the Nasdaq 100 Index, QQQ, informally called *triple-Qs* or *cubes,* is the ticker symbol for an index ETF that is rebalanced quarterly and reassembled annually. QQQ offers investors who do not want to pick their own stocks a liquid, cost-efficient way to invest in a set of companies that is heavily weighted with large-cap technology stocks but is not a technology-only investment.

Sector ETFs, less well known and generally with higher expense ratios than market ETFs, buy securities in a specific industry, which may be identified in the fund's name. Most, but not all, sector ETFs focus on U.S.-based stocks. An investor can purchase a sector ETF to include an industry in the investor's portfolio without selecting individual stocks. This can be done to "hedge," or reduce risk, through increasing diversification by entering an industry not included in the investor's portfolio. On the other hand, an investor can purchase a sector speculatively, risking a narrow focus, while hoping for a return larger than available elsewhere in a more diversified investment. Sector ETFs are sometimes used for short-term investment time frames. The Global Industry Classification Standard (GICS) defines sectors for the financial industry. The eleven major GICS sectors are as follows:

- Energy: **XLE**
- Materials: **XLB**
- Industrials: **XLI**
- Consumer discretionary: **XLY**
- Consumer staples: **XLP**

62

- Health care: **XLV**
- Financials: **XLF**
- Information technology: **SMH**
- Telecommunication services: **XTL**
- Utilities: **XLU**
- Real estate: **IYR**

All the above sectors have sector ETFs. Sectors are defined in other ways, including commodities such as corn; metals such as copper, gold, silver, platinum, and palladium; and the top thirty Mexican companies. The market improves for precious metals during inflationary periods. Sector ETFs allow investment in such assets without needing to take custody of them and keep them secure. Some sector ETFs try to replicate the return on sector use indexes maintained by companies such as S&P and Dow Jones. Sector ETFs using leverage can be purchased, with the goal of achieving a multiple of the return of the underlying index when advancing or declining. Investors review sector ETFs for their fees and trading volume.

With continued extremely high stock market volatility, investors have an opportunity to profit by purchasing volatility ETFs. The CBOE Market Volatility Index (VIX) is the reference for volatility ETFs (VIX ETFs). The VIX, referred to as the fear index, strives to measure the market's assumptions regarding future volatility on a real-time basis. It uses the implied volatilities on S&P 500 Index options (SPX), which show the market's anticipation of thirty-day future volatility of the S&P 500 Index. Investors who wish to build high-risk equity positions based on how VIX futures contracts will trade may use VIX ETFs, made for short-term estimates of changes in market volatility, not for long-term investing. Investors will find VIX ETFs have higher carrying charges than many other ETFs.

Exchange-Traded Notes (ETNs)

An **_exchange-traded note ETN_** is a type of unsecured debt instrument with which the issuer, usually a bank or financial institution, commits to pay on the maturity date of the note a return linked to the performance of an index, an asset, or a group of assets. An investor should be aware of the creditworthiness of the issuer when investing.

By purchasing an ETN, an investor can invest in a variety of investments that may not lend themselves to direct investment. ETNs are not necessarily appealing to long-term or strategy focused investors. They appeal more to traders, scouring the corners of markets for a quick advantage point when it comes to their investment decisions.

ETNs don't typically make interest payments like traditional bonds do. Rather, interest goes to the ETN in the form of credit as a result of market index performance, not including issuer's fees. Because ETNs do not represent ownership of an underlying investment, their valuation must be estimated using a formula instead of the NAV. The maturities of ETNs can range from ten to thirty years and sometimes longer.

ETNs can vary as to fees but can include both commissions paid when buying or selling ETNs and reoccurring costs, such as the daily investor fee. The term **_indicative value_** refers to the closing value at the end of a trading day and is the value of the reference asset or index minus the daily investor fee.

ETNs vs. ETFs

Like ETFs, ETNs trade on exchanges and are available in both inverse and leveraged varieties. As with inverse and leveraged ETFs, inverse and leveraged ETNs are designed to be short-term trading vehicles. Although ETFs and ETNs are both traded on exchanges, they are quite different. Like mutual funds, ETFs are registered investment companies, offering diversification, professional management, conventional investment strategies, a goal of matching an appropriate benchmark over a relatively intermediate-term or long-term period, and an underlying portfolio that can be valued throughout any trading day. ETNs are not registered investment companies, may not offer diversification, may have no active professional management, generally have no goal of matching any benchmark other than the reference asset(s), and are subject to the creditworthiness of the issuing institution.

Investment Risks

One definition of risk is the possibility of loss. ***Investment risk*** therefore could be defined as the possibility of loss of part or all of an investment. However, investments are made with a hope or an expectation of a return on investment. So, in an investor's mind, investment risk is expanded to mean the chance that the return on the investment will be less than the expected return. Therefore, investment risk can be viewed as the likelihood that the original principal value of the investment will eventually be recovered as well as the likelihood that the return on the principal will be realized.

Types of Risk

Capital Risk

Capital risk relates to the possibility that all or part of the original investment will be lost. The capital risk is more readily identifiable in an interest-bearing debt instrument, in which interest payments are made throughout the life of the debt and the capital, or face amount of the investment, is to be paid at maturity. The bondholder receives interest payments in advance of maturity, but until receiving the face amount at maturity, the receipt of interest payments is only a partial fulfillment of the goal of the investment.

Credit Risk

Credit risk names the uncertainty as to whether the party issuing the debt security will be financially able to fulfill the obligations of the debt, which is typically timely payment of interest payments and payment of the principal amount at maturity. In the case of foreign debts, a subcategory of credit risk could be sovereign risk, which names the potential complication of foreign exchange procedures.

Currency Risk

Currency risk, or exchange-rate risk, is the possibility that an investment may lose value because of one of the following:

- An investor uses domestic currency to purchase an investment denominated in a foreign currency. Although the foreign issuer pays interest or dividend payments as required or payment at maturity or liquidation, if the foreign currency decreased in value relative to the domestic currency, the value of payments to the investor are of less value in domestic currency than they would have been had the currency exchange rate not deteriorated.

- An investor attempts to trade an asset denominated in a foreign currency market after the exchange rate changed unfavorably. The loss in value is not due to the issuer's business operations but to the change in the exchange rate.

Inflationary/Purchasing Power Risk

Inflationary/purchasing power risk refers to the comparison between the nominal value of an investment and the change in price of the goods or services that would be purchased with the investment's proceeds. The market price of an investment typically changes to reflect inflation or interest rate changes relative to the investment, especially if the investment is denominated in currency units, such as U.S. dollars.

Interest Rate/Reinvestment Risk

Interest rate/reinvestment risk represents the uncertainty regarding the investor's future opportunity to reinvest cash received from the investment (such as interest or dividends) with the reasonable expectation of the same or greater return as that received on the original investment.

- For debt instruments such as bonds, this would be of special concern if interest rates were to fall. If the investment is callable by the issuer, the reinvestment risk will apply to the entire original investment. When interest rates fall, the issuer will likely call the bonds in order to obtain financing at a lower rate. If the investor chooses to reinvest in new bonds, the investor will receive a lower interest rate than on the original investment.

- For stocks paying dividends, this could be a concern if the issuer is not issuing additional shares. The cash must be used to purchase the issuer's shares on the open market. If the market price has risen to reflect the favorable dividend history, the dividend yield would be less than that of the original investment.

To reduce reinvestment risk, an investor may choose to invest in noncallable bonds even though they may have a lower interest rate than callable bonds. The investor may choose to purchase zero-coupon bonds, which have no inherent reinvestment risk. Finally, the investor may choose to purchase longer-term debt securities, deferring the reinvestment risk to a later point in time.

Liquidity Risk

Liquidity risk is the uncertainty that an asset can be sold or otherwise readily converted into cash within a short amount of time. The definition of liquidity risk often combines the ease and speed with which an asset may be sold with the ability to obtain a reasonable price for the asset.

Market/Systematic Risk

Market/systematic risk refers to a risk that is unrelated to the specific investment but instead related to the general direction of market prices. This risk can be greater in times of economic and political uncertainty. Although capital risk, currency risk, and liquidity risk may be mitigated through diversification, market risk is not so readily addressed. Investors generally consider market risk to be difficult to mitigate in the short term.

Non-Systematic Risk

Non-systematic risk represents a broad category of risks that are inseparable from the characteristics of the country, industry, issuer, or type of investment.

The typical investor seeks to mitigate non-systematic risk in the short term by using conventional methods, such as diversification and portfolio rebalancing, or by using not-so-conventional methods, such as hedging.

Political Risk

Political risk or geopolitical risk is the name for the influence that political changes, such as elections, changes in laws and regulations, coups, and military control, can have on investments in companies operating in a specific country. The exposure increases with the length of the investment because the initial investment decision is made based on current conditions.

Prepayment Risk

Prepayment risk, like reinvestment risk, refers to a debt instrument being redeemed prior to maturity. Callable bonds may be called by the issuer. In times of decreasing interest rates or increasing housing values, mortgage-backed securities may have significant levels of prepayment of mortgages due to refinancing and trading up.

Strategies for Mitigation of Risk

Investors seek to lower the expected risk of investments to reduce the likelihood of loss and/or reduce the level of fluctuation in the growth of the overall portfolio value.

Diversification

Diversification attempts to simply offset the non-systematic risk characteristics of one investment by holding an investment that has a lower level of the risk characteristics in the first investment. In a portfolio, a variety of investments with different sets of characteristics allows the opportunity to participate in favorable investment environments and lessen the impact of a single unfavorable match between the investment and the investment's environment. Diversification among issuers can reduce capital risk by investing in a variety of companies, industries, types of investments, and countries.

An investor may also diversify the timing of investments. Rather than investing an amount all at one time, the investment may be made by installments over time. The goal is that a lower cost per share will be attained than if the entire investment had been made all at once. The success of this strategy, known as dollar cost averaging, depends on both the market going down during some of the period of installments and the market ending up higher at the end of the holding period than it was at the beginning.

This strategy will likely not be successful if the investment is liquidated while the market is lower than it was at the time of the initial investment.

Portfolio Rebalancing

Portfolio rebalancing refers to an occasional review of the assets in an investment portfolio, with the purpose of adjusting the diversification to an original or preferred proportion. Although the word rebalancing suggests an equal proportion of two or more types of investments, such as 50 percent stocks and 50 percent bonds, the term has been used to refer to any deliberate proportional formula. The intention is to avoid the investor being unintentionally exposed to risks due to misallocation of investments by type. The assumption is that those investments that have risen in value more than the others—for example, stocks more than bonds—are more likely to be overweighted in the portfolio. Use of a predetermined formula does not respond to reasons for the change in the allocation or allow for estimates of future performance of stocks as compared with bonds. It also does not reflect the influence of changing interest rate environments on the market value of bonds or the anticipated level of economic growth on the market value of stocks. The graphic below demonstrates an example of portfolio rebalancing.

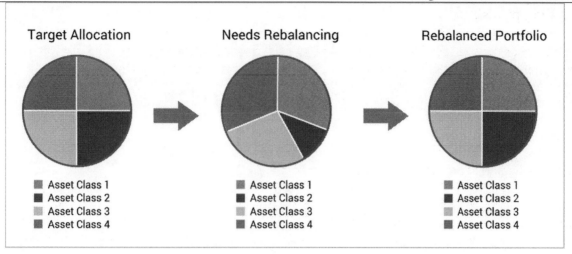

The frequency of rebalancing is subject to various factors, such as the time and cost involved, and does not necessarily result in proportionately better risk profiles. The most frequent rebalancing would typically be monthly, with quarterly reviews being reasonable. Annual rebalancing may be considered too infrequent because during that time, one or more assets could increase or decrease in value out of proportion to other assets. The result would be that the new allocation among assets is different from the intended allocation. This is called portfolio drift.

Hedging

Hedging attempts to match the risk characteristics of one investment with another investment that will perform well in the environment in which the first investment would perform poorly. This can be done by purchasing a derivative, such as an option. For example, buying a put on a stock that is owned allows the investor to have downside protection at the cost of the premium paid on the put. Another type of hedge is an index option, which allows the investor to participate in the performance of an index representing a certain section of the market. For example, an investor with currency risk holding an investment denominated in a foreign currency may benefit from purchasing a currency option, which allows the investor the prerogative to buy or sell a certain quantity of a foreign currency at a certain price on a certain day. For the duration of that option, the investor has some protection from market price changes that are unrelated to the performance of the company itself.

See our SIE Resource Page for links to current rules and regulations.

You can visit by going to https://www.apexprep.com/sie or by scanning the QR code.

Understanding Trading, Customer Accounts and Prohibited Activities

Trading, Settlement and Corporate Actions

Orders and Strategies

Types of Orders

For an investor to make a profit, the investor must typically sell a security for more than the amount for which the security was purchased. Many **securities** are offered for purchase at an asking price, and at the same time are offered for sale at a bid price. The difference between the bid price and the asking price is called the **spread**. The following distinguishes between a long sale and a short sale, and the variety of strategies that can be pursued.

An investor may anticipate the market price for a security rising during the period of time during which the investor plans to hold the security. In this case, the investor purchases the security (long purchase), generally by using the services of a broker-dealer, in anticipation of selling it later.

If the investor chooses to sell the security that is owned (long sale) at a time when the market price is higher than the purchase price, the investor realizes a gross profit. The gross profit will typically be reduced by compensation paid to the broker-dealer and other entities involved.

If the investor chooses to sell the security that is owned (long sale) at a time when the market price is less than the purchase price, then the investor suffers a gross loss on that investment. The gross loss will typically be increased by compensation paid to the broker-dealer and other entities involved.

On the other hand, an investor may anticipate the market price for a security falling during a period of time during which the investor plans to borrow the security. In this case, the investor borrows the security from an investor who owns it, generally by using the services of a broker-dealer. In this way, the investor sells a security the investor does not own (short sale) before purchasing it.

If the investor later chooses to purchase the security to cover a short position for less than the purchase price, the purchased security is returned to the investor who loaned the security, and the investor who made the short sale realizes a gross profit. The gross profit will typically be reduced by compensation paid to the broker-dealer and other entities involved, to include the cost of borrowing the security for the short sale.

If the investor who made the short sale chooses to purchase the security (to cover a short position) while the market price is higher than the sales price, the purchased security is returned to the investor who loaned the security. In this case, the investor who made the short sale suffers a gross loss on that investment. The gross loss will typically be increased by compensation paid to the broker-dealer and other entities involved, to include the cost of borrowing the security for the short sale.

Securities regulation intends the following:

- The investor will have the information needed to make an informed decision regarding the purchase and the sale.

- The decisions (buy orders and sell orders) the investor makes are carried out in a manner appropriate to the intention of the investor.

Investors choose to make buying and purchasing decisions, which are carried out as buy orders and sell orders. The explanations below display different ways for buy orders and sell orders to be placed. The use of some of the **order types** will depend upon whether the investor is in a long position, owning the security, or in a short position, having borrowed the security.

- A market order is to be completed as soon as practical at the best available price.

- A stop order is to be completed immediately after a specified stop price is available on the market, at which time it becomes a market order. A stop order typically expires at the end of the trading day unless a different time frame is specified.

- A limit order is to only be completed when it may be fulfilled at a price that is at least as favorable as the person placing the order specifies. Similar to a stop order, a limit order typically expires at the end of the trading day unless a different time frame is specified.

- A good-'til-canceled (GTC) order does not expire at the end of the trading day. It does not expire until fulfilled or cancelled by the investor.

- A discretionary order is an order for which the representative chooses a characteristic of the order other than the price or timing, such as one of the following:

  o Which security to buy or sell (asset)
  o The quantity to buy or sell (amount)
  o Whether to enter an order or not (action)

- A discretionary order placed in a discretionary account must be approved by the supervisory principal on the date the trade is made.

- A non-discretionary order is an order for which the representative chooses no characteristic of the order other than the price or timing. The investor with a non-discretionary account must authorize a discretionary order in writing.

- A solicited order is an order for which the investor acts upon a recommendation of the representative. This must be indicated on the order record.

- An unsolicited order is an order for which the investor specifies all characteristics of the order.

Buy and Sell, Bid-Ask

To **buy a security**, the investor typically asks a broker-dealer to complete a buy order. The broker-dealer contacts a clearing broker, who works with a market maker, who offers an ask price, at which the market maker is willing to sell a security.

To **sell a security**, the investor typically asks a broker-dealer to complete a sale order. The broker-dealer contacts a clearing broker, who works with a market maker, who offers a bid price, at which the market maker is willing to purchase a security. The market maker earns compensation for the difference between the bid and ask prices, as well as the difference between the historical price the market maker paid for a security as compared with the price for which it is later sold.

The following charts illustrate the characteristics of various types of orders. An order may be a market order, a GTC order, a non-discretionary order, or an unsolicited order, as the various categories of characteristics describe different dimensions of an order.

Order Type	Client specifies price	Timing	Liquid or illiquid securities	Spread	Buy Order	Sell Order	Certain to be ful-filled?	Purpose / Description
Market	No	Immediately	Liquid	Narrow	Yes	Yes	Yes	Immediate purchase or sale
Sell stop (loss)	Stop	When "stop" price reached, immediately	Liquid or illiquid	N/A	N/A	Yes	No	Long position, limit loss or protect profit
Buy stop	Stop	When "stop" price reached, immediately	Liquid or illiquid	N/A	Yes	N/A	No	Short position, limit loss or protect profit
Limit	Limit	If / when limit reached	Illiquid	Wide	Typically below current market	Typically above current market	No	Trade depends on minimally acceptable price
Buy stop-limit order	Stop and limit	If / when limit reached, then stop reached	Illiquid	Wide	Typically below current market	N/A	No	Sale depends on minimally acceptable price
Sell stop-limit order	Stop and limit	If / when limit reached, then stop reached	Illiquid	Wide	N/A	Typically above current market	No	Purchase depends upon minimally acceptable price

When the previous orders are placed:
- Additional conditions regarding timing may be imposed.
- Discretionary orders require written trading authorization.
- Orders must be marked as either solicited or unsolicited.

Order Condition	Price	Timing	Certain to be fulfilled?	Purpose / Description	Verbal or Written Authorization Required
Timing Condition					
Day Orders (Unless stated otherwise, all orders are day orders)	N/A	Only good until the end of the day (4:00 p.m. Eastern), then cancelled	No	Allows only one trading day for market to satisfy order's specified conditions	N/A
Good-'til-Canceled (GTC) or Open Order	N/A	Remains in effect until cancelled by investor	Yes	Allows time for market to satisfy order's specified conditions	N/A
Specified Time	N/A	For specified period, e.g., week, or other time frame	No	Allows time for market to satisfy order's specified conditions	N/A
Discretionary or Non-discretionary					
Discretionary	N/A	N/A	N/A	Investor authorizes representative to choose characteristic other than price and timing	Written
Non-discretionary or Not-Held	Discretion allowed for price	Discretion allowed for time during the current trading day (until 4:00 p.m. Eastern) then cancelled	N/A	Investor specifies security, whether to buy or sell, quantity of shares or units	Verbal

Solicited or Unsolicited					
Solicited	N/A	N/A	N/A	Investor's idea	N/A
Unsolicited	N/A	N/A	N/A	Influenced by representative's recommendation	N/A

Trade Capacity

If the broker-dealer is a party to the transaction, either selling the security being purchased by the investor, or purchasing the security being sold by the investor, the broker-dealer firm is acting in the **capacity of a principal**.

If the broker-dealer is not a party to the transaction, only facilitating the fulfillment of the order, the broker-dealer firm is acting in an **agency capacity**.

FINRA Rule 2120: Commissions, Mark Ups, and Charges includes a series of rules regarding compensation for a broker-dealer, whether acting in the capacity of an agent (who is not a party to the transaction), or in the capacity of a principal (who is a party to the transaction). Commission is the compensation received by a broker-dealer acting in an agency capacity.

Markup/markdown is the compensation received by a broker-dealer acting in a principal capacity and is calculated as follows:

- The difference between the lower price paid for a security to another party and the higher price at which it is sold to a customer (markup), or

- The difference between the lower price paid to a customer for a security and the higher price at which is later sold to another party (markdown).

FINRA Rule 2121: Fair Prices and Commissions requires a member to provide a reasonable price to a customer, taking into account various characteristics of the order.

- General Considerations: with five percent as a guideline, but not an absolute standard, depending upon other factors, some of which follow:
- Relevant Factors
    - Type of security
    - Availability
    - Price
    - Total monetary size of the transaction
    - Disclosure to the customer
    - A member's typical behavior in charging markups
    - The business in which the member typically engages

FINRA Rule 2122: Charges for Services Performed states that the cost of any services provided, such as handling cash and/or securities, is expected to be fair and consistent among customers.

FINRA Rule 2124: Net Transactions with Customers states that when a broker-dealer acts as a principal on a transaction, a market maker may purchase the security from another party at a certain price, in order to fulfill the order for the broker-dealer's customer at a different price. If the broker-dealer's customer is a non-institutional investor, the member must provide disclosure regarding the price difference involved. If the broker-dealer's customer is an investor, then more choices are available to assure the customer's knowledge and permission to fulfill a net transaction.

Long and Short, Naked and Covered

A ***long, or covered, position*** is a conservative one in which the customer purchases the security prior to selling it. The maximum possible loss is equal to the amount paid for the security were it to become worthless.

A ***short, or naked, position*** is one in which the customer borrows and sells a security before purchasing it. This is done in an anticipation of the price declining. This is a more aggressive strategy. The maximum possible loss is unknown and could be quite large if the price were to significantly increase.

Bearish and Bullish

A ***bearish (short or naked) position*** is one taken in expectation that the price for a security will decrease. A ***bullish (long or covered) position*** is one taken in expectation that the price for a security will increase.

FINRA 5210: Publication of Transactions and Quotations

Any published quote of an offered purchase or sale of any security must be based on a member's understanding that the bid price or asked price of the security is a real bid for, or offer of, the security.

MSRB G-13: Quotations

Municipal securities quotes published by dealers must present actual prices and amounts of securities that are currently offered by the quoting dealer.

FINRA 6438: Displaying Priced Quotations in Multiple Quotation Mediums

Members that publish real-time quotations for an over-the-counter equity security in more than one market must publish the same prices in each market, except in some cases for a customer limit order.

FINRA 5220: Offers at Stated Prices

A member must only make offers to buy any security from, or sell any security to, someone at a stated price if the firm will actually buy or sell at whatever share price level is stated, in accordance with the details of the offer.

FINRA 5290: Order Entry and Execution Practices

A member or associated person must process an order without dividing it into a number of smaller orders primarily to receive the most financial or other benefit, such as through transaction fees.

1934 Act Section 15: Rules Relating to Over-the-Counter Markets

A requirement that broker-dealers must follow is the ***penny stock rules***, by explaining the risks and adequate data about the market for penny stocks, and evaluating whether the customer is a match for investing in penny stocks. Specifically, the broker-dealer must do the following:

- Determine that the customer may reasonably place the specific penny stock order and receive from the customer written approval of the trade;

- Provide the customer with a risk disclosure document that explains the risks of trading in penny stocks;

- Reveal to the customer the bid and ask prices and the number of shares that apply to such bid and ask price for the penny stock; and

- Explain to the customer the dollar value of fees the firm and its broker will receive for the trade. In addition, after the order is fulfilled, the broker-dealer must transmit to its customer account reports each month showing the then current value of each penny stock held in the customer's account, based on the then-current market.

The ***penny stock risk disclosure document*** includes the following:

- An explanation of the risk in the market for penny stocks in both initial public offerings (IPOs) and subsequent secondary markets;

- An acknowledgement of the responsibility of the broker or dealer to the customer under the federal securities laws, and of the customer's rights in the event that the broker or dealer fails to carry out those responsibilities;

- A concise, clear explanation of how a dealer market works, where a dealer is a party to the trade, including bid and ask prices for penny stocks and the meaning of the difference between the bid and ask prices (spread);

- The toll-free telephone number for questions about enforcement actions in the case of violations;

- Definitions of important terms used in the disclosure document or in the process of trading in penny stocks; and

- In general, data required by the SEC, in the format determined by the SEC.

Rules about penny stocks can be found in Exchange Act Rules 15g-1 through 15g-100.

FINRA 5310: Best Execution and Interpositioning specifies that, in any trade for or with a customer or a customer of another broker-dealer, every broker-dealer will give conscientious attention to determine the best market for the security being traded, and handle the trade in the chosen market so that the customer gets the best price that is reasonably possible, given current market activity.

MSRB G-18: Best Execution specifies essentially the same care being given to customers who trade in municipal securities, as FINRA Rule 5310 specifies for securities supervised by FINRA.

MSRB G-14: Reports of Sales or Purchases directs brokers, dealers, and municipal securities dealers that handle trades in municipal securities to submit information about each trade to the MSRB's Real-time

Transaction Reporting System (RTRS) within fifteen minutes of the completion of the trade, with few exceptions.

Inv Co Act 1940 17a-6: Exemption for Transactions with Portfolio Affiliates

A mutual fund, or a company controlled by a mutual fund, and a portfolio affiliate of the mutual fund may trade securities, so long as none of a list of persons close to the fund is a party to the trade or would benefit financially from the trade.

Inv Co Act 1940 17a-7: Exemption of Certain Purchase or Sale Transactions Between an Investment Company and Certain Affiliated Persons Thereof

This rule is intended to allow purchasing and selling of securities between mutual funds and specific affiliated persons if it is unlikely that the purchase or sale will harm the fund.

Investment Returns

Components of Return

To calculate an ***investor's return***, cash received during the time the investor holds the security is added to the change in the price (unrealized gain or loss), or when sold, to the proceeds from the sale (realized gain or loss). Interest is typically paid by a company on money loaned by an investor, such as by purchasing a bond. Dividends are declared by the board of directors and paid to the stockholders. Commission or markups/markdowns on purchases and sales, costs of advice, securities custody, and recordkeeping are deducted to obtain the net return. The return on capital is:

$$\frac{Return - Amount\ Invested}{Amount\ Invested}$$

For example, if $100 of interest is received while the security was held, $1,050 is received at the sale, total costs are $50, and the amount paid was $1,000, the calculation would be as follows:

$$\frac{\$100 + \$1,050 - \$50 - \$1,000}{\$1,000} = \frac{\$100}{\$1,000} = 10\%$$

The return on capital may be calculated before income tax or after income tax. Until the investment is sold, and all expenses have been paid, the income tax can only be calculated on a contingent basis.

Different Types of Dividends

A board of directors may declare a ***dividend*** in cash or with stock. Stock dividends may dilute the value of existing stock.

Dividend Payment Dates

When a board of directors declares dividends, the board determines a date of ownership (record date), in order to determine which owners will be paid the dividend. The price of the stock may increase by the amount of the dividend after the dividend date. The rules of the exchange on which the stock is traded determines the ex-dividend date or ex-date, the first date that the stock trades without a right to the dividend. This is usually the first business day or trading day before the record date because one business day is needed in order to settle. An investor purchasing the stock on or after the ex-date will not be entitled to receive the dividend. The price of the stock will typically decrease by the amount of the dividend on the ex-date. The board of directors determines the payable date, which is the date the dividend is actually paid.

Concepts of Measurement

Yield is the amount of interest or dividends received during a period, generally a year, divided by the current price of the security. A quarterly payment may be multiplied by four, or a semi-annual payment may be multiplied by two, in order to extrapolate the payment in terms of current annual yield.

Yield to maturity (YTM) is calculated as follows, assuming timely interest payments are received, and interest payments may be immediately reinvested at the same rate as the original bond until the bond matures. The following calculation reflects a bond with the following:

- $Years\ to\ maturity = 8$
- $Coupon\ rate = 3\%$
- $Face\ value = \$1,000$
- $Purchased\ price = \$1,100$

$$\frac{\dfrac{(Coupon\ Rate \times Face\ Value \times Years\ to\ Maturity) + (Face\ Value - Purchase\ Price)}{Years\ to\ Maturity}}{\dfrac{Face\ Value\ at\ Maturity + Purchase\ Price}{2}}$$

$$\frac{\dfrac{(.03 \times 1000 \times 8) + (1000 - 1100)}{8}}{\dfrac{1000 + 1100}{2}}$$

$$\frac{\dfrac{240 + (-100)}{8}}{1050}$$

$$\frac{\dfrac{140}{8}}{1050}$$

$$\frac{17.50}{1050}$$

1.67% is the YTM for this example.

Yield to call (YTC) is calculated as follows, assuming timely interest payments are received, and interest payments may be immediately reinvested at the same rate as the original bond until the bond matures. The following calculation reflects a bond with the following:

- $Years\ to\ call = 5$
- $Coupon\ rate = 3\%$
- $Face\ value = \$1,000$
- $Call\ premium = \$30$
- $Call\ value = face\ value\ (\$1,000) + call\ premium\ (\$30) = \$1,030$
- $Purchased\ price = \$1,100$

76

$$\frac{(Coupon\ Rate \times Face\ Value \times Years\ to\ Call) + (Call\ Value - Purchase\ Price)}{Years\ to\ Call}$$
$$\frac{Call\ Value\ to\ be\ Received + Purchase\ Price}{2}$$

$$\frac{\frac{(.03 \times 1000 \times 5) + (1030 - 1100)}{5}}{\frac{1030 + 1100}{2}}$$

$$\frac{\frac{150 + (-70)}{5}}{1065}$$

$$\frac{\frac{80}{5}}{1065}$$

$$\frac{16}{1065}$$

1.5% is the YTC for this example.

Total return is a percentage calculated as follows:

- The numerator is obtained by adding all cash received from the investment, plus or minus any gain or loss on the sale. The gain or loss on the sale is the proceeds, when disposed of by sale or maturity, less the cost of the investment.

- The denominator is the purchase cost of the investment.

Basis points may be used to refer to the yield of an investment, with one percent equal to one hundred basis points. If one bond has a yield of 2.17 percent, and another bond has a yield of 2.78 percent, the second bond has a yield that is sixty-one basis points higher than the first bond $278 - 217 = 61$.

Cost Basis Requirements

A ***cost basis*** is used to calculate a trading profit for tax purposes, especially the capital gains realized when the security is sold. The cash received, whether interest or dividends, is typically taxed in the tax year in which they are paid. The various costs of acquisition are included, such as the purchase price, commissions, and markups. If multiple purchases have been made, if stock dividends have been declared, or if the firm has returned capital in some way, the identification of the cost basis may be move involved. To satisfy the IRS, the oldest shares purchased may need to be designated as the shares sold.

Benchmarks and Indices

Benchmarks and indices provide a method for comparing the return on a given security with similar securities, to determine whether the security's return on principal was reasonably equal to, unfavorably lower than, or unexpectedly higher than other similar investments. These are typically used to measure the performance of investment managers.

Trade Settlement

Trade settlement refers to the time (in business days) after the trade is agreed to (transaction date or trade date) until the following time:

- By which the seller's broker-dealer receives the purchase price and

- By which the purchaser's broker-dealer has received ownership of the security, by having the purchaser entered as owner on the books of the issuer (settlement date).

Settlement Time Frames

Regular-way settlement refers to the typical number of days required for settlement. Commercial paper and bank certificates of deposit (CDs) settle on the trade date (T). Treasury bonds, treasury bills, mutual funds, and option trades settle one day after the trade date (T+1). Corporate stock, corporate bonds, and municipal funds specified by MSRB rule G-15 settle two business days after the trade date (T+2).

If the purchaser or seller wishes to settle in a time frame other than regular-way (*special settlement*), this is agreed to before the trade takes place. If the purchaser and seller agree, a cash trade (*cash settlement*) may settle on the trade date. If the seller is not able to provide ownership in the regular-way time frame, the seller may request the settlement be done with extended time (*seller's option*).

MSRB G-47: Time of Trade Disclosure

This rule requires the dealer to let their customers know, either before the trade date or on the trade date, any significant characteristics of the security and the transaction.

Physical vs. Book Entry

Stock certificates formerly were typically printed. Transferring them from the seller to the buyer (delivery) would require a few days. Book entry is a way of maintaining record of the security's owner without a physical, printed certificate. This expedites trades by allowing electronic settlement.

Corporate Actions

A *corporate action* is an act that significantly modifies an organization and affects people involved, such as stockholders or bondholders, especially by affecting the market price of its stock. Such acts typically require approval by the board of directors. Some acts may require the stockholders' approval. Some corporate actions require shareholders to submit a response.

Types of Corporate Actions

In the case of a stock split, the shareholder is provided with new shares in exchange for old shares.

Example one: A stock split may be approved by the board of directors when the trading price is so high that it inhibits investors from purchasing, with the following results:

- The new shares may have one-half the par value of the old shares.
- Therefore, two new shares are provided in exchange for each old share.
- The new shares will begin trading at one-half the price of the old shares.

Example two: A reverse split may be approved by the board of directors when the stock price has fallen, with the following results:

- The new shares may have twice the par value of the old shares.
- Therefore, one new share is provided in exchange for two old shares.
- The new shares will begin trading at twice the price of the old shares.

The graphic below shows the effects of a stock split and a reverse split.

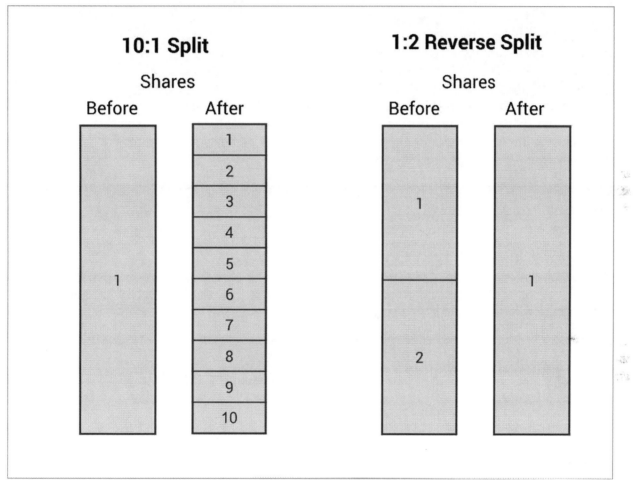

A corporation may purchase its own stock on the open market (buyback) to lessen the number of shares among whom ownership will be shared and for whom dividends will be paid. The reacquired stock is called **treasury stock**. It may not be voted, and it does not receive dividends.

A **tender offer** is a publicly-announced offer to purchase shares for a certain price if a certain quantity of shares is provided in acceptance of the offer. This is not necessarily approved by the board of directors.

An **exchange offer** is a type of tender offer in which the party making the offer would provide another security's shares in exchange for the desired shares.

A **rights offer** is approved by a board of directors to raise additional capital by offering current shareholders the opportunity to purchase enough shares to maintain the same proportional ownership as previously held.

Mergers and acquisitions (M&A) may be approved by a board of directors in order to combine the company with another company (merger) or to purchase another company (acquisition).

Regulation M is a regulation of the SEC to provide a fair market for a new issue of a security by a corporation, by preventing persons involved with the offering from artificially influencing the price.

Impact of Stock Splits and Reverse Stock Splits

A ***stock split*** typically decreases the market price and cost basis proportionally with the ratio of stock split.

A ***reverse stock split*** typically increases the market price and cost basis proportionally with the ratio of the reverse stock split.

Corporate Actions

A ***corporate action*** may require a change in the par value of the affected shares. In the case of a two-for-one stock split, each share of stock would be replaced with two shares, with the new par value being one-half what it was. The market price would become one-half of what it was, and the cost basis for each new share would become one-half of what it was.

In a one-for-two stock reverse stock split, two shares of stock would be replaced with one share, with the new par value being twice what it was. The market price would become twice what it was, and the cost basis for each new share would become twice what it was.

Delivery of Notices and Corporate Action Deadlines

When a board of directors approves a corporate action, notice is provided to the shareholders, with the timing and method depending upon where the shares are traded. An exchange will handle notices for shares traded on that exchange, assuring its deadline is met. For shares traded over-the-counter (OTC), FINRA communicates the notices to meet the appropriate deadlines.

Proxies and Proxy Voting

Proxy voting is when a shareholder may authorize another party to cast the votes which the shareholder is entitled to cast.

FINRA Rule 2251: Forwarding of Proxy and Other Issuer-related Materials provides direction for brokers regarding proxy materials for owners of stocks and owners of bonds other than municipal bonds. The MSRB regulates municipal bonds.

A member firm will forward the proxy materials to the beneficial owner when all of the following occur:

- The issuer provides enough copies of proxy materials, such as the proxy vote form and explanatory materials such as annual reports and information statements, to the member firm.

- The issuer requests that those materials be forwarded to the owners of the securities.

- The issuer provides assurance that payment will be made for the cost of the forwarding process.

1934 Act Section 14: Proxies provide guidance for boards of directors soliciting proxies, as to the following:

- Importance of giving data to owners
- Data to be provided to owners of securities
- Content of the proxy statement
- Method of solicitation
- Online access to proxy materials and online shareholder discussions
- Shareholder approval of executive compensation
- Roles of broker-dealers, banks, and other financial firms to forward data to actual owners of the securities

Customer Accounts and Compliance Considerations

FINRA specifies fair dealings with customers. This begins as early as opening a customer account.

FINRA 4512: Customer Account Information directs a member firm to keep the following data regarding each customer:

- Contact information
- Whether of legal age
- Representative(s) overseeing the account
- Signature of supervisor approving the establishment of the account
- If not a natural person, legal names of persons who can provide instructions for actions
- For a natural person, an alternative contact

For a natural person, if transactions include securities other than mutual funds of the customer's own choice, reasonable effort should be made to obtain the following:

- Social security number of tax identification
- Occupation and employer's name and address
- Whether the customer is a representative for another member firm

FINRA 2231: Customer Account Statements states that statements showing transactions since the last statement, securities owned, and cash balances should be sent to customers at least once every calendar quarter.

1934 Act 15c2-12: Municipal Securities Disclosure specifies that broker-dealers and municipal securities dealers who are assisting municipalities in offering municipal securities to the public make a good-faith effort to make sure the municipality has reported certain data to the MSRB, which would be of interest to an investor making a decision whether to purchase the security being offered. One type of data would be changes in the issuer's financial situation.

FINRA 4514: Authorization Records for Negotiable Instruments Drawn from a customer's account prohibits a representative from withdrawing cash or cash equivalents from a customer's account without that customer's written authorization.

Account Types and Characteristics

Cash

An account with which a customer pays for all transactions in full is a ***cash account***.

Margin

An account with which a customer does not pay for a transaction in full but borrows from the member firm is a ***margin account***.

Federal Reserve Board Regulation T provides a set of guidelines for cash accounts and margin accounts, including the following:

- Payments are made promptly, not later than T+2, for securities purchased with either account type.
- Short sales must be made in a margin account.
- The customer must pay at least fifty percent (or the amount over $500) of the cost of a security purchased on margin.

FINRA 4210: Margin Requirements: specifies the way to determine the amount of collateral required in a margin account.

1934 Act Section 11(d): Trading by Members of Exchanges, Brokers, and Dealers

"Prohibition on extension of credit by broker-dealer" generally prohibits a member of a national exchange from trading for the member's own account, or a registered representative's account, or an account for which a representative may act with discretion, allowing the following exceptions:

- Market makers
- Odd-lot dealer in an authorized security
- Stabilizing transactions during an IPO
- Certain arbitrage or hedge transactions
- Account, estate, or trust of a natural person
- Correction of an error
- Primarily underwriting and distributing securities for another party
- Selling to customers
- Acting as a broker if the broker's gross income is mainly from such activity
- Maintenance of "fair and orderly markets," giving priority to orders for persons who are not members or otherwise connected with the exchange

FINRA 2264: Margin Disclosure Statement states that the member will provide the customer with a margin disclosure statement before, or when, opening a margin account.

Options

Options provide the owner the opportunity, but not the responsibility, to purchase or sell a specific quantity of a specific security at a specific price, by a certain time on a certain date; alternatively, an option may provide the owner the results of performance of an underlying security or index.

Discretionary vs. Non-Discretionary

Discretionary indicates the customer authorized the representative to select some characteristic of an order other than price and timing. Other than the price and timing, the characteristics of a **non-discretionary** order are all specified by the customer.

FINRA 3260: Discretionary Accounts require written authorization for the representative to select one or more characteristics of an order, other than the price or timing. Prior written authorization is required for each trade in which the representative's discretion is used.

Fee-Based vs. Commission

Fee-based vs. commission are two general methods in which securities professionals are compensated. Fee-based industry professionals may charge for their advice, whether or not any transaction is completed. Commissioned industry professionals are paid by taking an order and assisting in its completion and are only compensated upon completion of the trade.

Educational Accounts

Educational accounts have tax advantages (growing tax-deferred until used, and not taxed when used if used for eligible educational expenses) to assist the beneficiaries in saving for future educational costs. These include the following:

- Coverdell Educational Savings Account (ESA) allows a wide choice of investments and may be used for college. When used for grades below college, school expenses other than tuition may be paid from the account.

- 529 College Savings Plan: Typically administered by a state and allows a choice of mutual funds from a set of investment portfolios. This plan may be used for college. When used for grades below college, only tuition may be paid from the account.

Customer Account Registrations

1934 Act 17a-14: Form CRS, for Preparation, Filing and Delivery of Form CRS Investment Company Act of 1940

In June 2019, the SEC adopted guidance that member firms provide the Form CRS (Customer Relationship Summary) to the SEC and also to non-institutional customers by June 30, 2020. This form should aid non-institutional investors in more fully understanding the differences among the various types of financial service firms and associated persons, and the services they can expect from a financial firm and its individual professionals. A fee-based account with an investment adviser is contrasted with a transaction-based account with a broker-dealer. The activities and responsibilities of an investment advisory representative are explained, as well as those with a registered representative, and those with a person who is also registered or affiliated with another broker-dealer, an investment adviser, or other financial services firm. Form CRS is intended to inform retail investors about:

- Various ways in which the customer may relate to the firm and use its services;
- Expense of doing business with the firm;
- Conflicts of interest;
- Any legal or disciplinary history which the firm or its associated persons has, that should be reported to the customer; and
- A way to get more data regarding the firm.

When a member firm opens an account for a customer, it will be one of the following types.

Individual

An ***individual account*** is for one person, who alone may determine activity, unless that person authorizes another person to act.

Joint

A ***joint account*** is for more than one owner, any of whom may determine activity, but all of whom must sign when a signature is needed.

Corporate/Institutional

A ***corporate/institutional account*** requires a corporate resolution specifying all persons who are authorized to open the account, and all persons who are authorized to determine activity in the account.

Trust (e.g., revocable, irrevocable)

A ***trust*** requires the trust agreement to be on file, as well as documentation of the trustee's authority to determine activity for the good of the beneficiary.

Custodial

A ***custodial account*** allows an adult under the Uniform Transfer to Minors Act (UTMA) to contribute money or investments for a minor's good, and then determines activity as custodian.

Partnerships

Partnerships require the following to be on file: each general partner's name, address, citizenship, tax identification number, and the partnership agreement, which specifies which partner(s) may determine activity.

Retirement

Types and Characteristics

A ***retirement account*** is for an individual and regulated by tax law with tax deferral until used. It may be either an individual retirement account (***IRA***), which is managed by the individual, or it may be a plan sponsored by an employer (***qualified plan***). Each may have withdrawals taken out beginning at age 59 $1/2$, paying ordinary income tax rates on the withdrawal. Unless exceptions are satisfied, withdrawals taken before age 59 $1/2$ may result in an additional ten percent penalty for early withdrawal.

Required Minimum Distributions

By the age of 70 $1/2$, the owner must begin taking a minimum distribution, or pay a fifty percent penalty calculated on the required minimum distribution.

Contributions

Contributions to an IRA or a qualified plan are not taxed in the year made. Each has an annual limit for contributions that may occasionally be adjusted for inflation.

Anti-Money Laundering (AML)

Anti-money laundering (AML) is the category of rules that help ensure that persons cannot use securities accounts and transactions to hide illegal sources of funds.

84

Definition of Money Laundering

Money laundering is hiding a source of money obtained through unlawful means. This is usually done by using it for legal transactions.

USA PATRIOT Act Section 314 – Cooperative Efforts to Deter Money Laundering allows the Financial Crimes Enforcement Network (FinCEN) to make available to financial firms a list of individuals or firms under suspicion of illegal activity and to require financial firms to provide information regarding persons on that list.

USA PATRIOT Act Section 326 – Verification of Identification is a Treasury rule that provides for banks and other financial firms to do the following:

- Establish procedures to ascertain the identity of persons opening accounts

- Keep records of certain information regarding persons who open accounts, including name, address, etc.

- Compare the information with lists provided by the Treasury and other agencies as required

USA PATRIOT Act Section 352 – Anti-Money Laundering Programs amended the Bank Secrecy Act to provide that financial firms, including member firms, set up anti-money laundering programs.

Stages of Money Laundering

Structuring is a way of making a large amount of money less visible to regulators and officials in the legal system by making a large number of small transactions. **Layering** involves processing the funds through a series of transactions and recordkeeping deception. **Placement** enters the funds into the reputable financial system.

AML Compliance Program

The following rules (FINRA 3310 and MSRB G-41) provide for firms to establish and maintain a documented anti-money laundering process to help ensure member's fulfillment of the Bank Secrecy Act and the U.S. Department of Treasury's rules that interpret the act. Each member's anti-money laundering process must be approved in writing by a high-level executive.

FINRA 3310: Anti-Money Laundering Compliance Program relates to member firms.

MSRB G-41: Anti-Money Laundering Compliance Program relates to brokers, dealers, and municipal securities dealer.

Suspicious Activity Report (SAR)

A **suspicious activity report (SAR)** must be submitted by a financial firm to the FinCEN within thirty days of the date when data is observed that could lead a person to reasonably expect an SAR to be filed, unless no suspect was identified. In that case, another thirty days may be used to attempt to identify a suspect. A SAR is required in the following situations:

- If it appears than an employee made a transaction of insider trading (trading with knowledge the general public would not know)

- If a money laundering activity possibly occurred

- If the Bank Secrecy Act, which has process, recordkeeping, and reporting requirements for financial firms, may have been violated

- If computer hacking is detected

- If a customer runs an unlicensed money services business

Currency Transaction Report (CTR)

A *currency transaction report (CTR)* is a form completed by a bank official when a customer asks to deposit or withdraw more than $10,000.

FinCEN

FinCEN is the part of the U.S. Department of Treasury that gathers and reviews data regarding monetary business to prevent financial crimes, including money laundering and terrorist financing.

Office of Foreign Asset Control (OFAC)

The *Office of Foreign Asset Control (OFAC)* is the part of the U.S. Department of Treasury which handles trade and economic sanctions based on foreign policy against certain countries, organizations, and persons. OFAC maintains a Specially Designated Nationals and Blocked Persons List (SDN), an updated list of persons and groups that are known, or suspected, to be involved in activities such as drug smuggling and terrorism.

Books and Records and Privacy Requirements

Books and Records Retention Requirements

The Securities Exchange Act of 1934, Section 17 specifies that broker-dealers are responsible to maintain data and submit reports to the SEC as determined by the SEC and specifies how long those records are kept. The SEC determined that the data maintained must satisfy the needs of self-regulatory organizations (SROs) to carry out examinations of the broker-dealers. FINRA also has rules specifying data to be maintained and enforces the related SEC rules, as well as data maintenance rules of the MSRB.

FINRA Rule 4511: General Requirements requires firms to keep records as directed by the following:

- FINRA rules
- Securities Exchange Act
- Rules related to the Securities Exchange Act

Records are to be kept in an arrangement and form in keeping with Rule 17a-4 of the Securities Exchange Act.

MSRB G-8: Books and Records to be Made by Brokers, Dealers, Municipal Securities Dealers, and Municipal Advisors specifies that records be kept of complaints or municipal advisory clients or persons representing them. The complaint data includes the following:

- Name
- Address
- Account number of municipal advisory client number/code
- Date complaint received
- Date of the incident that triggered the complaint
- Name of each person named in the complaint

- Description of the complaint
- Action taken, if any, by the firm receiving the complaint
- A code, coordinated with FINRA Rule 4530, to categorize the complaint

MSRB G-9: Preservation of Records provides flexibility in the format of maintained data, so it does not need to be recorded with paper and ink, so long as the firm has a way for the data to be reviewed upon request by a regulatory supervisor.

1934 Act 17a-3: Records to be Made by Certain Exchange Members, Brokers, and Dealers specifies that data be maintained for certain minimum periods of time, and mentions the format in which they may be kept. This is in regard to the following types of data:

- Orders and transactions
- Associated persons
- Customer accounts
- Customer complaints
- Compensation
- Public communication
- List of persons who can explain the data

1934 Act 17a-4: Records to be Preserved by Certain Exchange Members, Brokers, and Dealers specifies data to be maintained by the following firms:

- Member of a national securities exchange who handles securities transactions for parties that are not themselves members of a national securities exchange

- Broker or dealer who handles transactions with the services of a member of a national securities exchange

- Broker or dealer, including an over-the-counter derivatives dealer

- A broker or dealer who is a dealer in security-based swaps

- A major registered security-based swap participant who is a broker-dealer, including an over-the-counter derivatives dealer

Some data must be maintained for six years, and in a place readily available for the first two years. Other data must be maintained for three years, and in a place readily available for the first two years.

Confirmations and Account Statements
FINRA 2232: Customer Confirmations

In addition to the specifications in 1934 Act 10b-10 – Confirmation of Transactions, at or before the fulfillment of any order, a member firm must provide the customer with a written document (confirmation) with the following data.

- If the security is callable, that it is callable, and that the customer may receive additional data regarding the security form the member firm.

- Markup/markdown, calculated as specified in ***FINRA Rule 2121***: Fair Prices and Commissions, in dollars and as a percentage of the market price, if the member firm acted in a principal capacity (was a party to the transaction) with a non-institutional customer. Conditions and exceptions relate to the member firm handling the other side of the transaction through an affiliate, or if the non-institutional customer placed the order with a different trading desk than the trading desk handling the offsetting transaction, and the member firm has a policy in place to ensure that the trading desk handling the offsetting transaction had no knowledge of the customer transaction.

- For orders by non-institutional customers regarding government agency or corporate securities, 1) identification of a FINRA webpage with Trade Reporting and Compliance Engine (TRACE) publicly available information about market activity in the security for which the order was placed, and 2) the time at which the order was fulfilled to the specific second.

1934 Act 10b-10: Confirmation of Transactions

For securities other than U.S. savings bonds or municipal securities, this rule generally specifies that the customer be provided a document (confirmation) at or before the fulfillment of any order, including at least the following data:

- Date
- Identity
- Price
- Number of shares bought or sold
- The capacity of the broker-dealer
- The net dollar price and yield of a debt security
- Under specified circumstances, the amount of compensation paid to the broker-dealer and whether payment for order flow is received
- If callable, the call price and the maturity date fixed by the call notice

MSRB G-15: Confirmation, Clearance, Settlement, and Other Uniform Practice Requirements with Respect to Transactions with Customers

This rule specifies that broker-dealers include a description of the securities on the municipal security customer order confirmation documents, to include the following:

- Name of the issuer
- Interest rate
- Maturity date
- If callable, a note to that effect
- If revenue bonds, all of the following:
  o A note to that effect
  o Type of revenue
  o If needed for a reasonably complete description of the securities, the name of any company or other person besides the issuer who is guaranteeing the bonds, or if there is more than one such guarantor, the note "multiple obligors"

MSRB G-15 also specifies that if the municipal security is pre-refunded (to be replaced by a new issue), that is to be noted on the confirmation. If the security is about to be pre-refunded, though that is not required to be noted by G-15, it may be required by the MSRB Rule G-17 on fair dealing. Similarly, G-15 may not require how the bond proceeds will be used, but if that information is necessary for a customer to make a reasonable decision, Rule G-17 requires disclosure of how bonds proceeds will be used.

MSRB Rule G-17: Fair Dealing specifies that a dealer must explain all material facts about the security which would reasonably be expected to guide the investor's decision and would not leave out any "material" facts which would result in other explanations being misleading and incomplete.

Holding of Customer Mail

FINRA 3150: Holding of Customer Mail provides that a member firm may hold a customer's mail, if the following conditions are met:

- Written instructions are given to the member, describing the time period, and if longer than three months, explaining with good reason (not just convenience) the reason for the longer time period.

- The member notifies the customer in writing of other ways, such as online access or email, to review account transactions and data, and receives written acknowledgement by the customer of that notification.

- The member must have a way to contact the customer.

- The member makes a fair effort to keep the customer's mail secure, not used in any way contrary to the customer's interests, as defined by government securities laws or FINRA rules.

Business Continuity Plans (BCP)

FINRA Rule 4370: Business Continuity Plans and Emergency Contact Information specifies that member firms establish, and update as necessary, a business continuity plan (BCP) that outlines steps to take in the case of a business interruption, such as a natural emergency, to allow the firms to continue to provide the expected services to customers, other broker-dealers, and other parties. Updates to the BCP are expected to take into account changes in the broker-dealer's type of business, way of doing business, organizational structure, and place of operations. Even though some clearing firms provide access to account data to customers of some introducing firms, those introducing firms are also subject to the BCP rule.

Customer Protection and Custody of Assets

MSRB G-25: Improper Use of Assets

Under the Securities Exchange Act of 1934 Rule 15c3-3 (known as the Customer Protection Rule) registered broker-dealers must keep monies or specified securities belonging to customers in a separate reserve bank account in order to prevent the comingling of customers' and broker-dealers' assets. This is to make sure the broker-dealer does not make improper use of the customers' assets. It also helps ensure the safety of the customer's assets in case of the broker-dealer's business failure.

Privacy Requirements

SEC Regulation S-P – Privacy of Consumer Financial Information and Safeguarding Personal Information requires broker-dealers, Investment companies, and Investment advisers to develop written methods to keep customer data secure.

Nonpublic Personal Information

On November 12, 1999, a federal law called the Financial Modernization Act of 1999, otherwise named the **Gramm-Leach-Bliley Act (GLB Act)**, was enacted reforming the financial services industry and improving consumer financial privacy. It covers banks and other firms providing financial services and products, including securities and insurance products. It directs the Federal Trade Commission (FTC) and other government financial regulatory agencies to enforce the privacy part of the act, including the following:

- The *Financial Privacy Rule*, which guides how financial firms obtain and use customers' financial information

- The *Safeguards Rule*, which directs all financial firms to protect customer data

- A section intended to keep anyone or any party from obtaining consumers' financial information through "pretexting," that is, using deceit

The Financial Privacy Rule guards a consumer's nonpublic personal information (NPI). NPI includes personally identifiable financial information that a financial firm obtains in the process of serving a consumer with a financial product or service unless that information is otherwise publicly available.

Confidentiality of Information
Confidentiality of information is accomplished by providing a person's private information only to parties who need it to do that party's work, and only for purposes stated in relation to the person, or according to laws that specify how confidential information may be used.

Privacy Notifications
The Gramm-Leach-Bliley Act specifies the following:

- That privacy notifications be given
- To whom they are given
- What they include:
  - how the firm obtains NPI
  - how the firm shares NPI
  - how the firm guards NPI of consumers and customers, including former customers
- Their appearance
- Their delivery
- Provision of opt-out notices
- Exceptions

Safeguard Requirements
To put the GLB Act into effect, the FTC issued the *Safeguards Rule*. This rule directs financial firms that FTC supervises to develop and maintain processes to assure the security of customer information.

Communications with the Public and General Suitability Requirements

Communications with the Public and Telemarketing
Classifications and General Requirements
FINRA 2210: Communications with the Public classifies communications with the public into the three following categories:

- Retail communication is defined as written (including electronic) communication that is sent to, or made accessible to, more than twenty-five retail investors within any thirty-calendar-day period. Retail communication is approved before its use, or before its filing

90

with FINRA's Advertising Regulation Department by a registered principal who is qualified.

- Correspondence is defined as written (including electronic) communication that is sent to, or made accessible to, twenty-five or less retail investors within a thirty-calendar-day period. Each member firm establishes, maintains, and follows procedures as follows:

  o Review and approval procedures for incoming and outgoing written (including electronic) correspondence, to recognize and appropriately respond to any items for which the FINRA rules or federal securities laws specify action, such as customer complaints

  o If using risk-based selection of correspondence to review, then 1) indoctrination of associated persons regarding the firm's approach to correspondence, 2) records kept of the indoctrination, and 3) ongoing monitoring of the risk-based procedures to make sure they are carried out

- Institutional communication is defined as written (including electronic) communication that is only sent to, or only made accessible to, institutional investors, excluding a member's internal communications. Each member firm establishes, maintains, and adheres to procedures as follows:

  o Review of institutional communication by a registered principal who is qualified, depending upon the member firm's mix of business, size, organizational structure, and categories of customers

  o If review is not made of all institutional correspondence, then 1) indoctrination of associated persons regarding the firm's approach to institutional correspondence, 2) records kept of the indoctrination, and 3) ongoing monitoring of the risk-based procedures to make sure they are carried out, with records of these actions maintained for review when asked by FINRA

Do-Not-Call List

The Federal Trade Commission's National **Do-Not-Call List** is intended to give a consumer the choice about whether to receive telemarketing calls. It is not intended to prevent calls from survey companies, political groups, collection agencies, and charities.

Federal Trade Commission Telemarketing Sales Rule directs telemarketers to do, or not do, certain actions, as follows:

- Honestly disclose information the recipient needs
- Limit the time during which calls may be made
- Not call a person who has requested not to be called again

FINRA 3230: Telemarketing specifies the following for member firms and their associated persons, as well as directing each member firm to establish, maintain, and carry out procedures to assure their fulfillment:

- Time-of-Day Restriction: Calling residences only between 8 a.m. and 9 p.m. local time at the called residence, except in one of the following situations:

- The member has a business relationship with the person called.
- The member received the person's invitation or permission to call.
- The person called is a broker or dealer.
- Firm-Specific Do-Not-Call List
- No calling of any person on a list who asked not to be called by, or in the interest of, the member
- Federal Trade Commission's National Do-Not-Call List: No calling of any person on the list, except in one of the following situations:
- Established Business Relationship Exception, unless the person has asked to be added to the firm-specific do-not-call list
- Prior Express Written Consent Exception (which may be electronic) and includes the phone number to be called
- Personal Relationship Exception

MSRB G-39: Telemarketing specifies the following for brokers, dealers, and municipal securities dealers:

- Time-of-Day Restriction: calling residences only between 8 a.m. and 9 p.m. local time at the called residence, except in one of the following situations:
- The broker, dealer, or municipal securities dealer has a business relationship with the person called.
- The broker, dealer, or municipal securities dealer received the person's invitation or permission to call.
- The person called is a broker, dealer, or municipal securities dealer.
- Firm-Specific Do-Not-Call List
- No calling of any person on a list who asked not to be called by, or in the interest of, the broker, dealer, or municipal securities dealer
- Federal Trade Commission's National Do-Not-Call List: no calling of any person on the list except in one of the following situations:
- Established Business Relationship Exception, unless the person has asked to be added to the firm-specific do-not-call list
- Prior Express Written Consent Exception (which may be electronic) and includes the phone number to be called
- Personal Relationship Exception

MSRB G-21: Advertising provides that dealers selling municipal securities should only advertise in ways that are honest and accurate and include adequate explanation of risks involved. It is intended to protect investors and governmental units issuing securities and avoid or reduce financial loss from trading the securities. To be thorough, the rule even determines the font size and content of footnotes. Also included is the use of testimonials in case they may be affected by payment to the persons providing testimony, or they may report investment results not obtained by other investors. Important data should not be left out. The future return on an investment should not be stated.

Best Interest Obligations and Suitability Requirements

FINRA 2111: Suitability directs a broker-dealer or associated person to have a common-sense foundation for recommending a security transaction or approach to security transactions to a customer, with a foundation in the characteristics of the customer, determined through conscientious effort.

1934 Act 15l-1: Regulation Best Interest was adopted by the Securities Exchange Commission, effective September 10, 2019, as a new rule under the Securities Exchange Act of 1934. It specified a new and higher expectation for broker-dealers and associated persons when making a recommendation to a retail customer of any securities transaction or pattern of securities transaction. This is a higher expectation than suitability.

It draws on the foundations of fiduciary care, similar to the principles of care that apply to investment advisers under the Investment Advisers Act of 1940, commonly known as Advisers Act. Regulation Best Interest expects broker-dealers and associated persons to do the following:

- Offer objective recommendations to solely benefit the retail customer, without regard for the recommender's personal gain as a result of said recommendations

- Address conflicts of interest by developing, maintaining, and carrying out processes intended to recognize and disclose conflicts of interest

- Where disclosure is insufficient to adequately address, reduce, or eliminate the conflict

Know-Your-Customer (KYC)
FINRA 2090: Know Your Customer explains that a broker-dealer should make a conscientious effort during a relationship with a client to learn and document an adequate description of each customer, and identify each person who has the prerogative to determine activity in the client's account.

General Requirements
FINRA characterizes a recommendation, as referenced in **FINRA 2111:** Suitability, as an inquiry regarding facts and circumstances. Distributing market literature does not amount to a recommendation.

Prohibited Activities

Market Manipulation

Definition of Market Manipulation
If a person or firm uses improper methods to increase or decrease the market price of a security or somehow affect the actions of other investors for personal gain, it may be called price manipulation, stock manipulation, or market manipulation.

1934 Act Section 10: Regulation of the Use of Manipulative and Deceptive Devices

In general, this section defines a manipulative or deceptive device or contrivance as something a person does or fails to do, in violation of the rules of the Securities Exchange Commission using any of the following:

- Interstate commerce
- The mail
- Any national securities exchange

In regard to the purchase or sale of any of the following:

- Any security, whether registered on a national securities exchange or note
- Any securities-based swap agreement

To do any of the following in a way that violates a rule of the SEC:

- Place a short sale
- Enter any stop loss order in connection with the purchase or sale of any security other than a government security
- Be involved with a trade involving the loan or borrowing of securities in violation of SEC rules

Subsections of Section 10 offer some specific guidelines.

1934 Act Section 10b-1: Prohibition of use of manipulative or deceptive devices or contrivances with respect to certain securities exempted from registration.

This rule clearly defines manipulative or deceptive device or contrivance, to prohibit fraud in trading of securities that are exempt from registration, such as municipal securities.

1934 Act Section 10b-3: Employment of Manipulative and Deceptive Devices by Brokers or Dealers

This rule specifies that brokers-dealers may not commit fraud relating to securities. This rule is used, along with Rule 10b-5, as a legal foundation to charge persons with fraud.

1934 Act Section 10b-5: Employment of Manipulative and Deceptive Practices

This rule specifically identifies violating SEC rules as any person who defrauds another person in the purchase or sale of any security. This rule is used to charge a person with fraud. Rule 10b-5(1) allows for a person to show the intention to place an order before coming across material, confidential data as a defense against being held guilty of fraud under this section.

Types of Market Manipulation

Market rumors refer to false data being announced or published, such as in social media, regarding a company, in order to alter the price of its securities.

Pump-and-dump occurs when one or more investors holding a company's security starts market rumors with fictitious good news. The goal is to inflate the price (pump) so the security may be sold at a profit (dump).

Front running involves placing a large order that results in attention being given to a security, and the market responds with higher prices. If a person or firm is aware of a large order that has not yet occurred for a security, they may not enter an order for the firm's account or for a customer's discretionary account. To do so would be an attempt to make a quick profit by selling after the large order is complete, to take advantage of the anticipated price increase.

Excessive trading, or ***churning***, refers to trades made to generate commission to the representative, rather than for the benefit of the customer.

Marking the close/marking the open refers to a large quantity of transactions either immediately before the close of trading for the day, or immediately after the opening of trading for the day, which changes the value of a security from what typical supply and demand would have caused.

Since broker-dealers use the closing price of a security to calculate reserve requirements for margin accounts (accounts whose owners have borrowed from the broker-dealer), impacting the closing price affects the margin calls made on customers for that security. The closing price is published in various media. If the affected security is part of an index, artificially influencing the value of the security improperly affects that day's calculation of the index.

Backing away is the process of a market maker (a firm who offers a bid price and an ask price for a security) declining to fulfill an order placed in accordance with a published bid. This breaks rules of the SEC and FINRA. The firm may be required to pay a fine and discontinue serving as a market maker.

Freeriding refers to a customer buying a security and not paying for it until the security rises and sales proceeds are received. SEC Regulation T directs that a customer promptly pays for securities bought and defines "promptly" for various categories of securities. If settlement is made "regular way," settlement will occur within two trading days after the trade date (T+2), and payment will be made within two trading days after settlement (S+2). So typically, payment will be made within four trading days after the trade date (T+4), which is no later than two business days after settlement.

Insider Trading

Definition of Insider Trading
Insider trading typically refers to placing an illegal order based on important, relevant data that is not known to the public. Under certain restrictions and reporting requirements, persons technically identified as insiders may place trades.

Definition of Material Nonpublic Information
Material nonpublic information is important, relevant data that is not known to the public that, if known by the public, would result in a change in the market price of a security.

Insider Trading & Securities Fraud Enforcement Act of 1988 (ITSFEA) was passed in response to scandals in years prior to the act. It prohibited giving (by the "tipper") and receiving (by the "tippee") important, relevant data that is not known to the public in order to place an order.

Identifying Involved Parties
In order to identify parties to illegal insider trading, ITSFEA requires broker-dealers to do the following:

- Monitor employees' orders for themselves and their orders in the firm's accounts

- For firms that assist firms who issue securities, establish watch lists (maintained by supervisory and legal staff) and restricted lists (provided to employees) of securities about which the firm has insider information, and use them to monitor or limit employees' orders for securities on those lists

Penalties
1934 Act Section 21A: Civil Penalties for Insider Trading

As civil penalties for illegal insider trading, the SEC may levy fines as much as three times the profit obtained, or the loss averted. The SEC may also have the inside trader refund the increase on the trading.

As a criminal penalty for an individual, the U.S. Department of Justice (DOJ) may seek fines as large as $5 million. The DOJ may seek a fine for an organization of as much as $25 million per instance.

Following the FINRA Code of Procedure (COP), FINRA may expel or suspend a firm, or revoke the registration of a person associated with a member for a violation of FINRA rules, such as illegal insider trading. An expelled or suspended firm may not transact securities business while expelled or suspended. A person with a revoked registration may not receive payment for any securities-related actions, except for those earned before the revocation became effective.

As a criminal penalty for illegal insider trading, the DOJ may seek incarceration for as long as twenty years per instance for an individual.

1934 Act Section 20A: Liability to Contemporaneous Traders for Insider Trading

This provides that a person who, at the same time, bought or sold the same class of security as that transacted by a person guilty of illegal insider trading may bring suit in court against the guilty party asking for damages. A person who provided material nonpublic information to the guilty trader is also liable to a person who, at the same time, bought or sold the same class of security as the person guilty of illegal insider trading.

1934 Act 10b5-1: Trading on Material Nonpublic Information in Insider Trading Cases

This subsection describes when buying or selling a security equates to trading on the basis of material nonpublic information, in violation of an obligation of trust to the issuer, its shareholders, or the person who shared the information. The person who is aware of the material nonpublic information is considered to make the trade on the basis of that information, unless the following can be demonstrated:

- Before learning of the material nonpublic information, one of the following existed or occurred:
- A written plan for trading
- Instruction had been given to another person to trade
- A binding contract to trade the security
- The plan, instruction, or contract fulfilled one of the following conditions:
- Included the amount of securities to buy or sell, the price, and the date of the transaction
- Included a method to determine the amount, the price, and the date
- Did not permit the person to subsequently affect the trade, if any other person involved in the plan, instruction, or contract, was not aware of the material nonpublic information
- The transaction was "pursuant" to a plan, instruction, or contract, without deviating or acting in any way to hedge the security involved

1934 Act 10b5-2: Duties of Trust or Confidence in Misappropriation Insider Trading Cases enlarges the conventional view of insider trading to include a person using material nonpublic information in a way that betrays a duty owed to the party from whom the material nonpublic information was received.

Other Prohibited Activities

FINRA 2010: Standards of Commercial Honor and Principles of Trade uses broad language to require that all persons in the securities industry do business with high standards and fair principles of trade.

Restrictions Preventing Associated Persons from Purchasing Initial Public Offerings (IPOs)

FINRA 5130: Restrictions on the Purchase and Sale of Initial Equity Public Offerings prohibits members firms and their associated persons from being involved in selling initial public offering (IPO) shares to any customer account in which a restricted person has an interest, unless the sale qualifies for an exception. Restricted persons include FINRA member firms and non-member broker-dealer firms, associated persons of broker-dealer firms, persons assisting with the IPO in a material way, fund managers, persons who own broker-dealer firms, and immediate family members of the persons listed, as well as persons materially supported by the persons listed, including persons living in the same household.

A member firm of an associated person may not purchase IPO shares in an account in which the firm or the associated person has an interest, unless the purchase qualifies for an exception.

A member firm acting as an underwriter for the IPO may not hold the shares acquired in the capacity as an underwriter, unless the situation qualifies for an exception.

Exceptions include the following:

- Allowing a member firm in the selling group to sell IPO shares to another member of the selling group, in order to ultimately sell the shares to a non-restricted person

- Allowing a broker-dealer to buy or sell IPO shares at the offering price as an accommodation to a non-restricted person customer

- Allowing a broker-dealer or its owner, if a part of an investment partnership, to buy IPO shares at the offering price if those purchases are credited to the accounts of the partners, if the restricted person(s) accumulated interest are not more than ten percent of that partnership account

Use of Manipulative, Deceptive, or Other Fraudulent Devices

FINRA 2020: Use of Manipulative, Deceptive or Other Fraudulent Devices determines that no firm shall influence someone to buy or sell a security by using any manipulative, deceptive or other fraudulent device.

1934 Act 15c1-2: Fraud and Misrepresentation

The term ***manipulative, deceptive, or other fraudulent device*** is defined to include the following:

- Anything a person could do which would work "as a fraud or deceit" upon anybody

- Any untrue statement of important data that could be misleading, that is made with awareness or suspicion that the statement is untrue or could be misleading

- Any failure to share important data whose omission would be essential given the situational context, so that its omission could be misleading, made with the awareness or suspicion that failure to share could be misleading

- Other possibilities not limited by the above definitions

1934 Act 15c1-3: Misrepresentation by Brokers, Dealers, and Municipal Securities Dealers as to Registration

The term manipulative, deceptive, or other fraudulent device or contrivance includes insinuations by a broker, dealer, or municipal securities dealer that the commission has endorsed any of the following, regarding the broker, dealer, or municipal securities dealer:

- Financial strength
- Overall approach to securities activity
- Any specific service
- The value or suitability of any security or suitability of any trade or set of trades

The SEC is concerned that insinuations may be based on one of the following:

- The registration of a broker or dealer
- The registration of a municipal securities dealer
- The failure of the commission to deny or revoke a registration

FINRA 5230: Payments Involving Publications that Influence the Market Price of a Security

No member firm may use money to encourage any firm or person to publish something that could influence the market price of a security, except for the following:

- Communication that is obviously paid advertising
- Communication that announces the amount of compensation
- An article that qualifies as a research report

FINRA 5240: Anti-intimidation/Coordination

No member firm or associated person is allowed to do any of the following:

- Cooperate with any other member or any associated person of another member, or anyone else, regarding price levels in quotations or trade transactions

- Communicate to another member firm a request to change a price in a quotation or a trade transaction

- Use fear to change a price, affect trading behavior, or discourage competitive activities of another market maker or market participant

Provided that behavior is in keeping with all related laws and regulations, a member firm or an associated person may do the following:

- Determine its own quotes to buy or sell, both as to prices and quantity of shares

- Determine its own profit margin, pricing increment or number of shares for its quotations, and any formula that relates those characteristics to one another

- Announce its own quotes to buy or sell, along with the amount it is willing to buy or sell, relative to any security to any investor, as advertising, the opportunity to buy or sell a security, and to arrange details of a trade transaction

- Announce its own quote, or the price at or the quantity of shares at which it is willing to buy or sell any security, to any person with the intention of obtaining an agreement with that person to be an agent or subagent for the member firm or as a customer of the member firm (or with the intention of seeking to be retained as an agent or subagent), and to work out a buy or sale order

- Perform any underwriting (or work with any syndicate for the underwriting) of securities allowed by the securities regulations and laws

- Act on one's own behalf with the market makers with which it will trade and arrange conditions under which it will handle orders unless such acts are contrary to this rule

- Send an order to another member firm for processing

98

FINRA 5270: Front Running of Block Transactions

This is one of a set of rules that intends to help assure that brokers and market makers process trades at prices that are in the best interests of those who place the orders. It forbids brokers from dealing in securities-related orders for their own interest if they possess private knowledge that a block transaction (generally, an order for 10,000 shares or more) is imminent.

FINRA 5280: Trading Ahead of Research Reports

A member firm is not to place an order for a security or a derivative based upon that security which is founded on nonpublic advance knowledge of the information or scheduled release of a research report for that security. Each member firm is to make and update processes to restrict the interchange of data between persons in the research department and the persons in the trading department to eliminate the likelihood that persons in the trading department will have the use of nonpublic advance knowledge of the schedule of, or data in, a research report for any firm's or person's benefit.

FINRA 5320: Prohibition Against Trading Ahead of Customer Orders

This generally forbids a member firm that has a client's order to place an order like it for that security for its own interest, at a price that would fulfill the client's order, unless the firm promptly completes the client's order for at least as many shares and at least as favorable price as it submitted for its own interest. Orders of at least 10,000 shares, orders of at least $100,000 in value, orders from client firms, and not-held orders are excluded from this prohibition.

Improper Use of Customers' Securities or Funds

FINRA 2150: Improper Use of Customers' Securities or Funds; Prohibition Against Guarantees and Sharing in Accounts

This rule limits or prohibits any member or associated person from the following activities:

- Using a client's securities or money in an improper manner

- Guaranteeing a client against loss regarding any securities trade or any securities account

- Sharing personally in the gain or loss in a client's account at the member firm or any member firm, unless all of the following occur:

    o The associated person receives prior written permission from the member firm employing the associated person;

    o The associated person receives prior written permission from the client; and

    o The member firm or associated person splits the gains or losses in any account of a client with the same percentage as the investment made in that account by the member firm or the associated person.

An exception to this rule includes the associated person's parents, mother-in-law, father-in-law, husband, wife, children, or any relative to whose support the member or person associated with a member provides.

Also, a member firm or associated person who is acting as an investment adviser may receive compensation based on a share of gains or losses in an account if all of the following occur:

- The associated person receives prior written permission from the member firm employing the associated person;

- The associated person receives prior written permission from the client

- All conditions in Rule 205-3 of the Investment Advisers Act (as amended), which requires that the client be a qualified client, with qualified client referring to a client with either:

  - At least $1 million managed by the firm, or

  - Net worth (with a spouse, if applicable), in the opinion of the investment adviser, of $2.1 million before establishing the advisory contract.

Borrowing from Customers
FINRA 3240: Borrowing from or lending to Customers

This allows borrowing and lending arrangements between registered investment advisers (RIAs) and customers of their member firm only if certain conditions are met:

- The member firm must have set up a documented process.
- One of the following conditions must apply:
  - The customer is an immediate family member of the broker.
  - The customer is a bank or other financial firm that borrows and lends in the normal course of business.
  - The customer and broker are both employed at the same member firm.
  - The agreement must be built on a personal relationship that is outside the broker-customer relationship.
  - The agreement is because of an approved business relationship that is outside of the broker-customer relationship.
- The associated person must let the member firm know they are borrowing or lending, and the firm must provide approval. Proper notification must be given, and advanced approval must be received, as follows:
  - The details of the agreement are described to the member firm before funds are transferred.
  - Persons of the member firm's compliance department evaluate the agreement and decide whether to allow it.
  - If the agreement is not allowed, the lending arrangement does not happen.
  - The firm has the prerogative to disallow the transaction because if repayment were not made, the firm might be responsible for the payment.

Sharing in Customer Accounts
FINRA 2150 (above) addresses conditions for sharing in customer accounts.

FINRA 3210: Accounts at Other Broker-Dealers and Financial Institutions

This regulates how investment adviser firms and their adviser representatives begin trading in accounts at firms other than their own. These advisers and brokers report to their firm their plan (or a plan of their spouses, children, or other family members) to open an account at a firm other than the one by whom they are employed or registered. They only open the account after approval by their member firm.

FINRA 3250: Designation of Accounts

A member firm only opens and keeps an account in one of the following:

- The actual name of the account holder
- By a number or symbol, if the firm has a document signed by the customer acknowledging ownership of the account

Financial Exploitation of Seniors
FINRA 2165: Financial Exploitation of Specified Adults

This allows a member firm, for a short period of time, to prevent disbursement of money or investments on behalf of a specified adult customer if the firm has one of the following rational suspicions:

- Financial exploitation has happened.
- Financial exploitation is happening.
- Financial exploitation was attempted.
- Financial exploitation will be attempted.

Specified adults include the following:

- An individual who is sixty-five or older
- An individual who is at least eighteen, who the member rationally suspects has a mental or physical impairment that prevents the individual from making decisions in their own best interest

Activities of Unregistered Persons
Prohibition against Paying Commissions to Unregistered Persons
FINRA 2040: Payments to Unregistered Persons

Member firms and associated persons do not pay compensation based on securities accounts or transactions to any individual who is not registered as a broker-dealer with FINRA. Member firms and associated persons only pay compensation based on securities accounts or transactions to registered individuals by following all FINRA rules and securities laws, rules, and regulations.

Prohibition against Solicitation of Customers and Taking Orders
Unregistered persons may only communicate with prospective clients for the following actions:

- To invite a member of the public to a meeting scheduled by the firm
- To determine the customer's interest in having a conversation with a registered person about investments
- To determine the customer's interest in receiving documents about investments

Therefore, unregistered persons may not solicit customers or take orders.

Falsifying or Withholding Documents

Section 17(a)(1) of the Securities Exchange Act of 1934 (also known as Exchange Act or SEA) requires registered broker-dealers to produce and maintain certain data and make certain reports. These are required to be accurate and produced on a timely basis.

Signatures of Convenience

Under Rule 2010, FINRA has disciplined individuals who have had clients sign forms that were not completed, which the representative completed later, supposedly for the client's convenience.

Responding to Regulatory Requests

Securities Exchange Act Rules 17a-3 and 17a-4 set standards for data to be retained for minimum lengths of time. The Securities Exchange Commission directs member firms to have information available so that state securities regulators, self-regulatory organizations such as FINRA and MSRB, and the SEC are able to complete examinations of those member firms.

FINRA Rule 13507: Responding to Discovery Requests

In the case of arbitration, except when a different time frame is agreed upon, the firm or individual receiving a discovery request must, within sixty days, do one of the following:

- Produce the requested data by first-class mail, overnight service, courier, email, or facsimile

- Explain the reason that the requested data is not available in the requested time frame and make clear when the documents will be available

- Object to the request, naming document(s) and reasons per Rule 13508 Objecting to Discovery Requests; Waiver of Objection

The receiving party must use its best efforts to produce all requested data. If data is not available as requested, the firm or individual receiving a discovery request must provide a rational timeframe to produce the data. If any data is redacted (removed), the redacted data shall be labeled as redacted.

Prohibited Activities Related to Maintenance of Books and Records

Books and records include accounting information, securities accounts, data, notes, communications, and other data required by FINRA rules, federal securities laws, and by MSRB rules to be kept. This includes the following:

- Trade blotters (transaction logs)
- Accounting details
- Customer account details
- Securities records
- Order tickets
- Trade confirmations

FINRA Rule 4511 requires data to be kept for certain lengths of times (six years, if not specified) and in certain formats. Changing or destroying data in violation of FINRA rules are significant infractions, which may result in fines and other punitive steps.

See our SIE Resource Page for links to current rules and regulations.

You can visit by going to https://www.apexprep.com/sie or by scanning the QR code.

Overview of the Regulatory Framework

SRO Regulatory Requirements for Associated Persons

Registration and Continuing Education

SRO Qualification and Registration Requirements

The following are some items addressed in the FINRA By-Laws and Rules:

FINRA By-Laws Article I: Definitions

This article defines dozens of terms used throughout the by-laws.

FINRA By-Laws Article III: Qualifications of Members and Associated Persons

This article describes, in general, registration and other qualifications that may be established, activity in the profession, standards of behavior, and reporting requirements.

FINRA By-Laws Article IV: Membership

This article describes the application for membership, which includes the following:

- An agreement to follow laws, rules, and regulations of the SEC, MSRB, Department of the Treasury, and FINRA, and all rulings' orders and decisions and sanctions
- An agreement to make required payments, including annual amounts and others as determined
- Other reasonable information as may be included in the application from time to time

FINRA By-Laws Article V: Registered Representatives and Associated Persons

This article requires member firms to only allow qualified persons, who are not subject to disqualification, to perform securities activities or investment banking activities.

FINRA Rule 0100 Series: General Standards

These rules include the following topics:

- The FINRA rules' adoption is authorized by the FINRA By-Laws, Article VII, Section 1.
- The FINRA rules' effective dates are determined by the board as provided in the FINRA By-Laws, Article XI, Section 1.
- Interpretation of FINRA rules will be in keeping with FINRA's purposes.
- Definitions are specified for words and phrases used throughout the rules.
- FINRA will coordinate with the MSRB regarding registration and supervision of municipal securities brokers, municipal securities dealers, and municipal advisors.
- Members will become non-members for various reasons, effective as of the appropriate date.

FINRA Rule 1000 Series: Member Application and Associated Person Registration

These rules describe how a firm becomes a member and a person becomes registered.

FINRA Rule 1122: Filing of Misleading Information as to Membership or Registration

This rule prohibits member firms and their associated persons from providing false information in filings with FINRA.

The MSRB has rules relating to qualifications and behavior of representatives.

MSRB Rule G-2: Standards of Professional Qualifications

This rule requires that only qualified persons handle municipal securities transactions.

MSRB Rule G-3: Professional Qualification Requirements

This rule establishes qualification testing and continuing education (CE) requirements and specifies classification of principals and representatives.

MSRB Rule G-7: Information Concerning Associated Persons

This rule specifies that municipal securities brokers and municipal securities dealers will acquire information from their employees concerning their suitability to work in the municipal securities industry so that this information may be filed with the related governing SRO or other entity.

MSRB Rule G-10: Delivery of Investment Brochure

This rule states that a municipal securities dealer will provide the investor brochure to an investor when a written complaint from that investor regarding a municipal securities transaction has been received.

Definition of Registered vs. Non-Registered Person

The FINRA is the SRO that regulates broker-dealer firms in the United States. A registered person is a person who has passed a FINRA registration exam.

Permitted Activities of Registered and Non-Registered Persons

A registered person, when engaged by a FINRA member broker-dealer firm, is authorized to encourage a person, according to securities laws and regulations regarding suitability and other considerations, to buy or sell a security appropriate to the representative's registration. A registered person serves under the supervision of an appropriately registered supervisor.

A non-registered person may do the following without close supervision:

- Invite members of the public to a meeting for which the firm is responsible
- Ask whether a member of the public is interested in reviewing possible investments with a registered person of the firm
- Ask whether a member of the public is interested in receiving printed materials about investments

A non-registered person is not allowed to discuss investments with a member of the public.

FINRA Rule 2060: Use of Information Obtained in Fiduciary Capacity

This rule provides that no member firm who serves in a recordkeeping role for the issuer during a securities distribution receives contact information regarding owners of securities that may be used to promote transactions with those owners unless the issuer directs the member firm to do so.

FINRA Rule 2263: Arbitration Disclosure to Associated Persons Signing or Acknowledging Form U4

This rule states that a member firm, when asking an associated person to sign a U4 filing, furnish that person with a printed document clarifying that, by signing, the person is agreeing to arbitration of disputes.

FINRA Rule 2267: Investor Education and Protection

This rule provides the following annually for each customer:

- FINRA BrokerCheck Hotline number
- FINRA website address
- Notice of the opportunity to obtain a document that describes FINRA BrokerCheck

FINRA Rule 4330: Customer Protection—Permissible Use of Customers' Securities

This rule specifies that a member firm must receive permission in writing from a customer before lending that customer's securities.

FINRA Rule 4530: Reporting Requirements

This rule requires member firms to do the following:

- Create quarterly summary reports of investor complaints made in writing
- Immediately report (within thirty calendar days after the firm could have been expected to know) specified significant events
- Provide a copy of certain criminal and civil actions

Ineligibility for Membership or Association

The FINRA By-laws, Article III, Section 3, states that no dealer or broker shall continue in membership if the firm does any of the following:

- No longer satisfies the requirements of Article III, Section 2, which broadly allows the FINRA board to establish requirements
- Is subject to a disqualification under Article III, Section 4, which refers to Section 3(a)(39) of the Securities Act of 1934 and includes such things as discipline by a state securities commission
- Does not file all forms as required

Background Checks

FINRA Rule 3110(e): Responsibility of Member to Investigate Applicants for Registration Members' Supervisory Obligations

This rule provides that each member firm will have a documented process to use for background checks, before it asks to register a person with FINRA, to determine that the applicant possesses integrity and other characteristics appropriate for activity in the securities industry. This anticipates that the firm will make a reasonably thorough review of information available to the public, including the current Form U5. At least some parts of Rule 3110 may have been superseded by the 4510 Series rules.

Fingerprinting
SEC Rule 17f-2: Fingerprinting of Securities Industry Personnel

This rule directs that, unless an exemption applies, every broker, dealer, registered transfer agent, and registered clearing agency must have each partner, director, officer, and employee fingerprinted. These fingerprints are submitted as determined by the attorney general of the United States.

CBOE Rule 7.10: Fingerprint-Based Background Checks of Exchange Directors, Officers, Employees, and Others

This rule explains that the CBOE performs fingerprint-based background checks on its personnel for the safety of its buildings and information.

Statutory Disqualification
Securities Exchange Act of 1934 Section 3(a)(39): Definitions and Application of Title (Statutory Disqualification)

This subsection refers to several possible situations in which a firm may not hire an individual, including the following:

- Disciplinary action taken by organizations such as an SRO or a corresponding foreign regulatory organization, securities exchange, Commodity Futures Trading Commission (CFTC), or foreign financial regulatory authority

- Conviction of certain offenses, including a felony, within ten years prior to an application for membership or participation

However, statutory disqualification may be appealed to the SEC.

Failing to Register an Associated Person
FINRA Rule 1011 lists those who are associated persons, which includes persons who work with a member firm in almost any capacity unless the person performs only "clerical and ministerial" functions. Those persons must be registered for the roles they fulfill.

FINRA may impose a penalty for failure to properly register an associated person for the activities that person performs. FINRA defines several registration categories and the roles that an associated person having each registration may perform.

FINRA Rule 1220: Registration Categories

This rule lists the following registration categories:

- General Securities Principal
- Compliance Officer
- Financial and Operations Principal
- Introducing Broker-Dealer Financial and Operations Principal
- Investment Banking Principal
- Research Principal
- Securities Trader Principal
- Registered Options Principal

- Government Securities Principal
- General Securities Sales Supervisor
- Investment Company and Variable Contracts Products Principal
- Direct Participation Programs Principal
- Private Securities Offerings Principal
- Supervisory Analyst
- General Securities Representative
- Operations Professional
- Securities Trader
- Investment Banking Representative
- Research Analyst
- Investment Company and Variable Contracts Products Representative

FINRA Rule 8310: Sanctions for Violation of the Rules

This rule states that FINRA may impose a penalty on a member firm or associated person for each infraction of any of the following:

- Federal securities laws, rules, or regulations
- Rules of the MSRB
- FINRA rules
- Direction based on the FINRA rules

The penalty may include one or more of the following:

- Censure
- Fine
- Suspend membership of firm
- Suspend registration of associated person
- Expel member
- Cancel membership of firm
- Revoke or cancel registration of associated person
- Suspend or bar member or associated person from association with all members
- Temporary or permanent cease and desist order against member or associated person
- Any other appropriate penalty

Therefore, failing to register an associated person can result in a severe penalty.

State Registration Requirements

In some ways, the SEC itself administers laws regarding the securities industry. In other ways, the SEC administers these laws through the exchanges and FINRA.

In Hall v. Geiger Jones Co., 242 U.S. 539 (1917), relating to the states being able to regulate securities without violating the U.S. Constitution, Justice Joseph McKenna wrote the following:

"The name that is given to the law indicates the evil at which it is aimed, that is, to use the language of a cited case, 'speculative schemes which have no more basis than so many feet of blue sky' ..."

Each state has been able to regulate the securities industry within its own state, except where federal law exempts a security or a transaction from state jurisdiction. Those state laws have been referred to as "Blue

Sky" laws. To sell a security in a state, the transaction, the representative, and the firm must be registered, or exempt from registration, in that state. Many state laws are similar to the Uniform Securities Act (USA) of 1956, but many have significant differences, and although the NASAA promotes some coordination among all fifty states and the District of Columbia, as well as the U.S. Virgin Islands, Puerto Rico, Canada, and Mexico, even the same language may be interpreted differently in different states and territories.

Continuing Education (CE) Requirement

FINRA Rule 1250: Continuing Education Requirements

FINRA oversees continuing education for securities persons. Other SROs and the Securities Industry/Regulatory Council on Continuing Education provide input. FINRA Rule 1250 lists two components to this CE requirement: firm element and regulatory element.

Firm Element

The ***firm element*** is a systematic instruction process developed by each member firm. The following associated persons are generally required to fulfill this requirement:

- Registered persons having communication with customers
- Registered operations professionals
- Research analysts
- Immediate supervisors of any of these persons

Each firm annually assesses its needs and organizes its process in a document, taking into account the following:

- Number of associated persons in the firm
- Their functions
- Their achievement in the regulatory element
- Changes in the industry's oversight
- Supervisors' need for updated supervisory knowledge and skill

The firm develops content regarding morals, investment characteristics, suitability, sales activities, and industry oversight to improve the participants' expertise, competence, and thoroughness.

Regulatory Element

The ***regulatory element*** was developed by FINRA, with input from the other organizations mentioned above. This element must be fulfilled within 120 days after the second anniversary of registration and within 120 days after every third anniversary. Otherwise, unless FINRA grants more time, the representative's registration will be considered inactive. FINRA rules describe penalty actions for becoming inactive and remediation of those actions.

Employee Conduct and Reportable Events

Employee Conduct

Form U4 and Form U5

Form U4 (Uniform Application for Broker-Dealer Registration) is used by associated persons' firms to register associated persons with SROs and oversight authorities, such as states. The firms typically submit U4 information electronically on the Central Registration Depository (CRD). Registered investment adviser representatives and broker-dealer agents are required to update the U4 when certain events occur. U4 information is available to the public through the BrokerCheck website at https://brokercheck.finra.org/. An updated Form U4 is submitted within thirty days after significant information changes.

Form U5 (Uniform Termination Notice for Security Industry Registration) is used by associated persons' firms to end the registrations of associated persons with SROs and oversight authorities, such as states and territories. Firms ending the registration of an associated person must answer some questions regarding the circumstances. A firm is required to amend a formerly submitted Form U5 if new information about certain events becomes known. A firm typically submits U5 information electronically on the CRD.

Issuers' agents, some persons submitting to stock exchanges, and specific investment adviser representatives may find it necessary to submit U4 or U5 information on paper documents. A firm may need to file paper Form U4 to accompany a new membership application.

Consequences of Filing Misleading Information or Omitting Information

Firms or natural persons that file or encourage the filing of an erroneous Form U5 may be penalized by FINRA through fines and suspensions. Disciplinary actions have cited the following as a basis for penalties:

- Article V, Section 3, of the FINRA By-Laws requires member firms to submit Form U5 no later than thirty days after ending an associated person's registration.

- FINRA Rule 1122 states: "No member or person associated with a member shall file with FINRA information with respect to membership or registration which is incomplete or inaccurate so as to be misleading, or which could in any way tend to mislead, or fail to correct such filing after notice thereof."

- FINRA Rule 2010 states: "A member, in the conduct of its business, shall observe high standards of commercial honor and just and equitable principles of trade."

For filing erroneous U4 or U5 forms or amendments, FINRA's Sanction Guidelines have suggested the following:

- Against the responsible supervisory person and/or member firm: a monetary fine of $5,000 to $146,000 and suspension of the responsible supervisory person from all supervisory functions for ten to thirty business days

- Against an individual: a monetary fine of $2,500 to $37,000 and suspension of the individual from all related business activities for five to thirty business days

Customer Complaints

FINRA Rule 4513: Written Customer Complaints

This rule requires each member firm to preserve, for a period of at least four years, a file of the following:

- Written customer complaints that have to do with that office
- Written customer complaints that have to do with activities supervised from that office
- Action, if any, taken by the member

Customer complaint refers to any dissatisfaction expressed in writing by a customer or a customer's authorized representative regarding activities related to encouragement, or completion of, any purchase, sale, or final handling of securities or funds of that customer.

Potential Red Flags

The Bank Secrecy Act requires broker-dealers, among other financial firms, to establish and maintain documented Anti-Money Laundering (AML) processes, approved by a senior manager of the firm. FINRA Rule 3310 provides guidance for this process.

FINRA Regulatory Notice 19-18 lists ninety-seven examples of "money laundering red flags" in the following categories, including possible scenarios:

- Potential Red Flags in Customer Due Diligence and Interactions with Customers: Customer provides unexpected identification documents.

- Potential Red Flags in Deposits of Securities: Customer opens a new account and deposits a large quantity of rarely traded securities or "penny stocks."

- Potential Red Flags in Securities Trading: Trading volume of relatively rarely traded securities or penny stocks suddenly increases.

- Potential Red Flags in Money Movements: Customer often deposits substantial amounts of cash or cash equivalents.

- Potential Red Flags in Insurance Products: Customer cancels an insurance policy and requests that the proceeds be sent to someone else.

- Other Potential Red Flags: Customer prefers not to disclose facts required to submit necessary reports for the transaction.

Reportable Events

Outside Business Activities

FINRA Rule 3270: Outside Business Activities [OBAs] of Registered Persons require the following:

A registered individual reports in writing an OBA, in addition to work for their member firm, for which compensation is or might reasonably be expected to be received.

The member firm reviews the written notice with the following considerations:

- Will the OBA interfere with the registered individual's duties to the member firm and the member firm's customers?

- Will the OBA be perceived by outsiders as part of the member's activities?

Then, the member firm considers whether any conditions need to be placed upon the OBAs.

Private Securities Transactions

FINRA Rule 3280: Private Securities Transactions of an Associated Person

This rule provides the following two alternatives for an associated person, prior to being involved in one, or a set of, private securities transactions:

- The associated person must provide written notice to the member firm describing the private securities transaction and the person's role and stating the amount of commission or that no commission will be received.

- If the associated person is to be involved in a set of related private securities transactions for which a commission will not be received, the associated person must provide a single written notice to the member firm.

In the case of a commissioned transaction, the member responds in writing to the associated person regarding the person's involvement as follows:

- If approved, the transaction is recorded by the member, and the member supervises the person's involvement as for any transaction done for the member.
- If disapproved, the person is prohibited from involvement in the transaction.

In the case of a non-commissioned transaction, the member responds immediately in writing, confirming receipt of the associated person's notice and, if the member chooses, states any specified mandatory or prohibited behavior by the person during involvement in the private securities transaction.

Political Contributions

FINRA Rule 2030: Engaging in Distribution and Solicitation Activities with Government Entities

A broker-dealer to which FINRA Rule 2030 will apply is referred to as a covered member.

FINRA Rule 2030 will apply to the following:

- A broker-dealer acting on behalf of any investment adviser registered or required to be registered under the Investment Advisers Act of 1940 (the "Advisers Act")

- A "foreign private adviser" exempt from registration under Section 203(b)(3) of the Advisers Act

- An "exempt reporting adviser" under Advisers Act Rule 204-4(a).

- A FINRA member that implores a government entity as acting representative of an associated investment adviser

- A placement agent that encourages a government entity to invest in a pooled investment vehicle such as a private investment fund or a mutual fund included as part of an overall governmental investment plan

112

Accordingly, FINRA Rule 2030 will not apply to the following:

- A broker-dealer acting as a representative of an investment advisor in compliance with state securities authorities

- An investment adviser relying on additional absolution from SEC registration

- A broker-dealer taking part in activities that would necessitate municipal advisor registration and alignment with the pay-to-play rule of the MSRB

This rule requires a covered member to refrain from "distribution or solicitation activities for compensation" with any governmental unit for two years after a political contribution is made to a person in that governmental unit by the covered member or a covered associate.

A de minimis exception allows a "covered associate that is a natural person" to contribute as follows:

- No more than $350 per candidate, per election, to a candidate for whom the person was qualified to vote at the time of the payment

- No more than $150 per candidate, per election, to a candidate for whom the person was not qualified to vote at the time of the payment

MSRB Rule G-37: Political Contributions and Prohibitions on Municipal Securities Business

The MSRB issued different requirements for firms and their municipal financial professionals (MFPs). This rule defines the following:

- Activity: "municipal securities business"
- Political contribution: "any item of value"
- Person: "MFP"
- Payments: whether to a political account or to non-political accounts that might free up funds for political activities

If one of a number of certain persons of a firm or a political action committee (PAC) administered by the firm or its persons makes a payment to a person of an issuer of municipal securities, the firm of the payer may be prohibited from participating in municipal securities business for two years.

If a firm is assisting, or seeking to assist, an issuer with its municipal securities issue, the firm and its MFPs are not allowed to request political contributions or assist persons of the issuer in obtaining political contributions.

The MSRB interprets the rule to prohibit actions that would involve payments to political groups or other organizations that would be indirect contributions to persons of the issuer. The dealer would need to learn from the receiving organization how contributed funds would be used. Providing a restriction with the payment would not, in itself, prevent transgression of the rule. The MSRB further directed that dealers develop and adhere to supervisory processes to ensure compliance with the rule, including no indirect payments or payments for non-political accounts that would free up funds for political purposes. The MSRB did allow that making payments to a non-political account and providing a restriction with the payment might be part of an overall supervisory process if the overall situation justifies it.

Dollar and Value Limits for Gifts and Gratuities

FINRA has separate, but similar, rules regarding non-cash compensation paid by persons or entities providing products for sales and distribution by representatives who do the following:

- Participate in direct participation programs ("unlisted" investments, not listed on the exchanges) unless FINRA otherwise provides an exemption in a particular case (FINRA Rule 2310(c) – Non-Cash Compensation)

- Sell and distribute variable contracts (FINRA Rule 2320(g)(4) – Non-Cash Compensation—Variable Contracts)

- Sell mutual funds (FINRA Rule 2341(l)(5) – Non-Cash Compensation—Investment Company Securities/Mutual Funds)

- Sell public offerings unless FINRA otherwise provides an exemption in a particular case (FINRA Rule 5110(h) – Non-Cash Compensation—Public Offerings)

Each of the above rules establishes the following categories of guidelines for non-cash compensation:

- The amount is not linked to a level of sales and does not exceed that fixed by FINRA, currently $100 per person per year.

- Non-frequent meals or tickets to entertainment events may be provided as long as they are not costly enough to seem inappropriate or linked to a certain level of sales.

- Firms offering investment products may share the cost of informational meetings as long as the following conditions are met: The member firm gives advance agreement; the location is appropriate; no guests of the representatives have their way paid; and payment is not conditioned on a level of sales. The firm must keep records of these transactions.

- Payments come from the member firm or a firm controlling the member firm, and no non-member firm participates in any way in the transaction. The firm must keep records of these transactions.

- In certain situations, a non-member firm or a member firm other than the representative's member firm may contribute to, but not assist in, the structure of the transaction. The firm must keep records of these transactions.

MSRB Rule G-20: Gifts, Gratuities, and Non-Cash Compensations

This rule establishes the following categories of guidelines for non-cash compensation for representatives who sell municipal securities:

- Rule G-20 allows gifts as long as they are not linked to a level of sales and their value does not exceed a certain amount (currently $100 per person per year).

- Rule G-20(d) provides an exclusion for promotional items that are of nominal value and display the issuing entity's business or other corporate logo.

- Rule G-20(d)(vi) states that "… personal gifts given upon the occurrence of infrequent life events, such as a wedding or birth of a child, are not subject to the $100 limit so long as the gift(s) do not otherwise give rise to any apparent or actual material conflict of interest." The classification would depend on whether the representative had any previous personal or family relationship with the recipient and whether the representative or the firm paid for the gift. If the firm paid for the gift, it would be classified as business related and not subject to the exemption.

- Non-frequent meals or tickets to entertainment events may be provided as long as they are not costly enough to seem inappropriate or linked to a certain level of sales.

- Firms offering municipal securities may share the cost of informational meetings as long as the following conditions are met: The member firm gives advance agreement; the location is appropriate; no guests of the representatives have their way paid; and payment is not conditioned on a level of sales. The firm must keep records of these transactions.

- Payments may come from the member firm or a firm controlling the member firm, and no non-member firm participates in any way in the transaction. If the payment is linked to the sale of municipal securities, it is linked to the total production of municipal securities sales of that firm's representatives, and each municipal security is given equal consideration. The firm must keep records of these transactions.

- In certain situations, a non-member firm or a member firm other than the representative's member firm may contribute to, but not assist in, the structure of the transaction. The firm must keep records of these transactions.

The MSRB has issued rules determining supervisory procedures for ensuring that the giving and receiving of gifts, gratuities, and non-cash compensation follows MSRB rules.

Business Entertainment
FINRA Rule 3220: Influencing or Rewarding the Employees of Others

This rule (the Gifts Rule) prohibits an associated person of a member firm from giving, directly or indirectly, a gift worth more than $100 per year to any person linked to the member firm's business.

Felonies, Financial-Related Misdemeanors, Liens, Bankruptcy
Form U4 requires the disclosure of certain items, including the following, and must be updated when disclosable events occur:

- All felony charges and convictions
- Misdemeanor charges and convictions involving investments or an investment-related business
- Bankruptcy within the last ten years
- An action by the SIPC within the last ten years, short of a bankruptcy liquidation, in which customer claims are paid directly without a formal liquidation proceeding
- Compromise with creditors within the last ten years
- Currently unsatisfied judgments and liens

Below is the listing of Form U4, Section 14, disclosure questions.

Criminal Disclosure
- 14A (Felony Criminal Disclosure)
- 14B (Misdemeanor Criminal Disclosure)

Regulatory Action Disclosure
- 14C (Regulatory Action by SEC or CFTC)
- 14D(1) (Regulatory Action by other federal regulator, state regulator, or foreign financial regulator)
- 14D(2) (Final order of state securities commission, state authority that supervises or examines banks, savings associations, or credit unions, state insurance commission, appropriate Federal Banking agency, or National Credit Union Administration)
- 14E (Regulatory Action by SRO 14F—Professional Suspension)
- 14G (Formal Pending Action/Investigation)

Civil Judicial Disclosure
- 14H (Civil Judicial Actions)

Customer Complaint/Arbitration/Civil Litigation Disclosure
- 14I (Customer Complaints)

Termination Disclosure
- 14J (Terminations for Cause)

Financial Disclosure
- 14K (Bankruptcy, SIPC, and Compromise with Creditors within the last ten years)
- 14L (Bonding Payouts or Revocations)
- 14M (Unsatisfied Judgments and Liens)

FINRA Rule 8312: FINRA's BrokerCheck Disclosure

This rule provides that, in general, FINRA will disclose data, including the following, about current and former member firms, their current and former associated persons, and persons associated with member firms sometime within the most recent ten years:

- Any data from the most recently submitted registration forms
- Current registrations
- Summary data regarding particular arbitration awards against a member firm related to a dispute with a public customer
- Relevant portion of the most current comment provided by the person who is a subject of the data
- Qualification exams passed and date passed
- Whether the person is subject to having business phone conversations taped under Rule 3170 (the Taping Rule)
- Certain complaints
- Names of member firms, if changed
- Data regarding a person who was implicated in a final regulatory action as defined in Form U4 and reported to the CRD system

In general, FINRA will disclose the following data about a person previously associated with a member firm, but not for ten years, who was implicated in a final regulatory action as defined in Form U4 and reported to the CRD system, or registered with FINRA or a CRD Exchange on or after August 16, 1999:

- Convicted or pleaded guilty or nolo contendere to a crime

- Subject of a non-criminal restriction regarding investment-related activity, a non-criminal court determination of involvement in a violation of any securities-related law or rule, or similar non-criminal charge brought by a state or foreign investment supervisory entity
- Accused in a securities-related arbitration or non-criminal lawsuit of an illegal sales practice and had an arbitration award of non-criminal judgment

FINRA will not release information that is prohibited by federal law, such as social security number, home address, and physical characteristics.

FINRA By-Laws Article XII: Disciplinary Proceedings

This article states FINRA's authority to establish disciplinary processes relative to member firms and their associated persons, including the following:

- Prerogative for the person or member firm who is the subject of the process to receive an opportunity to speak or have someone, such as an attorney, speak to the accusation
- Exact charges
- Notice to the accused with opportunity to respond
- Record kept of the process
- Decision regarding the specific infraction, the rule or law that was broken, how the decision was made, and the penalty

FINRA By-Laws Article XV: Limitations of Power

This article states the following:

- FINRA will not make any political contributions.
- FINRA will not use its name for any political purpose.
- FINRA's name will not be used other than as allowed by the rule.
- FINRA's personnel will make no expenditures not authorized by the board.
- FINRA's governors and committee members will avoid conflicts of interest.
- FINRA's rules regarding municipal securities will not be in effect for member firms or their associated persons if not consistent with Section 15 of the Securities Exchange Act of 1934, which establishes the MSRB.

See our SIE Resource Page for links to current rules and regulations.

You can visit by going to https://www.apexprep.com/sie or by scanning the QR code.

Practice Test #1

Knowledge of Capital Markets

1. Which of the following is the main reason the Securities Act was enacted?
   a. To prevent investors from losing their principal
   b. To help investors improve their return on investment
   c. To provide issuers of bonds a larger number of bondholders
   d. To bring stability to the capital market

2. Which of the following best describes the role of self-regulatory organizations (SROs)?
   a. To promote public knowledge of investment principles
   b. To prevent criminals from purchasing securities
   c. To prevent felons from selling securities
   d. To develop and enforce industry standards

3. Which of the following is the primary role of the Department of the Treasury?
   a. To establish monetary policy
   b. To enforce fiscal policy
   c. To administer federal finances
   d. To prevent political corruption

4. Which of the following takes orders from a client and passes the order to an entity that is qualified to match the buy order with a sell order from another person?
   a. Hedge fund
   b. Prime broker
   c. Introducing broker
   d. Clearing broker

5. Which of the following is a function of the Options Clearing Corporation?
   a. Guaranteeing all listed stock option contracts in the United States
   b. Guaranteeing all options purchased through clearing brokers
   c. Guaranteeing the accounts of investors' holdings with bankrupt brokers
   d. Guaranteeing all futures contracts bought or sold through clearing brokers

6. Which of the following describes the fourth market (dark pools)?
   a. Initial public offerings
   b. Companies trading without broker commissions
   c. Over-the-counter market
   d. Penny stocks

7. Which of the following is a method by which the Federal Reserve implements monetary policy?
   a. Using open market activities
   b. Enforcing securities laws
   c. Lobbying Congress
   d. Nominating judicial candidates

8. What is the primary purpose of financial statements?
   a. To inform investors of management's future plans
   b. To affirm compliance with SEC registration
   c. To report on historical events and values
   d. To justify the purchase of stock

9. Level of new business start-ups is an example of which of the following?
   a. Leading economic indicator
   b. Lagging economic indicator
   c. Coincident economic indicator
   d. Seasonal economic indicator

10. Which of the following is correct?
   a. Exchange rates are the proportion of one country's goods and services that are purchased with cash as compared with all goods and services purchased with cash and credit.
   b. The gross domestic product reflects the total of a country's goods and services produced and used or consumed in that country during a period of time.
   c. The gross international product reflects the total of a country's goods and services produced during a period of time.
   d. A trade deficit is enacted by Congress as a tool of fiscal policy.

11. Which of the following may agree to a best efforts agreement for an initial public offering (IPO)?
   a. Securities Exchange Commission
   b. Underwriting syndicate, led by the lead underwriter
   c. Lead underwriter for "standby" agreement
   d. Securities commissioner of the state in which the security is offered

12. Which of the following is typically issued by a governmental entity other than a state?
   a. Prospectus
   b. Official statement
   c. Program disclosure document
   d. Partnership agreement

Understanding Products and Their Risks

13. Which of the following is the main reason that a company issues stock?
   a. To increase diversification of ownership
   b. To raise capital for beginning or expanding business operations
   c. To lower the number of dividends to pay
   d. To take advantage of lower interest rates

14. Which of the following is considered a debt security?
   a. Common stock
   b. Convertible preferred stock
   c. Nonconvertible debenture
   d. Put on a warrant

15. A broker-dealer is required to be a member of which of the following organizations?
    a. Financial Industry Regulatory Authority (FINRA)
    b. Securities Exchange Commission (SEC)
    c. New York Stock Exchange (NYSE)
    d. Better Business Bureau (BBB)

16. Which of the following satisfies an anti-dilution provision?
    a. Rights
    b. Warrants
    c. Puts
    d. Calls

17. Which of the following is a method used by the U.S. government to implement fiscal policy to stimulate the economy?
    a. Increasing the discount rate
    b. Decreasing the fed funds rate
    c. Increasing lock-up period on initial public offerings (IPOs)
    d. Financing deficit spending

18. Which of the following is a benefit of owning a Treasury zero-coupon bond?
    a. Typically declines in price when the Federal Reserve cuts rates
    b. Decreases price responsiveness to interest rate changes as the term to maturity increases
    c. Makes quarterly interest payments
    d. Eliminates reinvestment risk

19. Which of the following is an agency of the federal government?
    a. Federal Home Loan Mortgage Corporation (FHLMC, or Freddie Mac)
    b. Government National Mortgage Association (GNMA, or Ginnie Mae)
    c. The Federal Farm Credit Banks (FFCBs)
    d. The Federal National Mortgage Association (FNMA, or Fannie Mae)

20. Which of the following is an effect of municipal bond insurance?
    a. A private insurance company pays the municipal government for shortfalls in project revenue.
    b. A private insurance company pays the municipal government for shortfalls in tax revenue.
    c. An insured bond issue will have a higher credit rating than a noninsured issue.
    d. An insured bond issue will have no credit rating.

21. Which of the following is true of an option?
    a. The holder (buyer) is obligated to execute the option.
    b. The writer (seller) is obligated to fulfill the option if exercised.
    c. The issuer of the underlying security must grant permission for an option to be traded.
    d. The SEC guarantees performance of the option.

22. Which of the following is a characteristic of an option that is traded over the counter?
    a. Terms may be negotiated.
    b. Terms will be standardized.
    c. Stock indexes will not be the underlying basis.
    d. The holder must provide notification of intention to exercise by 4:00 p.m. eastern time on the third Friday of the expiration month.

23. What is the exposure of the writer of an uncovered (naked or short) call option?
    a. Limited to the premium exchanged
    b. Limited to the strike price multiplied by the quantity of shares
    c. Negligible
    d. Unlimited

24. Which of the following is a similarity between a mutual fund and a closed-end investment company?
    a. Shares may be purchased throughout the day.
    b. Shares may only be sold after the close of business.
    c. Shares are based on a portfolio of investments.
    d. Shares of preferred shares are redeemed by the issuer.

25. Which of the following mutual fund share class would be expected to have the highest cumulative sales charge, considering the longest reasonably possible investment horizon?
    a. Class A
    b. Class B
    c. Class C
    d. Class T

26. Which of the following is common to a unit investment trust (UIT) and mutual funds?
    a. Trustees
    b. Ongoing management fee
    c. Board of directors
    d. Sales charges

27. Which of the following is common to mutual funds and municipal fund securities?
    a. The issuer is not primarily involved in holding or trading securities.
    b. The investment portfolios may hold similar securities.
    c. The funds have private individuals and companies as investors.
    d. The funds are managed by private investment companies.

28. Which of the following is considered a municipal fund security?
    a. College savings plans (commonly known as 529 plan)
    b. Prepaid tuition plans (PTPs)
    c. Municipal revenue bond
    d. Municipal general obligation bond

29. Which of the following is a tax benefit of the investment structure of direct participation programs (DPPs)?
    a. Accelerated depreciation
    b. Exemption of some income from taxation
    c. Avoidance of double taxation
    d. Extended tax reporting deadlines

30. Which of the following is common to both limited partnerships and tenant in common (TIC) transactions?
    a. They may involve investment in real estate.
    b. Each investor may sell interest to another investor with approval by the general partner.
    c. Significant decisions are decided by a majority of ownership interest.
    d. The IRS code limits the number of owners to thirty-five.

31. Which of the following is a requirement of real estate investment trusts (REITs) in order to avoid double taxation on dividends?
    a. It must hold all dividends, interest, and realized capital gains until maturity.
    b. At least 90 percent of its ordinary income must be distributed to investors.
    c. At least 95 percent of its gross income must be derived from dividends, interest, and rents from real property.
    d. At least 75 percent of its gross income must be derived from real property income.

32. Which type of REIT has the broadest range of cash flow types?
    a. S corporation
    b. Mortgage
    c. Equity
    d. Hybrid

33. Which of the following describes the goal of hedge funds defined as "absolute return"?
    a. Favorable returns in good markets and bad markets
    b. Closely matching the performance of the S&P 500 Index (within plus or minus 0.5 percent)
    c. Closely matching the performance of the S&P 500 Index (within plus or minus 0.5 percent) and always having a positive return on a calendar year basis
    d. Never having the fund's value go down from the end of one calendar quarter to the end of the next calendar quarter

34. Which of the following is a typical characteristic of a mutual fund but not a hedge fund?
    a. Short selling
    b. Leverage
    c. Registered investment adviser
    d. Arbitrage

35. Which of the following is a characteristic of a qualified client?
    a. An accredited investor
    b. A qualified purchaser
    c. An individual who has two years of income greater than $200,000 annually and reasonably expects the same level of income to continue
    d. An individual who has two years of income greater than $300,000 annually and reasonably expects the same level of income to continue

36. Which of the following is an example of a hedge fund manager's annual fee?
    a. 8.5 percent of the fund's offering price
    b. Two-and-twenty
    c. 12b-1 fee
    d. Contingent deferred sales charge (CDSC)

122

37. Which of the following aspects of a performance fee is intended to motivate a hedge fund manager to demonstrate consistently higher values?
    a. High water mark
    b. Hurdle rate
    c. Withdrawal fee
    d. Lock-up period

38. Which of the following would be a good practice both for an investor considering a mutual fund and an investor considering a hedge fund?
    a. Choose the share class whose sales charges match one's investment horizon.
    b. Know on what national exchanges the shares are traded.
    c. Select one's annuitization option.
    d. Match the fund's investment strategies and associated risks with one's personal investment goals, time horizons, and risk tolerance.

39. Which of the following is included on a firm's Form ADV?
    a. Names under which the firm does business and states in which it does business
    b. Better Business Bureau rating
    c. YouTube channels used for marketing services
    d. Each investment adviser representative's client list

40. Which of the following most closely relates to illiquidity of a hedge fund's assets?
    a. Use of derivatives
    b. Number of years during which the fund manager has managed those types of assets
    c. Calculation method for the performance fee
    d. Discretion allowed the hedge fund for asset valuation

41. Which of the following correctly states a current trend?
    a. Mutual funds are developing momentum to become more attractive than ETFs.
    b. ETFs are developing momentum to become more attractive than mutual funds.
    c. ETNs are developing momentum to become more attractive than mutual funds.
    d. ETNs are developing momentum to become more attractive than ETFs.

42. Which of the following is the recent regulatory change that most significantly improved the viability of actively managed ETFs in the market by allowing them to maintain confidential evidence of their proprietary management style?
    a. Commodity Futures Modernization Act of 2000
    b. Investment Company Act of 1940
    c. SEC Rule 6c-11 (called the ETF Rule), implemented in 2019
    d. SEC approval of the Precidian ActiveShares ETF model in 2019

43. Which of the following risks is most related to the successful operation of an issuer of a security?
    a. Currency risk
    b. Inflationary/purchasing power risk
    c. Credit risk
    d. Interest rate/reinvestment risk

44. Which of the following correctly states the typical relationship between a change in the general level of interest rates and a change in the market value of bonds?
    a. When interest rates stay the same, corporate bond values rise and treasuries decline.
    b. When interest rates stay the same, long-term bond values decline and short-term bond values rise.
    c. When interest rates decline, bond values rise.
    d. When interest rates decline, dollar-denominated bonds remain the same and foreign bond values decline.

45. Which of the following is considered difficult to mitigate in the short term through diversification, portfolio rebalancing, or hedging?
    a. Political/geopolitical risk
    b. Prepayment risk
    c. Market/systematic risk
    d. Non-systematic risk

Understanding Trading, Customer Accounts, and Prohibited Activities

46. Which of the following does a stop order become after the stop price is available on the market?
    a. Market order
    b. Good-'til-cancelled order
    c. Discretionary order
    d. Solicited order

47. Which of the following is a short sale?
    a. A sale of less shares than the quote with the best price
    b. A sale during the last hour of trading
    c. A sale of a security borrowed from another party
    d. A sale of an inverse option

48. Which of the following will calculate the return on an investment?

    a.
    $$\frac{Cash\ received + Realized\ gain\ or\ loss - Amount\ invested}{Amount\ invested}$$

    b.
    $$\frac{Cash\ received + Realized\ gain\ or\ loss}{Amount\ invested}$$

    c.
    $$\frac{Cash\ received + Realized\ gain\ or\ loss - Amount\ invested}{Sales\ proceeds}$$

    d.
    $$\frac{Sales\ proceeds}{Amount\ invested}$$

49. Which of the following will calculate the yield to maturity?

a.

$$\frac{\frac{(Coupon\ Rate \times Face\ Value \times Years\ to\ Call) + (Call\ Value - Purchase\ Price)}{Years\ to\ Call}}{\frac{Call\ Value\ to\ be\ Received + Purchase\ Price}{2}}$$

b.

$$\frac{\frac{(Coupon\ Rate \times Face\ Value \times Years\ to\ Maturity) + (Face\ Value - Purchase\ Price)}{Years\ to\ Maturity}}{\frac{Face\ Value\ at\ Maturity + Purchase\ Price}{2}}$$

c.

$$\frac{\frac{(Coupon\ Rate \times Face\ Value \times Years\ to\ Maturity) + (Face\ Value - Purchase\ Price)}{Years\ to\ Maturity}}{\frac{Face\ Value\ at\ Maturity + Purchase\ Price}{2 \times Years\ to\ Maturity}}$$

d.

$$\frac{\frac{(Coupon\ Rate \times Face\ Value \times Years\ to\ Maturity) + (Face\ Value - Purchase\ Price)}{Years\ to\ Maturity}}{\frac{Face\ Value\ at\ Maturity + Purchase\ Price}{Years\ to\ Maturity}}$$

50. What is the payment date for regular way settlement on corporate stock, corporate bonds, and municipal funds specified by MSRB rule G-15?

a. S+4
b. T+4
c. T
d. T+2

51. Which type of corporate action results in the following adjustment to securities: five shares of the firm's common stock are replaced by two shares of the firm's common stock?

a. Stock split
b. Reverse stock split
c. Tender offer
d. Exchange offer

52. Which of the following would represent the impact a three-for-one stock split would have on the par value of a share of stock?

a. The par value would be the same as the old share.
b. The par value would be one-third as much as the old share.
c. The par value would be one-third more than the old share.
d. The par value would be three dollars per share.

53. Which of the following account types is used to make a short sale?

a. Cash account
b. Margin account
c. Option account
d. Discretionary account

125

54. A discretionary account has which of the following features?
   a. Borrowed money is used to buy a security.
   b. A borrowed security is sold.
   c. A characteristic of an order other than price and timing is selected by the representative.
   d. The counterparty of an order is selected by the representative.

55. Which of the following describes a joint account?
   a. A corporate resolution is needed to specify who may open the account and who may initiate activity.
   b. The trust agreement must be on file, along with documentation of the trustee's authority to determine activity for the good of the beneficiary.
   c. The partnership agreement is required.
   d. Any owner may determine activity, but all owners must sign when a signature is needed.

56. Which of the following is a characteristic of a retirement account?
   a. It is opened by a person who is retired.
   b. It is opened by a person who is an employee of a corporation.
   c. It is opened by a person who owns an annuity to place in the account.
   d. It is opened by a person who desires tax deferral on the investment return.

57. Which of the following describes money laundering?
   a. Concealing the source of illegally-obtained money
   b. Embezzling money from an employer
   c. Extortion through threatened exposure of another person's misdeeds
   d. Bribery of an elected official through hidden political contribution

58. Which of the following reports is to be submitted by a financial firm to the FinCEN within thirty days of observing a person's suspicious action?
   a. Suspicious Activity Report
   b. Currency Transaction Report
   c. OFAC Report
   d. Customer Account Statement

59. Which of the following is true of the books and records requirements for member broker-dealers?
   a. Requirements must allow for self-regulatory organizations to carry out examinations of broker-dealers.
   b. Data must be kept on electronic media.
   c. Records must be kept ten years, unless specifically designated for a different time frame.
   d. A registered principal must regularly sign an inventory of records.

60. Which of the following best describes nonpublic personal information (NPI)?
   a. Personally identifiable information that would be obtained in the course of serving a financial services consumer, but which may be publicly available
   b. Personally identifiable information that is publicly available, and that is kept in a company's nonpublic storage area
   c. Personally identifiable financial information that a financial firm obtains in the process of serving a consumer with a financial product or service unless that information is otherwise publicly available
   d. Personally identifiable financial information that specifically relates to a financial service consumer's real estate property purchase price

126

61. According to FINRA Rule 2210 – Communications with the Public, which of the following is sent to twenty-five or less retail investors within a thirty-day calendar period?
    a. Institutional communication
    b. Proxy information
    c. Retail communication
    d. Correspondence

62. Which is the highest obligation of a securities professional?
    a. Most favorable price
    b. Suitability
    c. Best interest
    d. Highest return on investment

63. Which of the following is the act of using improper methods to increase or decrease the market price of a security or somehow affect the actions of other investors for personal gain?
    a. Market manipulation
    b. Insider trading
    c. Freeriding
    d. Backing away

64. Which of the following types of market manipulation is also referred to as "churning"?
    a. Market rumors
    b. Pump-and-dump
    c. Front running
    d. Excessive trading

65. Which of the following involves the inappropriate use of material nonpublic information?
    a. Intimidation
    b. Borrowing from customers
    c. Insider trading
    d. Exploitation of specified adults

66. Which of the following is addressed by 1934 Act Section 15c1-2 – Fraud and Misrepresentation?
    a. Short selling
    b. Virtually any deceptive act
    c. Stop order
    d. Asking to deposit or withdraw more than $10,000

67. Which of the following is forbidden to unregistered persons?
    a. Receiving compensation from a member firm based on securities accounts or transactions
    b. Inquiring whether the customer wishes to receive investment marketing materials
    c. Inviting the customer to a firm-sponsored golf tournament
    d. Asking whether the customer would like to discuss investments with a registered person

68. Which of the following correctly describes the situation of FINRA's discipline of registered representatives regarding a customer's signatures under FINRA Rule 2010?
   a. The registered representative had a client sign a form that was not completed, which the representative completed later, without knowledge and approval of a registered principal.
   b. The registered representative had a client sign a form that was not completed, which the representative completed more than one year later.
   c. The registered representative had a client sign a form that was not completed, which the representative completed later, resulting in a trade that lost money for the customer.
   d. The registered representative had a client sign a form that was not completed, which the representative completed later.

Overview of the Regulatory Framework

69. Which of the following is required to be a member of the Financial Industry Regulatory Agency (FINRA)?
   a. A bank that wishes to make loans to a governmental unit
   b. A public official who wishes to be appointed to the Federal Reserve
   c. A company that wishes to issue an initial public offering (IPO)
   d. A firm that wishes to take orders for securities

70. Which of the following may only be done by a person registered with FINRA?
   a. Inviting members of the public to a meeting for which the firm is responsible
   b. Asking whether a member of the public is interested in reviewing possible investments with a registered person of the firm
   c. Encouraging a person to buy or sell a security
   d. Asking whether a member of the public is interested in receiving printed materials about investments

71. Which of the following is a part of the FINRA continuing education requirements?
   a. State element
   b. Federal element
   c. Regional element
   d. Firm element

72. Which of the following is the Application for Securities Industry Registration or Transfer?
   a. Schedule A
   b. Form BD
   c. Form U5
   d. Form U4

73. Which of the following constitutes a reportable customer complaint?
   a. A letter written by a customer's neighbor who overhears a conversation in which the customer is critical of service received
   b. An in-person comment by a customer saying the advice received regarding purchasing an investment was incomplete and misleading
   c. A text received from an executor of a customer's estate saying the final handling of the securities was improper
   d. A phone call by a customer saying the order was not completed as requested

74. Which of the following does FINRA Rule 3270 (Outside Business Activities of Registered Persons) require a member firm to consider before approving an outside business activity (OBA)?
   a. Will the OBA be perceived by outsiders as part of the member's activities?
   b. Will the OBA take too much of the registered person's time away from that person's family?
   c. Will the OBA lead to the registered person initiating similar, additional OBAs?
   d. Will the OBA lead to the registered person leaving the association with the member firm?

75. Which of the following connects a registered person's political contributions with the ability to perform certain activities for compensation?
   a. FINRA Rule 2030 – Engaging in Distribution and Solicitation Activities with Government Entities
   b. FINRA Rule 3270 – Outside Business Activities of Registered Persons
   c. FINRA Rule 4513 – Written Customer Complaints
   d. FINRA Rule 3280 – Private Securities Transactions of an Associated Person

Answer Explanations #1

Knowledge of Capital Markets

1. D: The Securities Act was enacted after the stock market crash of 1929 to bring stability to the capital market. Choice *A* may be an indirect result of fair disclosure of new stock issues through registration with the Securities Exchange Commission (SEC). Choice *B* is not a main purpose of the Securities Act, although it could be an indirect benefit. Choice *C* could be an indirect result of the Securities Act if investors wishing to buy bonds feel greater confidence through reading the disclosures required by the 1933 act.

2. D: Promoting public knowledge of investment principles best describes the role of self-regulatory organizations (SROs). Choice *A* is not a primary role of SROs, although SROs may assist the public in having the facts that would help them apply investment principles. Choice *B* is not a significant role of SROs, although the Anti-Money Laundering law is intended to reduce, or even prevent, the laundering of terrorist money through investment transactions. Choice *C* may partly be a result of some activity by SROs, but it is not an absolute mandate for SROs.

3. C: The primary role of the Department of the Treasury is administering federal finances, which involves receiving taxes through the IRS, paying bills, managing currency, and handling the federal government's accounts, including the public debt. Choice *A* is handled by the Federal Reserve. Choice *B* is handled by Congress. Choice *D* may be an indirect result of the Department of Treasury following laws and referring infractions that come to its attention to the Department of Justice.

4. C: A clearing broker may take orders but does not have characteristics, such as amount of invested capital, that qualify it to complete the trade. Choice *A* is a pooled investment firm and does not typically take orders from other persons or firms as one of its primary activities. Choice *B* refers to a firm that handles a variety of services for institutions or individuals with a high net worth. Choice *D* refers to the firm that would accept the order placed by an introducing broker and match it with a counterparty willing to complete the transaction.

5. A: Guaranteeing all listed stock option contracts is a function of the OCC. Choices *B* and *D* are not functions of the OCC, although the OCC does guarantee listed stock options contracts in the United States, which are purchased through clearing brokers. Choice *C* is a function, on a limited basis, of the Securities Investors Protection Corporation.

6. B: The fourth market (deep pools) refers to companies trading with each other with a wide range of securities, even customized derivatives, without broker commissions. Choice *A* occurs directly between the issuer and the investment broker and/or investors. Choice *C* refers to various venues in which computerized trading occurs, including part of the trading of exchanges. Choice *D* refers to low-priced equity securities that may be thinly traded and highly speculative and may not meet the qualifications.

7. A: Using open market activities is a method by which the Federal Reserve implements monetary policy. Choice *B* is a function of the Department of the Treasury, Securities Exchange Commission, the states and territories, and some self-regulatory organizations, but not the Federal Reserve. Choice *C* is not a method of implementing monetary policy. Choice *D* is a function of the president, not the Federal Reserve.

8. C: The primary purpose of financial statements is to fairly report a firm's financial activities during a period of time and/or to state the assets, liabilities, and net worth of a firm as of a specific point in time. Generally accepted accounting principles make up the main set of guidelines for financial statements of

130

companies whose securities are traded in the United States. Choice A is not the primary purpose of financial statements, although notes regarding management's future plans may be included. Choice B is not the primary purpose of financial statements, although financial statements are an important component of compliance with SEC registration. Choice D is also not the primary purpose of financial statements, although they may be useful during a decision-making process regarding the purchase of stock.

9. A: The level of new business start-ups is an example of a leading economic indicator. New business start-ups generally are followed by additional jobs, new products, and new services. The level of new business start-ups is not a lagging or coincident economic indicator, Choices B and C. Choice D, seasonal economic indicator, is not a relevant term.

10. B: The gross domestic product reflects the total of a country's goods and services produced and used or consumed in that country during a period of time. Choices A, C, and D are not correct. Exchange rates reflect the value of one country's money that may be exchanged for a given amount of another country's money. The gross national product reflects the total of a country's goods and services produced during a period of time. Deficit spending is enacted by Congress as a tool of fiscal policy.

11. B: An underwriting syndicate, led by the legal underwriter, may agree to a best efforts agreement for an IPO. Choice A, the Securities Exchange Commission (SEC), may review the underwriting agreement but will not be a party to it. Choice C, a "standby" agreement, is typically entered into by the issuer and an investment bank, which may not be a lead underwriter or party to the underwriting syndicate. Choice D, the Securities Commissioner of the state in which the security is offered, may review the underwriting agreement but will not be a party to it.

12. B: An official statement is typically issued by a state or municipality issuing a municipal security. Choice A, a prospectus, is typically offered by a private rather than public or governmental entity. Choice C is typically offered by a state regarding a 529 college saving plan. Choice D is typically offered by a partnership.

Understanding Products and Their Risks

13. B: Raising capital to begin or expand business operations is the main reason for issuing stock. Choice A is not typically a concern of companies. Choice C would be a reason for repurchasing company stock. Choice D would be a reason for issuing bonds.

14. C: A nonconvertible debenture is a debt security that cannot be converted into an equity security. Choices A and B represent ownership and therefore are included in the category of equity securities. Choice D represents an option that provides the opportunity, but not the obligation, to sell a warrant, which is an equity security.

15. A: A broker-dealer is required to be a member of the Financial Industry Regulatory Authority (FINRA). Choice B is the organization that regulates the securities industry and does not require a broker-dealer to be a member. Choice C is a stock exchange regulated by the SEC and does not require a broker-dealer to be a member. Choice D is a nonprofit corporation that reflects whether complaints have been issued regarding businesses, charities, and nonprofit organizations and does not offer memberships.

16. A: Rights preserve the right of first refusal so that a stockholder may purchase shares to maintain the same percentage of ownership. Choice B may be offered as an incentive to purchase stocks and bonds. Choices C and D are options that are not typically issued pursuant to an anti-dilution provision.

17. D: Financing deficit spending is a way the government can stimulate the economy through borrowing to support spending in excess of receipts. Choices *A* and *B* are ways in which the Federal Reserve implements monetary policy to stimulate growth without undue inflation. Choice *C* is intended to prevent insiders who acquired stock before it went public from profiting from the increase in the share price until a certain amount of time has passed and is not directly related to stimulating the economy.

18. D: Eliminating reinvestment risk is the benefit of constant reinvestment of interest because no payments are made prior to maturity. Choice *A* is incorrect because their price typically increases when the Federal Reserve cuts rates. Choice *B* is incorrect because it will have an increasing price responsiveness to interest rate changes as the term to maturity increases. Choice *C* is incorrect because it makes no interest payments prior to maturity.

19. B: The Government National Mortgage Association (GNMA, or Ginnie Mae) is an agency of the federal government. Choices *A, C,* and *D* are government-sponsored enterprises (GSEs).

20. C: An insured bond issue having a higher credit rating than a noninsured issue is an effect of municipal bond insurance. Choices *A* and *B* are not effects of municipal bond insurance because the insurance protects the bondholder against default on the bond by the municipality. Choice *D* is incorrect because the bond issue would continue to have a credit rating, which would be higher.

21. B: The writer (or seller) is obligated to fulfill the option. Choice *A* is incorrect because the holder (or buyer) has no obligation to execute the option. Choice *C* is incorrect because the issuer is typically not involved in the initiation of an option. Choice *D* is incorrect because the Options Clearing Corporation, not the Securities Exchange Commission, guarantees all options traded on U.S. exchanges.

22. A: Terms may be negotiated in an option that is traded over the counter. Choice *B* reflects exchange-traded options. Choice *C* is incorrect because stock indexes may be the underlying basis. Choice *D* is incorrect because the holder must provide notification of intention to exercise by 5:30 p.m. eastern time on the third Friday of the expiration month.

23. D: The writer of an uncovered call option has unlimited exposure and is required to purchase the shares, no matter how high they have risen, and sell at the strike price. Choice *A* is the maximum potential loss of the purchaser of the option. Choice *B* is the amount the writer would receive at exercise. Choice *C* is incorrect because the loss could be quite large.

24. C: Shares are based on a portfolio of investments. Choice *A* is true of closed-end investment company shares but not mutual funds. Choice *B* is true of mutual funds but not closed-end investment company shares. Choice *D* is not true of mutual funds because they do not issue preferred shares and is likely not true of investment company shares, even though preferred shares may be issued, because the closed-end investment company does not stand ready to redeem shares like a mutual fund does.

25. C: Class C has fewer sales charges early in the holding period, but the unending, ongoing 12b-1 fees can be expected to accumulate to more than any up-front sales charge, combined with the relevant contingent deferred sales charge (CDSC). Choice *A* reflects shares with a potentially higher up-front sales charge, 12b-1 fees that will stop, and no CDSC. Choice *B* reflects shares that have no up-front sales charge or CDSC and, if held long enough, 12b-1 fees that are waived. Choice *D* reflects shares with a lower maximum up-front sales charge, lower 12b-1 fees, and no CDSC.

26. D: Both a UIT and a mutual fund may have front-end sales charges and CDSCs. A mutual fund may also have 12b-1 fees. Choice *A* is a characteristic of a UIT but not a mutual fund. Choices *B* and *C* are not characteristic of a UIT, which is not actively managed.

27. B: The investment portfolios of both mutual funds and municipal fund securities may hold similar securities. Choice *A* is true of municipal fund securities but not mutual funds. Choices *C* and *D* are true of mutual funds but not municipal funds.

28. A: College savings plans were authorized by Section 529 of the IRS code and are considered municipal fund securities. Choice *B*, PTPs, are not considered to be municipal fund securities. Choices *C* and *D* are municipal securities but not municipal fund securities.

29. C: DPPs have pass-through tax treatment, which avoids double taxation, as occurs with corporate dividends. Choice *A*, accelerated depreciation, Choice *B*, exemption of some income from taxation, and Choice *D*, extended tax reporting deadlines, are not accomplished by using a DPP.

30. A: Limited partnerships (LPs) and tenant in common (TIC) transactions often involve investment in real estate. Choice *B* is true of LPs, but change in TIC participants requires acceptance of the new investor by the bank making the loan. Choice *C* is true of LPs, but TICs require unanimous consent. Choice *D* is true of TICs, whereas LPs may be limited to fewer than five hundred investors by securities law.

31. B: The Internal Revenue Code requires substantially all (90 percent) of ordinary income to be distributed to investors to merit pass-through tax treatment, which eliminates double taxation of dividends. Otherwise, the REIT would pay income tax on its income, and the investor would then pay income tax on dividends from the REIT. Choice *A* is incorrect because 90 percent of ordinary income from assets must be distributed to investors. Choices *C* and *D* are requirements in order for 20 percent of the income distributed by an REIT to be nontaxable, which is another attractive REIT tax benefit to investors.

32. D: Hybrid REITs use both mortgage interest rate spreads and rents and capital gains from ownership of commercial buildings to generate cash flow. An S Corporation, Choice *A*, is a way for a group of one hundred or fewer investors to have flow-through tax treatment (as a partnership has) with limited liability. Mortgage REITs, Choice *B*, receive cash flow from the interest rate spread from borrowing from investors at a lower interest rate and issuing mortgages at a higher interest rate. Equity REITs, Choice *C*, generate cash flow through purchasing ownership in and managing business properties.

33. A: Absolute return refers to the goal of having favorable returns in good markets and bad, usually by hedging, or generating favorable returns by matching an investment with another investment that will do well when the original investment does not. Index mutual funds may pursue the return of an index, such as the S&P 500 Index, by investing in substantially the same stocks although not with the specifics of Choice *B* or Choice *C*. Choice *D* may be a hope for a fund but is not typically stated as a specified goal.

34. C: A mutual fund is required to be registered with the SEC as a registered investment adviser (RIA) in which hedge funds are not required to register as an RIA. Therefore, hedge funds are not allowed to advertise freely but must target their distribution to accredited investors who are considered to be knowledgeable about investments. Short selling, Choice *A*, is borrowing an investment one does not own and selling it. This is done in anticipation of the investment declining in value so that it may be bought for less than the price for which it was sold. The investment purchased is returned to the entity that loaned the investment. Hedge funds may frequently sell short, whereas mutual funds generally do not. Leverage, Choice *B*, is borrowing to increase the return on investment. In this way, gains or losses are expanded, relative to the capital position of the fund. Hedge funds regularly use leverage. Mutual funds generally do not. Arbitrage, Choice *D*, is simultaneously buying and selling the same investment to profit from the inefficiencies in the market. Hedge funds may use arbitrage to some extent. Mutual funds generally do not.

35. B: A qualified purchaser can be an individual who is a super-accredited investor due to having at least $5 million in invested assets; a trust, if not set up mainly to invest in the fund; or a professional person or firm controlling at least $25 million in invested assets. A hedge fund may only charge performance-based fees to qualified clients, of which a qualified purchaser is a subcategory. An accredited investor, Choice *A*, has different and somewhat fewer requirements, such as Choices *C* and *D*. Accredited investors may invest in a hedge fund if the fund does not plan to charge performance-based fees.

36. B: A typical hedge fund manager's annual fee is 2 percent of the assets under management, charged quarterly, and a performance fee of 20 percent of the profits. Because of the competitive market for accomplished fund managers, the performance fee may be even higher for larger funds. Choices *A*, *C*, and *D* are sales and distribution charges for mutual funds but are not typically part of the hedge fund manager's annual fee.

37. A: The high water mark prohibits performance fees from being paid until a new record high value (for the fund) is attained. Although the hedge fund manager is not charged for a decrease in value, no performance fee will be paid until all losses are recovered by the fund reaching a new record high value. Hurdle rate, Choice *B*, is a minimum acceptable rate of return but is not intended to motivate a hedge fund manager to constantly increase fund values. Withdrawal fee, Choice *C*, and lock-up period, Choice *D*, are methods of discouraging investors from making casual withdrawals, which could frustrate the implementation of long-term strategies, but are not intended to motivate the hedge fund manager.

38. D: Matching an investment's strategies and associated risks with one's personal investment goals, time horizons, and risk tolerance is appropriate for any person and any investment, including a mutual fund and a hedge fund. Share classes, Choice *A*, are choices of sales charges a mutual fund offers investors with different time horizons. Neither mutual funds nor most hedge funds are traded on national exchanges, Choice *B*. Choosing an annuitization option, Choice *C*, is done at the end of the accumulation period of an annuity after all investment funds have been submitted, typically to plan a level of income for life or a certain period, whichever is longer.

39. A: The Form ADV shows all names under which the firm does investment advisory business as well as whether the firm provides the following services: broker-dealer, bank, insurance broker or agent, commodity pool operation or commodity trading adviser, registered municipal adviser, accountant or accounting firm, or lawyer or law firm. It also shows the states in which business is done under each name. Although the Better Business Bureau rating, Choice *B*, is not on the Form ADV, one could contact the Better Business Bureau because it indicates a business's good faith effort to respond to customer complaints. Although YouTube channels, Choice *C*, are not on the Form ADV, it does list social media websites, including website addresses for accounts on publicly available social media platforms where the firm or its representatives control the content (including, but not limited to, Twitter, Facebook and/or LinkedIn). Client lists, Choice *D*, are confidential and are not to be made public.

40. D: Hedge funds may invest in assets without a ready market, hindering frequent and accurate valuation. Use of derivatives, Choice *A*, may still allow liquidity because many derivatives and their underlying securities are traded on national exchanges. The number of years during which the fund manager has managed those types of assets, Choice *B*, would typically have no correlation to the liquidity of fund assets. The calculation method for the performance fee, Choice *C,* is only indirectly related to the liquidity of the assets.

41. B: ETFs are developing momentum to become more attractive than mutual funds due to their retaining popular features of mutual funds, such as diversification, professional management, conventional investment practices, and comparative benchmarks, while adding the features of lower internal fees, intraday liquidity, and fewer taxable events. Mutual funds have been dominant in the past but are not currently developing momentum to become more attractive than ETFs, Choice *A,* due to their valuation being only once daily, their sales charges, their higher internal fees, and their more frequent taxable events because of income distributions to shareholders.

ETNs are not developing momentum to become more attractive than mutual funds, Choice *C,* or to become more attractive than ETFs in general, Choice *D,* because ETNs have almost none of the features that make mutual funds and ETFs popular and none of the additional features that are making ETFs develop momentum to become more attractive than mutual funds. Instead, ETNs have limited appeal because they are not directly related to ownership of underlying securities, are subject to the creditworthiness of the issuer, and are appealing mainly to a limited set of investors seeking exposure to relatively exotic investments not readily available through stocks, bonds, or mutual funds.

42. D: SEC approval of the Precidian ActiveShares ETF model in 2019 allowed ETFs to publish a list of their holdings quarterly, as mutual funds do, rather than daily, allowing their proprietary trading strategies to be more private. The Commodity Futures Modernization Act of 2000, Choice *A,* updated the definition of equity security originally contained in the Securities Exchange Act of 1934 § 240.3a11-1 to include a security future. The Investment Company Act of 1940, Choice *B,* defined investment companies (closed-end and open-end, known as mutual funds), unit investment trusts (UITs), and face-amount certificate companies. The SEC Rule 6c-11 (called the ETF Rule) issued in 2019, Choice *C,* allowed ETFs to come to market more quickly by allowing exemptions to be approved more quickly for redeemable securities, NAV trading, and transactions with affiliated persons but did not materially address the confidentiality of ETF holdings.

43. C: Credit risk is directly related to the ability of the security's issuer to operate successfully and fulfill its obligations. Currency risk, Choice *A,* is related to the change in relative value between two countries' currencies and may have no relationship to the business success of the company. Inflationary/purchasing power risk, Choice *B,* relates to inflation in the economy, and interest rate/reinvestment risk, Choice *D,* relates to the general level of interest rates. Neither choice relates to the business success of the issuer, so even if the issuer pays interest and principal as promised, the cash received may have declined in value in relation to the amount of goods and services it can buy.

44. C: Bond values typically change inversely compared with changes in the general level of interest rates. For example, if a company issues a bond with a 5 percent coupon and the general level of interest rates declines from 5 percent to 4 percent, the market value of the bond will typically rise. The original bond will be paying 25 percent more in interest than a newly issued bond with the same face, or principal, value with a 4 percent coupon. Longer-term bonds typically have a greater percent change in market value than short-term bonds with the same coupon, given the same change in the general level of interest rates. When the general level of interest rates is stable, unlike stated in Choices *A* and *B,* bond values typically do not rise or decline in response. In that scenario, changes in bond values would be more likely related to something specific to the issuer, such as a change in its credit rating. Choice *D* would typically result in dollar-denominated bonds rising. Because the dollar would be decreasing in value, foreign bonds would typically rise.

45. C: Market risk, also known as systematic risk, is related to the value of most securities changing in the general direction of the market, with the change not related to characteristics of each specific security. This risk is more apparent when economic or political uncertainty increases. Market risk is generally considered to be difficult to manage in the short term using strategies such as diversification, portfolio rebalancing, or hedging, which are typically considered effective to help manage non-systematic, non–market-related risks. A strategy for mitigating political/geopolitical risk, Choice *A*, could include diversification among various countries. A strategy for mitigating prepayment risk, Choice *B*, could include diversification among maturity dates, types of debt instruments, and a sheer quantity of debt investments, as is available in a diversified mutual or ETF bond fund. Choice *D*, non-systematic risk, covers a wide variety of risks other than market risk, including capital risk, credit risk, currency risk, inflationary/purchasing power risk, interest rate/reinvestment risk, liquidity risk, as well as political/geopolitical risk, Choice *A*, and prepayment risk, Choice *B*. These are generally considered to be lessened through the use of diversification as well as portfolio rebalancing and hedging.

Understanding Trading, Customer Accounts, and Prohibited Activities

46. A: Choice *A* correctly indicates that a stop order is to be executed promptly when the stop price is available on the market. Unlike a limit order, a stop order does not need to be executed at a price at least as favorable as the stop price. Choice *B* relates to the length of time the order waits for execution but does not relate to the price. Choice *C* relates to whether the representation may select any characteristic of the order other than the timing or price. Choice *D* relates to whether the client accepted any recommendation from the representative about any characteristic of the order.

47. C: Choice *C* refers to borrowing a security and selling it, typically with the assistance of the seller's brokerage firm. The seller hopes the price will decline, allowing it to be purchased at a price lower than the selling price. At that time, the seller would purchase the security and return it to the party who loaned the security. This is speculative, with an unlimited maximum possible loss, because the price could rise without limit, resulting in a significant loss. Choices *A*, *B*, and *D* are unrelated to the borrowing of a security in order to sell it.

48. B: Choice *B* appropriately displays the factors in calculating return on an investment. Choice *A* duplicates the subtraction of the amount invested, which is already subtracted from the sales proceeds to obtain realized gain or loss. Choice *C* uses sales proceeds as the denominator, which is incorrect. Choice *D* would in some cases have the same result as *B*, when no cash is received while the investment is held, such as in the case of a zero-coupon bond. However, it is not a reliable formula for investments producing cash during the holding period.

49. B: Choice *B* correctly displays the calculation of yield to maturity. Choice *A* displays the calculation of yield to call. Choice *C* should have the numeral "2" instead of "2 x Years to Maturity" at the very bottom of the equation. Choice *D* should have the numeral "2" instead of "Years to Maturity" at the very bottom of the equation.

50. B: Choice *B* properly indicates payment date for corporate stock, corporate bonds, and municipal funds specified by MSRB rule G-15 as T+4, which is equal to S+2, since the settlement date is T+4. Choices *A*, *C*, and *D* are incorrect.

51. B: Choice *B* reflects an exchange of current shares of a security for a lesser number of new shares of the same security. Choice *A* would result in an exchange of current shares of a security for a greater number of new shares of the same security. Choice *C* would reflect a public offer of a certain monetary

136

price for current shares of a firm. Choice *D* would reflect a public offer of a certain quantity of another security for current shares of a firm.

52. B: Choice *B* expresses the change in the par value from a three-for-one stock split. Choices *A* and *C* are incorrect. Choice *D* would be correct only if the par value was three dollars before the stock split.

53. B: Choice *B* correctly indicates that a short sale, accomplished by borrowing the security, is executed only in a margin account. Choice *A* may be used for purchases when no money is borrowed, and no security is borrowed. Choice *C* is used to trade options and requires risk disclosures. Choice *D* refers to an account in which the customer allows the representative to select a characteristic of an order other than price and timing.

54. C: Choice *C* reflects the representative's prerogative to choose an order's characteristic other than price and timing. Choices *A* and *B* occur in a margin account. Choice *D* is not a typical occurrence in any account.

55. D: Choice *D* correctly reflects the actions regarding a joint account. Choice *A* describes a corporate account. Choice *B* describes a trust account. Choice *C* notes one characteristic of a partnership account.

56. D: Choice *D* reflects a significant attraction of retirement accounts: tax deferral. Choice *A* is not necessarily true, and a retired person may not need tax deferral. Choice *B* may be true of an employee-sponsored retirement account, such as a 401k. However, not every retirement account is opened by an employee. It may be opened by a self-employed person, or the spouse of a person with income. Choice *C* does not reflect the typical use of a retirement account. A person with an annuity already has tax deferral. Many teachers may begin contributing to a retirement annuity in a 403b account.

57. A: Choice *A* describes money laundering. Choices *B, C,* and *D* describe improper uses of money other than money laundering.

58. A: Choice *A* must be submitted when a person takes an action that is suspicious. If something suspicious occurs, but a suspect is not identified, another thirty days may be used to research the situation, in order to identify a suspect. Choice *B* is prepared by a bank official when a customer asks to complete a transaction greater than $10,000. Choice *C* refers to the Office of Foreign Asset Control (OFAC), which maintains a Specially Designated Nationals and Blocked Persons List (SDNs), against which new customer's names are compared. Choice *D* refers to statements that are provided to the customer at least once every calendar quarter.

59. A: Choice *A* is a books and records requirement for member broker-dealers. Choice *B* is not a requirement. Some data must be readily accessible, and the rest must be eventually accessible. Choice *C* is not a requirement. Records must generally be kept six years, unless specifically designated for a different time frame. Choice *D* is not a requirement, though a registered principal may be required to oversee the process of record retention.

60. C: Choice *C* describes nonpublic personal information (NPI). Choices *A, B,* and *D* fail to describe NPI because they include information that may be publicly available.

61. D: Choice *D* is sent to twenty-five or less retail investors within a thirty-day calendar period. Choice *A* is only provided to institutional investors. A firm's internal communications is excluded from this definition. Choice *B* is a category of communications with the public in FINRA Rule 2210. Choice *C* is sent to more than twenty-five retail investors within a thirty-day calendar period.

62. C: Choice *C* describes the highest obligation of a securities professional. Recommendations of security trades or investment strategies are to be made according to what is in the client's best interest, and without regard to the effect on the securities professional's compensation. Choice *A* may be a part of serving the customer's best interest, but the selection of the wrong security obtained at the most favorable price may not be in the consumer's best interest. Choice *B* is a standard that requires an investment be appropriate for some persons, and to be appropriate for the specific consumer, but does not necessarily reflect what is in the specific consumer's best interest. Choice *D*, high return on investment, may be part of a consumer's goal. However, an annuity may have the highest return, but its surrender fee may make it not in the consumer's best interest.

63. A: Choice *A* is defined as using improper methods to increase or decrease the market price of a security or somehow affect the actions of other investors for personal gain. Choice *B* typically refers to placing an illegal order based on material nonpublic information that is not known to the public and may not significantly affect the market value of the security in that order. Choices *C* and *D* are only two types of market manipulation—neither is a broad enough definition.

64. D: Choice *D* involves placing multiple orders to increase the compensation of the representation placing the orders rather than promoting the interest of the customer. Choice *A* involves false information about a company being spread in order to artificially increase or decrease the market value of its securities. Choice *B* happens when one or more investors holding a firm's security or securities start favorable, false market rumors in order to positively influence the market value of those securities, in order to sell them soon afterward at a profit somewhat unrelated to the actual economic health of the company. Choice *C* involves taking advantage of nonpublic knowledge that a large block transaction is about to be completed, by placing an order for a discretionary account or for the firm's account.

65. C: Choice *C* typically refers to making an illegal trade based on material nonpublic information. Choice *A* refers to trying to influence another member firm or another member firm's associated person through fear, to change their behavior in the market, but does not necessarily use material nonpublic information. Choice *B* is restricted by FINRA Rule 3240 but does not necessarily involve the use of material nonpublic information. Choice *D* is prohibited by FINRA Rule 2165 but does not necessarily use material nonpublic information.

66. B: Choice *B* expresses the broad range of 1934 Act Section 15c1-2. Choice *A* refers to borrowing a security in order to sell it. This does not necessarily involve deceit. Choice *C* refers to an order which is to be executed promptly after the stop price is available on the market. This does not necessarily involve deceit. Choice *D* reflects the need to file a Currency Transaction Report (CTR). This does not necessarily involve deceit.

67. A: Choice *A* is forbidden to an unregistered person. Choices *B, C,* and *D* are allowed actions by unregistered persons.

68. D: Choice *D* reflects the FINRA's discipline of registered representatives regarding a customer's signatures under FINRA Rule 2010, without any additional consideration. Choices *A, B,* and *C* mention additional conditions. If those conditions had not been present, the use of incomplete forms signed in advance by a customer would still be a disciplinary offense.

Overview of the Regulatory Framework

69. D: A firm that wishes to take orders for securities must be a member of the Financial Industry Regulatory Agency (FINRA). Choices *A*, *B*, and C do not represent a firm or person that is required to be a member of FINRA.

70. C: Only a person registered with FINRA, when engaged by a FINRA member firm and serving under an appropriately registered supervisor, may encourage a person to buy or sell a security. Choices *A*, *B*, and *D* may be done by an unregistered person without close supervision.

71. D: The firm element is a part of the FINRA continuing education requirement that is developed and administered each year to its FINRA-registered associated persons as appropriate. Choices *A*, *B*, and *C* are not parts of the FINRA continuing education requirements. The other part is the regulatory element, which FINRA updates and administers.

72. D: Form U4 is the Application for Securities Industry Registration or Transfer. In addition to its use in the initial application for registration, it is to be updated within thirty days of any significant changes. Choice *A*, Schedule A – Schedule of Information Required in Registration Statement, is a supplement required by the SEC when filing a registration of a securities issue of a U.S. company. Choice *B*, Form BD – Uniform Application for Broker-Dealer Registration, is the form to initiate registration for a broker-dealer with regulatory authorities such as FINRA and the Securities Exchange Commission. Choice *C*, Form U5 – Uniform Termination Notice for Security Industry Registration, is the form to end registration with FINRA, states, and territories. A firm is to update the form when it learns of pertinent data.

73. C: A text received from an executor of a customer's estate stating that the final handling of the securities was improper is a reportable customer complaint; it is dissatisfaction expressed in writing by a customer's authorized representative regarding activities related to final handling of that customer's securities. Choice *A*, although it is in writing, is not reportable because it is not by the customer's authorized representative. Choices *B* and *D* are not reportable because they are not in writing.

74. A: Before approving an outside business activity (OBA), a member firm must consider whether the OBA could be perceived by outsiders as part of the member's activities. Choices *B*, *C*, and *D* are not required by FINRA to be considered even though they may be reasonable considerations.

75. A: FINRA Rule 2030 – Engaging in Distribution and Solicitation Activities with Government Entities prohibits a registered person from "distribution or solicitation activities for compensation" with any governmental unit for two years if political contributions over a certain amount are made to a certain person's political activities. Choices *B*, *C*, and *D* do not connect political contributions with a registered person's ability to perform activities for compensation.

Practice Test #2

Knowledge of Capital Markets

1. Which of the following statements is true regarding stock market regulation?
   a. One purpose of the 1933 Securities Act was to discourage investment in the stock market.
   b. One purpose of the 1934 Securities Exchange Act was to repeal the 1933 Securities Act, which had led to an increased level of speculation in the stock market.
   c. During the late 1920's, business expansion was accompanied by a declining level of speculation in the stock market, which led to increased regulation in the early 1930's.
   d. One purpose of the 1933 Securities Act was to provide fair disclosure of new stock issues.

2. Which of the following was previously named the National Association of Securities Dealers (NASD)?
   a. New York Stock Exchange LLC (NYSE)
   b. American Stock Exchange (Amex)
   c. Financial Industry Regulatory Authority (FINRA)
   d. The Options Clearing Corporation (OCC)

3. Which of the following statements is true regarding the named organization?
   a. The CBOE's jurisdiction for trading is limited to the United States, Canada, Mexico, Puerto Rico and the U.S. Virgin Islands.
   b. FINRA's role was originally defined by Congress to include banks and broker-dealers.
   c. MSRB's function was originally defined to include municipal advisors.
   d. NYSE is the stock exchange with access to the largest selection of companies in the world, when considering the market capitalization of their listed stock.

4. In what year was the central banking system in the U.S. established by Congress?
   a. 1789
   b. 1865
   c. 1913
   d. 1933

5. Which of the following statements is true regarding the Federal Reserve?
   a. The system is overseen by a board that is called both the Federal Reserve Board and the Board of Governors.
   b. The system has ten branch banks, each with its own board and president.
   c. The system has twenty-four regional banks, each with its own board and president.
   d. The member banks receive dividends from stock they hold in Reserve banks and can trade that stock.

6. Which is a true statement regarding the Securities Investor Protection Act of 1970 (SIPA)?
   a. It required filing a prospectus with the SEC.
   b. It encouraged investors to consider enhancing their returns by investing more in options and futures.
   c. It created the Securities Investor Protection Corporation including a Board of Directors, some of whom are appointed by the President.
   d. It added a guarantee that an investor's stock value would not fall more than twenty percent in a given trading day.

140

7. Which of the following statements is true regarding FINRA Rule 2266 - SIPC Information?
   a. The members are required to inform investors in written form of the investor's ability to learn about SIPC, and obtain the SIPC brochure by contacting SIPC.
   b. The members are required to inform investors in written form, and give an oral explanation to each one, of the investor's ability to learn about SIPC, and obtain the SIPC brochure by contacting SIPC.
   c. The members are required to orally inform investors of the investor's ability to learn about SIPC, and obtain the SIPC brochure by contacting FINRA or the SEC.
   d. The members are required to inform investors in written form of their ability to learn about SIPC, and obtain the SIPC brochure by contacting FINRA in writing.

8. In what year was the Federal Deposit Insurance Company (FDIC) established by Congress?
   a. 1789
   b. 1865
   c. 1913
   d. 1933

9. Which of the following statements is true regarding banks?
   a. In times of high interest rates, bank customers chose to put more of their idle liquid assets into mutual funds.
   b. Some banks arranged for brokerage firms to set up business in the banks' offices.
   c. When the FDIC was established, it began assuring depositors that they may withdraw their funds at any time, up to $250,000 per depositor.
   d. FDIC required that banks let their customers know that mutual funds purchased on their premises guaranteed the value of the mutual funds, up to the limit set by the FDIC.

10. Which of the following statements is true regarding banks in relationship to the stock market?
   a. During and immediately after the stock market crash of 1929, liquid assets in banks were safe, as contrasted with the stock that lost value in the stock market crash.
   b. After the stock market crash of 1929, many banks were not able to provide depositors their money upon request.
   c. Making bank depositors' funds safe was the only purpose for establishing the Federal Reserve.
   d. The stock market crash of 1929 was the only time in American history when depositors had significant concerns because of their inability to withdraw their funds upon demand.

11. What category of investors is defined by regulators as trading investments such as stocks and bonds without enough frequency to receive discounted fees?
   a. Ordinary
   b. Retail
   c. Accredited
   d. Institutional

12. Which of the following is the main role of a broker?
   a. Brokers typically buy or sell on their own behalf.
   b. Brokers have the knowledge and financial strength to buy investments on behalf of the customer.
   c. Brokers offer bid and ask prices that do not change for 72 hours.
   d. Brokers eliminate the need for a customer to have a registered representative.

Understanding Products and Their Risks

13. Which of the following acts included a security future in the definition of an equity security?
    a. 1933 Securities Act
    b. 1934 Securities Exchange Act
    c. 2000 Commodity Futures Modernization Act
    d. 2002 Sarbanes-Oxley (SOX) Act

14. Which of the following describes a requirement in FINRA Rule 2261 - Disclosure of Financial Condition?
    a. When requested by a customer, the member broker firm provides its financial condition from its most recent balance sheet.
    b. When a customer purchases securities representing a 10% increase in his portfolio, the broker dealer automatically provides its most recent year-to-date income statement.
    c. When the member broker firm is owned by a parent company, whenever the parent company declares a dividend, the broker firm automatically provides the amount of dividend per share.
    d. When a customer opens a margin account, the broker dealer discloses the total amount of loans the broker dealer has outstanding to all customers.

15. Which of the following is true?
    a. Preferred shareholders typically are most interested in prospects of growth in share value.
    b. Bondholders typically are most interested in prospects of interest rates decreasing.
    c. Common shareholders typically are not interested in prospects of growth in share value.
    d. Creditors are typically not interested in the financial strength of the company.

16. Which of the following conversions typically occurs?
    a. Convertible preferred stock converts to senior bonds.
    b. Convertible senior bonds convert to subordinated debentures.
    c. Convertible preferred stock converts to common stock.
    d. Convertible common stock converts to preferred stock.

17. Which of the following scenarios represents a stockholder fully exercising the Right of First Refusal?
    a. Of 1,000,000 common shares issued, a shareholder owns 500,000 common shares and purchases 5,000 shares of a new issue.
    b. Of 1,000,000 common shares issued, a shareholder owns 500,000 common shares and purchases 5% of a new issue.
    c. Of 1,000,000 common shares issued, a shareholder owns 500,000 common shares and purchases 50% of a new issue.
    d. Of 1,000,000 common shares issued, a shareholder owns 500,000 common shares and purchases 500,000 shares of a new issue.

18. Which may typically occur with a rights issue?
    a. The subscription price will typically be higher than the current market price.
    b. The market value will typically rise when a rights offering is announced.
    c. Multiple rights may be needed to purchase a share of stock.
    d. Non-renounceable rights may be sold by current shareholders.

19. Which of the following is a typical scenario for a company providing an incentive for current bondholders or stockholders to purchase additional preferred stocks or bonds?
   a. Offered in combination with the bond or preferred stock, a stock call warrant provides an opportunity, but not an obligation, for the purchaser to exercise the warrant, but not resell the warrant to anyone else.
   b. Offered in combination with the bond or preferred stock, a stock call warrant provides an opportunity, but not an obligation, for the purchaser to exercise the warrant at a price lower than the current market price.
   c. Offered in combination with the bond or preferred stock, a stock call warrant provides an opportunity, but not an obligation, for the purchaser to exercise the warrant within a specific period, beginning at some point, as much as six months or a year after the issue.
   d. Offered in combination with the bond or preferred stock, a stock call warrant provides an obligation for the purchaser to exercise the warrant within a specific period, beginning at issuance and lasting as much as six months or a year.

20. Which of the following is true regarding characteristics of Treasury securities?
   a. T-Bills are issued with face values of one thousand dollars or more.
   b. T-Bonds are issued with face values of one thousand dollars or more.
   c. The level of inflation affects the earning power of Treasury Inflation-Protected Securities (TIPS), just as other Treasury securities' interest payments do.
   d. Auctions for 10-year notes are held monthly.

21. A firm planning to make an offering of a bond issue engages which of the following to advise on characteristics of the issue, such as the interest rate?
   a. Broker-dealer firm
   b. Investment bank
   c. Member of the NYSE
   d. Depositary bank

22. Since a competitive sale would typically be more advantageous to the issuer than a negotiated sale, why would an issuer user a negotiated sale?
   a. The issuer has a weak credit rating.
   b. The economy is unusually strong.
   c. The bond issue is especially simple and straightforward.
   d. The size of the bond issue is small.

23. Which of the following is a prominent agency that rates municipal bonds but is not one of the top two?
   a. Fitch Ratings
   b. Moody's Investors Service
   c. Standard & Poor's Global Ratings
   d. Municipal Securities Rulemaking Board (MSRB)

24. Which of the following would generally be considered most likely to fulfill its debt service?
   a. Special Tax Bond
   b. Double-Barreled Bond
   c. Moral Obligation Bond
   d. Private Activity Bond

25. Which of the following is an attractive characteristic of purchasing a stock call option?
    a. Call options are regulated by the Securities and Exchange Commission (SEC), rather than by the Financial Industry Regulatory Authority (FINRA).
    b. The purchaser of a call option may possibly gain more profit from changes in market value of the underlying asset with less original cash outlay than if purchasing the underlying security.
    c. Call options may be traded on the New York Stock Exchange (NYSE), which is the exchange with the highest option trading volume.
    d. Options are relatively unknown in the investment community, as they began selling in 1973.

26. Which of the following is a disadvantage of writing a naked stock call option?
    a. The strike price is not stated when the option is sold to the buyer.
    b. The writer of a naked stock call option has an unlimited risk.
    c. The expiration date is not stated when sold to the buyer.
    d. The buyer of the option may choose which company's stock to buy.

27. Which of the following is correct regarding all listed options, since are all guaranteed?
    a. All obligations of the options contracts are fulfilled.
    b. No investor who exercises a contract will ever be "out of the money" for more than the premium paid for the option.
    c. Every investor who exercises a contract will be "in the money" or "at the money."
    d. No company will be bankrupt on the exercise date of its stock options.

28. How is an open-end investment company, also known as a mutual fund, the same as closed-end investment companies?
    a. Both are traded at NAV, with possible adjustments for a sales load, redemption, and/or commission.
    b. Both are regulated by the Investment Company Act of 1940.
    c. Both issue their shares when organized, as typical public companies do.
    d. Both typically have a standing offer to redeem their shares for cash.

29. Which of the following is correct regarding the Expense Ratio?
    a. The largest proportion is the up-front sales load.
    b. The management fee is usually a smaller percentage of net asset value (NAV) in a small mutual fund, as compared with a large fund.
    c. The company does not calculate the performance of the investor's shares.
    d. The Expense Ratio includes the cost of record-keeping, which can help the investor when filing taxes.

30. Which share class would be most suitable to an investor with a short-term to medium-term time horizon and may be open to eventually changing to a long-term investment?
    a. Class A shares which convert to Class C shares
    b. Class B shares which convert to Class A shares
    c. Class C shares which convert to Class T shares
    d. Class T shares which convert to Class B shares

31. Which share class allows investors to see fees most clearly?
    a. Class A
    b. Class B
    c. Class T
    d. Clean shares

32. Which of the following statements is NOT true regarding mutual funds and UITs?
    a. The units of many UITs trade throughout the trading day on an exchange, whereas a mutual funds' orders are executed only after the trading day ends.
    b. A UIT's assets are typically fully invested, whereas a mutual fund's assets are usually not.
    c. Mutual funds and UITs both issue an initial public offering (IPO), and both may occasionally have a follow-on offering.
    d. A mutual fund's share value is determined daily, but its shares do not trade on an exchange, as a UIT may.

33. Which of the following is correct regarding variable contracts?
    a. They typically have less guarantees than mutual funds or UITs, so their internal fees are lower.
    b. Representatives are typically paid lower commissions for selling variable contracts than for other investment products.
    c. FINRA Rule 2330 requires the company issuing the variable contract and the representative soliciting and recommending the variable contract to assure the suitability of the contract as a whole and the suitability of the selection of specific investment choices (subaccounts) for the investor.
    d. An owner of a variable contract typically does not need to hold cash equivalents because of the availability of policy loans from the variable contract.

34. Which of the following is NOT an expected part of recommending an investor replace an annuity or life insurance product in order to fund the purchase of a variable contract of EIC?
    a. The replaced product is less than thirty-six months old.
    b. The representative provides no comparison of the benefits of the replaced product and the new product.
    c. The representative is expected to know enough about the investor's overall financial objectives, liquidity, and net worth to determine the suitability for recommending a variable annuity.
    d. The representative may be expected to document that the investor owns liquid assets equal to living expenses for a certain period of time, such as one year.

35. An equity indexed contract holder has chosen a minimum guaranteed rate of 4%, along with a limited upside potential of 80% of the increase in the S&P Index, up to a maximum of 8%. If the S&P Index increases by 7%, what would the contract be credited with?
    a. 4%
    b. 5.6%
    c. 7%
    d. 8%

36. An equity indexed contract holder has chosen a minimum guaranteed rate of 4%, along with a limited upside potential of 80% of the increase in the S&P Index, up to a maximum of 8%. If the S&P Index decreases by 7%, by what percentage would the contract be adjusted?
    a. -5%
    b. -4%
    c. 4%
    d. 5%

37. Which of the following is correct about how a municipal fund security is like an open-end investment company (mutual fund)?
    a. Neither is issued by a governmental unit.
    b. Both hold only municipal bonds.
    c. Their value varies with the sum of the market values of all securities held.
    d. They both can be local government investment pools (LGIPs).

38. Which of the following is correct regarding "direct-sold" or "advisor-sold" 529 plans?
    a. No states offer "direct-sold" 529 plans by mail or through a website.
    b. No states offer 529 plans through broker-dealers.
    c. "Direct-sold" investors may pay lower fees, and not have professional advice provided.
    d. States typically offer "advisor-sold" 529 plans, which provides profession investment advice with no fees.

39. Which of the following is correct regarding Local Government Investment Pools (LGIPs)?
    a. They are mutual funds.
    b. Multiple state agencies or municipalities may pool their cash reserves into an LGIP.
    c. LGIPs are established under federal securities laws.
    d. LGIPs do not provide diversification.

40. Which of the following is correct regarding trading in Direct Participation Programs (DPPs)?
    a. The ability to sell ownership units of DPP products is like selling a stock on a registered exchange.
    b. The issuer of a DPP redeems the ownership units within two years of issue, or earlier, if an earlier date is specified when the units are issued.
    c. DPP products are traded the NYSE and on over-the-counter markets.
    d. Though DPP products are not traded on national exchanges, in some cases another purchaser may be found.

41. In which of the following Acts was a direct participation program (DPP) described?
    a. Securities Act of 1933
    b. Securities Exchange Act of 1934
    c. Investment Company Act of 1940
    d. Investment Advisers Act of 1940

42. Which of the following qualifies as a direct participation program?
    a. Real estate investment trust
    b. Subchapter S corporation
    c. Internal Revenue Code 401 and 403(a) tax qualified pension and profit sharing plan
    d. Internal Revenue Code 403(b) tax sheltered annuity

43. Which of the following is correct regarding tax consequences of a Direct Participation Program (DPP)?
   a. The owners are taxed at a lower rate, in consideration of the DPP income already being taxed.
   b. The owners are taxed on profits reported as passive income, but the DPP is not taxed.
   c. The owners are taxed on profits reported as actively participating, but the DPP is not taxed.
   d. The DPP is taxed, and the owner receives tax-exempt dividend income from the DPP.

44. Which of the following would NOT be a direct participation program?
   a. Subchapter C corporation
   b. Subchapter S corporation
   c. Limited partnership
   d. Limited liability company

45. How is a direct participation program that is a real estate limited partnerships traded?
   a. If listed, it would trade on any national exchange.
   b. They may only be traded with other limited partners in the same partnership.
   c. They are only traded after market value is determined at the close of trading each day.
   d. Investors may find broker-dealers who stay aware of such investments and receive compensation for doing so.

Understanding Trading, Customer Accounts, and Prohibited Activities

46. Which of the following is not accomplished with an expectation of profit if the security's price declines?
   a. Short sale
   b. Sale of a put
   c. Purchase of a call
   d. Purchase of a security

47. Which of the following refers to the position of an investor who owns a security?
   a. Liquid position
   b. Contingent position
   c. Long position
   d. Short position

48. Which of the following would involve a broker-dealer acting in the capacity of a principal?
   a. The broker-dealer advised the investor to sell the security.
   b. The broker-dealer advised the investor to sell the security when it reaches a certain price.
   c. The broker-dealer purchased the security from the investor.
   d. The broker-dealer loaned the security to the investor.

49. FINRA Rule 2120 – "Commissions, Mark Ups and Charges" relates to which of the following situations?
   a. The broker-dealer advises the customer to make no trades until the following day.
   b. The broker-dealer has a conflict of interest because of personally owning the security being considered.
   c. The broker-dealer is acting in an agency capacity.
   d. The broker-dealer is closing the agency and will not be able to provide future service.

50. Markup/markdown is the compensation earned by the broker-dealer in which of the following circumstances?
    a. Providing advice when no trade is completed
    b. Acting in a principal capacity
    c. Acting in an agency capacity
    d. Acting as a Registered Investment Adviser

51. Which of the following is not allowed as a consideration of compensation under FINRA Rule 2121 – Fair Prices and Commissions?
    a. Occupation of the customer
    b. Type of Security
    c. Price
    d. Total monetary size of the transaction

52. Which of the following FINRA Rules requires a broker-dealer to disclose to a customer when the broker-dealer participates in the transaction by arranging for a security to be purchased at a lower price and sold to the customer at a higher price?
    a. FINRA Rule 2121 – Fair Prices and Commissions
    b. FINRA Rule 2122 – Charges for Services Performed
    c. FINRA Rule 2124 – Net Transactions with Customers
    d. FINRA 5210 – Publication of Transactions and Quotations

53. In FINRA Rule 2121 – Fair Prices and Commissions, 5 percent compensation is provided as which of the following?
    a. Minimum
    b. Maximum
    c. Guideline
    d. Absolute

54. Which of the following pairs are commonly-used references for the same positions?
    a. Open or naked
    b. Long or covered
    c. Short or open
    d. Long or naked

55. Which of the following are covered by both of the following rules: FINRA 5210 – Publication of Transactions and Quotations and MSRB G-13 – Quotations?
    a. Over-the-counter equity securities with prices published in multiple markets must be published with the same prices in each market, unless a customer submits a limit order.
    b. Published quotes must represent prices that investors can actually pay when buying or receive when selling.
    c. A broker-dealer must only make offers to buy or sell if willing to actually buy or sell at the prices offered.
    d. A member must process an order without separating it into multiple orders if the main cause for the multiple orders is to receive higher compensation.

148

56. As provided in the Securities Exchange Act of 1934, Section 15 – Rules Relating to Over-the-Counter Markets, how frequently must a broker-dealer report to the customer the current value of each penny stock held in the customer's account?
   a. Annually
   b. Monthly
   c. Weekly
   d. Quarterly

57. Which of the following are covered by both of the following rules: FINRA 5310 – Best Execution and Interpositioning and MSRB G-18 – Best Execution?
   a. Information about each trade will be submitted promptly to the Real-time Transaction Reporting System (RTRS)
   b. Inv Co Act 1940 17a-6 – Exemption for Transactions with Portfolio Affiliates
   c. Inv Co Act 1940 17a-7 – Exemption of Certain Purchase or Sale Transactions Between an Investment Company and Certain Affiliated Persons Thereof
   d. A broker-dealer will be conscientious in finding the best market and handling the trade to provide the best price practical to a customer.

58. Investment return is calculated in which of the following ways?
   a. The difference between the sales proceeds and the purchase price
   b. Cash received while the security is held
   c. The excess of net cash received over what was expected
   d. Cash received while the security is held, plus the difference between the sales proceeds and the purchase price, less any commissions, adviser fees, custody fees and recordkeeping costs, less income tax

59. Which of the following is the most accurate calculation of return on investment?
   a. Difference between the sales proceeds and the cost when purchased
   b. Cash received while the security is held, plus the difference between the sales proceeds and the purchase price, less any commissions, adviser fees, custody fees and recordkeeping costs
   c. Cash received while the security is held, plus the difference between the sales proceeds and the purchase price, less any commissions, adviser fees, custody fees and recordkeeping costs less estimated income tax
   d. Cash received while the security is held, plus the difference between the sales proceeds and the purchase price, less any commissions, adviser fees, custody fees and recordkeeping costs less actual income tax

60. Which of the following is determined by the rules of the exchange on which the stock is traded?
   a. Record date
   b. Payment date
   c. Declaration date
   d. Ex-dividend date or ex-date

61. Which of the following measures of bond interest is determined when the bonds are issued?
   a. Yield to maturity
   b. Yield to call
   c. Nominal yield
   d. Current yield

62. Which of the following is used to calculate a trading profit for tax purposes?
    a. Basis points
    b. Bid price
    c. Ask price
    d. Cost basis

63. Which of the following is NOT included in cost basis of a security?
    a. Commissions
    b. Markups
    c. Sales proceeds
    d. Purchase price

64. Which rules may require the cost basis to use the oldest shares purchased?
    a. Internal Revenue Code
    b. Securities Exchange Commission Act of 1934
    c. FINRA Rules
    d. MSRB Rules

65. Which of the following situations would NOT make determination of cost basis more complicated than usual?
    a. The issuing firm changed its name.
    b. Multiple purchases were made.
    c. Stock dividends were declared.
    d. The firm returned capital to shareholders.

66. Which of the following statements is NOT true regarding benchmarks and indices?
    a. They are not usually used to measure investment managers' performance.
    b. They allow comparison of a security's return with that of similar securities.
    c. They allow comparison of a security's return with that of investments other than securities.
    d. They allow comparison of a security's return with compensation threshold conditions.

67. Which of the following statements correctly defines trade settlement?
    a. Trade settlement refers to the time in business days between the date the trade is agreed to, until the seller's broker-dealer receives payment and the buyer's broker-dealer receives ownership.
    b. Trade settlement refers to the time in business days during which a security is held.
    c. Trade settlement refers to the time in calendar days between the declaration date for stock dividends and the ex-dividend date.
    d. Trade settlement refers to the time in calendar days between the first trade for which an investor places a market order and the confirmation of the order's execution is reported to the investor's broker-dealer.

68. Ownership of a security is changed by which of the following actions?
    a. The purchaser is entered as owner on the books of the issuer.
    b. Publication in the Wall Street Journal
    c. Publication in a local newspaper of legal record
    d. Communication from the broker-dealer of the seller to the broker-dealer of the buyer

Overview of the Regulatory Framework

69. In which of the following Articles are standards of behavior for FINRA members and associated persons described?
   a. FINRA By-Laws Article I – Definitions
   b. FINRA By-Laws Article III – Qualifications of Members and Associated Persons
   c. FINRA By-Laws Article IV – Membership
   d. FINRA By-Laws Article V – Registered Representatives and Associated Persons

70. In which of the following Articles is an agreement for FINRA members to follow laws; rules and regulations of the SEC; rules and regulations of the MSRB; rules and regulations of the Treasury Department; FINRA By-laws; NAS Regulation; NASD Dispute Resolution; FINRA Rules; and all FINRA rulings, orders, decisions, and sanctions?
   a. FINRA By-Laws Article I – Definitions
   b. FINRA By-Laws Article III – Qualifications of Members and Associated Persons
   c. FINRA By-Laws Article IV – Membership
   d. FINRA By-Laws Article V – Registered Representatives and Associated Persons

71. Which of the following statements is true regarding MSRB Rule G-10 – Delivery of Investment Brochure?
   a. The investor brochure will be provided to an investor who submits a written complaint regarding a municipal securities transaction.
   b. The investor brochure will be provided once each calendar year to every municipal securities customer.
   c. Every broker, dealer, and municipal securities dealer shall annually provide a statement that the firm is registered with the Department of the Treasury.
   d. Every municipal adviser shall annually provide a statement that that the firm is registered with the Federal Reserve.

72. Which of the following is true regarding non-registered persons?
   a. A non-registered person may meet with a member of the public to discuss risk tolerance and financial goals as they relate to investing in securities.
   b. A non-registered person may ask whether a member of the public is interested in reviewing possible investments with a registered person of the firm.
   c. A non-registered person may review the current investment portfolio of a member of the public.
   d. A non-registered person may have passed a FINRA registration exam.

73. Which of the following statements is true regarding FINRA Rule 2060 – Use of Information Obtained in Fiduciary Capacity?
   a. A member firm may not use information from its customers to send marketing information to them.
   b. A member firm may not use information about its associated person to send them business-related correspondence.
   c. A member firm may not correct errors in customer account profile records without written permission from its customers.
   d. A member firm serving in recordkeeping during a securities distribution may not use that information to encourage transactions with the owners unless the issue instructs the firm to do so.

74. Which of the following statements is correct regarding FINRA Rule 2263 – Arbitration Disclosure to Associated Persons Signing or Acknowledging Form U4?
    a. A person signing a U4 filing must be informed that arbitration will be used for disputes.
    b. A person signing a U4 filing must be informed that arbitration will not be used for disputes.
    c. A person signing a U4 filing must be informed that arbitration may be used for disputes.
    d. A person signing a U4 filing must be informed that arbitration will not be used for disputes involving felonies.

75. Which of the following statements is correct regarding what FINRA Rule 4330 – Customer Protection – Permissible Use of Customers' Securities requires a member firm to receive permission in writing from a customer before doing?
    a. Changing that customer's security records from paper to digital
    b. Publishing that customer's security holdings
    c. Lending that customer's securities
    d. Sharing information about that customer's securities with governmental agencies

Answer Explanations #2

Knowledge of Capital Markets

1. D: Choice *D* correctly describes one requirement of the 1933 Securities Act, fair disclosure of new stock issues. Choice *A* is incorrect because the 1933 Securities Act was enacted to encourage investment in the stock market. It was the first act of Congress to regulate securities at a national level. Choice *B* is incorrect because the 1933 Securities Act did not encourage more speculation, and the 1934 Securities Exchange Act did not replace the 1933 Securities Act. The 1933 Act regulated the primary market by requiring, for each primary offering, complete and honest documentation to the investor community about the security to be issued by an issuer. Choice *C* is incorrect because, during the 1920's, business expansion was accompanied by an increasing level of speculation in the stock market.

2. C: Choice *C* is correct because the Financial Industry Regulatory Authority (FINRA) was formerly the National Association of Securities Dealers (NASD). The NASD was established by the 1938 Maloney Act, which was amending the Securities Exchange Act of 1934. Choices *A*, *B*, and *D* are incorrect.

3. D: Choice *D* is correct. Of American exchanges still in existence, the New York Stock Exchange (NYSE) is the oldest. Based on market capitalization of securities traded, it is the largest stock exchange in the world. Choice *A* is incorrect because the Chicago Board Options Exchange's (CBOE's) jurisdiction for trading includes several other countries. The CBOE's trading volume is second-largest in the United States. Choice *B* is incorrect because FINRA's role was not originally defined by Congress to include banks. Choice *C* is incorrect because municipal advisors were added to the oversight responsibility of the Municipal Securities Rulemaking Board (MSRB) in 2010.

4. C: Choice *C* is correct. The Federal Reserve System was established in 1913 as the central banking system in the U.S. to promote a stable financial setting across the country. Choices *A*, *B*, and *D* are incorrect.

5. A: Choice *A* is correct. The Board of Governors and the Federal Reserve Board are both names for the same board, which supervises the system. Choices B and C are incorrect because the system has twelve regional banks and twenty-four branch banks. Choice D is incorrect because, though they do receive dividends from stock they hold in Reserve banks, they may not sell or trade that stock.

6. C: Choice *C* is correct. Five out of the seven directors are appointed by the President. They must also be approved by the Senate. One is appointed by the Secretary of the Treasury. One is appointed by the Federal Reserve Board. Choice *A* is incorrect because prospectus filing is required by the Securities Act of 1933, not the SIPA. Choice *B* is incorrect because it was re-establishing the willingness of investors to buy securities by protecting them, with limits, from bankruptcy of their broker-dealer. Choice *D* is incorrect because it did not guarantee against loss of market value.

7. A: Choice *A* is correct. The information must be provided in written form. It is not required to be provided orally. Oral notification is inadequate without the written form. The information may be obtained from the SIPC, not necessarily from FINRA or the SEC. Choices *B*, *C*, and *D* are incorrect.

8. D: Choice *D* is correct. The FDIC was established in 1933 to insure depositors' funds and encourage prudent management of bank. Choices *A*, *B*, and *C* are incorrect.

9. B: Choice *B* is correct. As mutual funds consistently provided higher returns than the interest earned on Certificates of Deposit (CDs), bank customers were moving liquid funds from CDs to mutual funds. So some banks made arrangements with brokerage firms to assist their banking customers on the bank's own premises. Choice *A* is incorrect, as low interest rates were the catalyst driving bank customers to increasingly use mutual funds. Choice *C* is incorrect, because the first limit was $2,500. Later limits were $5,000, $10,000, $15,000, $20,000, $40,000, and $100,000. In 2008, it was raised to $250,000. Choice *D* is incorrect because banks were strictly required to make quite clear to their customers investing in mutual funds on the bank's premises that those investments were not insured by the FDIC, and all or part of their investment could be lost.

10. B: Choice *B* is correct and that led to the formation of the FDIC to help assure bank customers that they could have confidence in their bank deposits up to a stated limit. Choice *A* is incorrect because many banks were not able to satisfy depositors' requests for withdrawals of their account balances. Choice *C* is incorrect because the Federal Reserve was also established to moderate the fractional reserve rate to encourage or discourage banks from making loans, which affects the money supply. Choice *D* is incorrect because in the late nineteenth century many banks were unable to satisfy their customers' request to withdraw funds.

11. B: Choice *B* is correct because regulators make a distinction between investors who have limited experience, knowledge, and ability to sustain a large loss and those that have more experience, knowledge, and ability to sustain a large loss. Investors who do not trade frequently enough to obtain discounted fees are retail investors. Choice A is incorrect because ordinary is not a regulatory category for investors. Choice *C* is incorrect because, according to the SEC's Rule 501(a) of Regulation D, a firm, natural person, or two natural persons, who have adequate knowledge to investment reasonably, and have assets to sustain a loss more than a firm or person who does not meet the stated standards, is an accredited investor. Choice *D* is incorrect because an organization that has invested assets from other persons or firms and invests those funds on behalf of them is an institutional investor.

12. B: Choice B is correct because brokers are registered persons or firms with one or more registered persons, who have invested capital that qualifies them to act on behalf of customers to purchase securities. Choice *A* is incorrect because brokers are only required to have enough invested capital to buy securities on behalf of the investor. A higher level of capital is required to buy or sell on their own behalf. If they had the higher invested capital, they would be known as dealers. Choice C is incorrect because bid and ask prices may change in less than 72 hours. A broker is a registered representative or a firm with one or more registered representative. Only a registered person may advise a customer regarding securities.

Understanding Products and Their Risks

13. C: Choice *C,* the 2000 Commodity Futures Modernization Act, modified the definition of security to include a security future**.** Choice *A* regulates initial public offerings (IPOs). Choice *B* established the SEC and regulates the secondary market. Choice *D* clarified audit rules and CEO's responsibility for accuracy of financial statements.

14. A: Choice *A* correctly describes a requirement of the rule. The disclosure of financial condition may be electronic or printed. Choices *B, C,* and *D* are not requirements of this rule.

15. B: Choice *B* is correct because bondholders expect to see the market value of bonds rise when interest rates decline. Choice *A* is incorrect because preferred shareholders are typically focused on dividends and preference in the event of liquidation. Choice *C* is incorrect because an attraction of common stock is

154

increase in the market value as bond holders and preferred stockholders have limited claims on the value of the company. As the company grows, common shareholders have claims on the increase of market capitalization value. Choice *D* is not true because creditors depend upon the financial strength of the company to enable it to make payments when due.

16. C: Choice *C* is correct because convertible preferred stock is often issued, which may be converted to common stock. In this case, the market value of the preferred stock may be similar to that of the common stock, proportionate to the par value of each. Choice *A* is incorrect because convertible preferred stock typically does not convert to senior bonds as that would diminish its claim on dividends. Choice *B* is incorrect because convertible senior bonds are not typically issued, and subordinated debentures have a later claim on net assets in the case of liquidation and would not be a desirable conversion. Choice *D* is incorrect because convertible common stock is not typically issued.

17. C: Choice *C* is correct since the common shareholder owns 50% of the outstanding shares, the shareholder may purchase 50% of the new issue. Choices *A* and *D* do not indicate what portion of the new issue 5,000 shares, or 500,000 shares, represents. Choice *B* is incorrect as the shareholder has only exercised 5% of the new issue and is entitled to 50% of the new issue.

18. C: Choice *C* is correct because a company may issue a right with a fractional ability to purchase a share of common stock. Choice *A* is incorrect because the subscription price will typically be lower than the current market price. Choice *B* is incorrect because the market price will typically fall when a rights offering is announced, as future dividends will be distributed among a larger quantity of common shares--unless the future profits are expected to soon increase proportionate to the increase in outstanding shares. Choice *D* is incorrect because non-renounceable rights may be exercised, or not used, as they cannot be sold.

19. C: Choice *C* is correct because a stock call warrant provides an opportunity, not an obligation, to purchase a stock at a price generally higher than the market price at issue, but hopefully below the market price during the exercise period. Choice *A* is incorrect because a stock call warrant can generally be resold on the open market. Choice *B* is incorrect because the exercise price is typically higher than the market price at issue. Choice *D* is incorrect because a stock call warrant typically provides an opportunity, but not an obligation, to purchase stock during a period beginning sometime in the future.

20. B: Choice *B* is correct because T-Bonds are issued with face values of one thousand dollars or more. If purchased directly from the Treasury, they may be purchased in increments of one hundred dollars, starting at one thousand dollars. Choice *A* is incorrect because T-Bills are usually issued with face values of one thousand dollars but are also issued with face values of one hundred dollars or multiples of one hundred dollars. Choice *C* is incorrect because the effective interest rate for Treasury Inflation-Protected Securities (TIPS) is adjusted, based on changes in the Consumer Price Index (CPI). The effective interest rate for TIPS is adjusted by changing the principal amount used to calculate the interest payments. Choice *D* is incorrect because auctions for ten-year notes are held in the last two months of each quarter: February, March, May, June, August, September, November, and December.

21. B: Choice *B* is correct because a firm planning to make an offering of a bond issue typically engages an investment bank to advise on characteristics of the issue, such as selecting the interest rate and increasing its marketability by offering convertible bonds. Choice *A* is incorrect, though one or more broker-dealer firms may assist, sometimes as part of a syndicate, to market the bond issue. Choice *C* is incorrect, though a member of the New York Stock Exchange (NYSE) may be involved in auctioning bonds. Choice *D* is incorrect, though a depositary bank assists in issuing ADRs on behalf of foreign companies.

22. A: Choice *A* is correct because, though an issuing municipality would typically benefit from a competitive sale, a negotiated sale may occur because of uncertainty in the financial markets, creative characteristics of the issue, the newness of the municipality, high total value of the bonds, or a weak credit rating. Choices *B, C,* and *D* are incorrect because a competitive sale would be more likely in these situations.

23. A: Choice A is correct because Fitch Ratings is a prominent agency that rates municipal bonds, with an approximate market share of 15%. It is not as widely used as Moody's Investors Service and Standard & Poor's Global Ratings. Therefore, Choices *B* and *C* are incorrect. Choice *D* is incorrect because the Municipal Securities Rulemaking Board (MSRB), is a regulatory board and not a rating service.

24. B: Choice *B* is correct because a double-barreled bond receives revenue from a project, as a revenue bond does, but is also backed by the full faith and credit of the issuing authority, as GO bonds are. Choice *A* is incorrect because a special tax bond is backed by specific taxes, does not have income from a revenue stream, and is not backed by the full faith and credit of the issuing authority. Choice *C* is incorrect because a moral obligation bond is a kind of revenue bond, which is not backed by the full faith and credit of the issuing authority. Choice *D* is incorrect because a private activity bond is a type of revenue bond, which is not backed by the full faith and credit of the issuing authority.

25. B: Choice *B* is correct because the owner or holder of a stock call option may exercise the option by purchasing the underlying stock any time before expiration and need not disburse the purchase price until the exercise date. If the stock price rises a significant amount, the option owner may receive as much profit as if the stock were purchased on the option purchase date, without having cash tied up in the amount of the purchase price for the period from the option purchase until the exercise date. Choice *A* is incorrect because options are regulated by FINRA. FINRA rule 2360 lists definitions and requirements related to trading in options. Choice *C* is incorrect because the Chicago Board Options Exchange (CBOE) is the largest option exchange in the United States. Based on the sum of market capitalization, the NYSE is the largest equities-based exchange in the world. Choice *D* is incorrect because options had previously been trading over-the-counter, and in 1973, the Chicago Board of Options Exchange (CBOE) began handling standardized options transactions, which were cleared and guaranteed by the newly-established Options Clearing Corporation.

26. B: Choice *B* is correct because the writer of a naked stock call option does not own the stock but promises to sell the stock at a certain price on or before a given date. If the stock goes up, the writer is obligated to purchase the stock at a loss in order to fulfill or cover the option, no matter how high the share price has risen. Choice *A* is incorrect because the strike price is stated when the option is sold to the buyer. Choice *C* is incorrect because the expiration is stated when the option is sold to the buyer. Choice *D* is incorrect because the option states the specific stock to buy.

27. A: Choice *A* is correct because the OCC guarantees all listed options in the event that the writer fails to perform, in order to promote financial integrity and stability in the marketplace. Choices *B* and C are incorr4ect because the guarantee does not relate to the market price being favorable to, or equal to, the strike price when exercised. Choice *D* is incorrect because the financial strength of the issuer of the underlying security is not guaranteed by the OCC.

28. B: Choice *B* is correct because the Investment Company of 1940 regulates open-end and closed-end investment companies, face-amount certificate companies, and unit investment trusts. Choice *A* is incorrect because mutual funds trade at NAV, with possible adjustments for sales charge or redemption fees, whereas closed-end investment companies trade throughout the trading day, according to supply and demand. Choice *C* is incorrect because open-end investment companies (mutual funds) issue new shares on an ongoing basis, whereas closed-end investment companies make an initial offering of stock, and do not issue shares on a continuing basis. Choice *D* is incorrect because only open-end investment companies (mutual funds) constantly offer to redeem their shares for cash. The closed-end investment companies do not offer to do so.

29. D: Choice *D* is correct because the cost of record-keeping is covered by the service fee. Choice *A* is incorrect because the up-front sales load is not included in the calculation of the Expense Ratio, as the Expense Ratio is made up of ongoing fees: the management fee, service fee, and 12b-1 fee. Each of these is an annual percentage of NAV, deducted from the fund on a daily basis. Choice *B* is incorrect because, due to economies of scale, the management fee is usually a smaller percentage of net asset value (NAV) in a large fund, as compared with a small fund. Choice *C* is incorrect because the company does calculate the performance of the investor's shares. The cost of doing this is covered by the service fee.

30. B: Choice *B* is correct because Class B shares charge no up-front sales charge, incur 12b-1 fees, and charge a CDSC if sold within eight years or so. If the investor holds the shares longer than intended (for as many as eight years), Class B shares that convert to Class A shares after that time will no longer have 12b-1 fees or CDSC, resulting in lower sales-related fees over the time horizon. Choice *A* is incorrect because Class A shares are typically appropriate for an investor who has a long-term time horizon at the time of purchases. Choice *C* is incorrect because Class C shares typically have a higher combination of up-front sales load and permanent 12b-1 fees, because of the permanent 12b-1 fees. Choice *D* is incorrect because Class T shares, typically with an up-front sales charge of 2.5% and a 0.25% 12b-1 fee, do not convert to Class B shares, which typically have higher 12b-1 fees for up to eight years, and a CDSC unless held for eight years or so.

31. D: Choice *D* is correct because clean shares have no sales load or 12b-1 fees. Advisors may charge for their advice when recommending this share class. The advisor's fees are readily seen, as they are separate from the mutual fund's fees. Choices *A*, *B*, and *C* are incorrect because these fees, directly related to the mutual fund, are not so readily seen as the fees of an advisor recommending clean shares.

32. C: Choice *C* is correct because, rather than a follow-on offering, mutual funds have what amounts to a continual initial public offering (IPO), which means they continually offer newly-issued shares when investors place buy orders. Mutual funds continually redeem those shares when offered for sale by investors. UITs have an initial public offering and may have a follow-on offering. Choice *A* is incorrect because the units of many UITs trade throughout the trading day on an exchange, whereas a mutual funds' orders are executed only after the trading day ends. Choice *B* is incorrect because a UIT's assets are typically fully invested and have no active investment management. In contrast, a mutual fund's assets are usually not fully invested but are actively managed, so cash equivalents are held after investments are sold, while waiting for target investment purchases. Choice *D* is incorrect because a mutual fund's share value is determined daily after the close of the market. Its shares do not trade on an exchange, but a UIT's units typically trade on an exchange.

33. C: Choice *C* is correct because FINRA Rule 2330 requires the company issuing the variable contract and the representative soliciting and recommending the variable contract to assure the suitability of the contract as a whole and the suitability of the selection of specific investment choices (subaccounts) for the

157

investor. Choice *A* is incorrect because variable contracts typically have more guarantees than mutual funds or UITs, so internal fees are higher. Choice *B* is incorrect because representatives are typically paid higher commissions for selling variable contracts than for other investment products. Choice *D* is incorrect because variable contracts typically do not allow policy loans. Withdrawing funds during the surrender period incurs surrender charges. Therefore, the owner of a variable contract should hold adequate cash equivalents in case of emergency, in order to avoid needing premature withdrawals from the variable contract.

34. B: Choice *B* is correct because the representative is expected to provide a comparison of the benefits of the replaced product and the new product. Choice *A* is incorrect because if a representative is recommending the replacement of an annuity or life insurance product that is less than thirty-six months old, justification is expected, especially if the replaced product incurs a surrender charge. Choice *C* is incorrect because the representative is expected to know enough about the investor's overall financial objectives, liquidity, and net worth to determine the suitability for recommending a variable annuity. Choice *D* is incorrect because the representative may be expected to document that the investor owns liquid assets equal to living expenses for a certain period of time, such as one year, in order to be reasonably certain that the investor will not need to make a premature withdrawal, which would incur a surrender charge.

35. B: Choice *B,* 5.6%, is correct because 80% of 7% equals 5.6%, which is greater than the guaranteed minimum of 4% and less than the maximum upside potential of 8%. Choice *A,* 4%, is incorrect because the calculated amount of 5.6% is greater than the guaranteed minimum of 4%. Choice *C,* 7%, the increase in the S&P Index, is incorrect because that is multiplied by 80% to obtain the calculated amount. Choice *D,* 8%, is incorrect because the calculated amount is 5.6%, which is less than the maximum.

36. C: Choice *C,* 4% is correct because, even though the S&P Index decreased, the guaranteed minimum is 4%. Choice *A* -5% is incorrect because, even though the S&P Index decreased, the guaranteed minimum is 4%. Choice *B* -4% is incorrect because, even though the S&P Index decreased, the guaranteed minimum is 4%. Choice *D* 5% is incorrect because when the S&P Index decreases, the contract is credit with the guaranteed minimum, which in this case is 4%.

37. C: Choice *C* is correct because a municipal fund security and a mutual fund are both valued by the sum of the market values of the securities in the fund. Choice *A* is incorrect because municipal fund securities are issued by governmental units, and mutual funds are issued by companies. Choice *B* is incorrect because municipal fund securities and mutual funds can hold equities. Choice *D* is incorrect because municipal fund securities can be LGIPs, whereas mutual funds cannot be LGIPs.

38. C: Choice *C* is correct because direct-sold investors may pay lower fees and not have professional advice provided. Choice *A* is incorrect because some states offer direct-sold 529 plans by mail or through a website only to their own residents. Choice B is incorrect because "advisor-sold" 529 plans are sold through broker-dealers. Choice D is incorrect because "advisor-sold" plans may have higher fees and offer investment advice from a professional advisor.

39. B: Choice *B* is correct because this is the primary purpose of LGIPs, so cash reserves may be available on short notice, with a favorable rate of return. Choice *A* is incorrect because LGIPs are developed by one or more government entities for use by governmental entities. Mutual funds are developed by companies for the use of the general public. Choice *C* is incorrect because LGIPs are formed according to a given state's laws. Choice *D* is incorrect because LGIPs do provide diversification.

40. D: Choice *D* is correct because another buyer may be found, even though DPPs are not traded on national exchanges. Choice *A* is incorrect because selling DPP products is not like selling a stock on a registered exchange, and DPP products are sometimes quite illiquid. Choice *B* is incorrect because the issuer of a DPP generally does not redeem the ownership units during the time frame of the undertaking, which could be lengthy. Choice *C* is incorrect because ownership units of DPPs are not traded on national exchanges, and some DPPs may not be traded on over-the-counter markets.

41. A: Choice *A* is correct because the Securities Act of 1933 was concerned with the primary market, which includes direct participation programs, which allow pass-through to owners of the tax consequences of the program. Choice *B* is incorrect because the Securities Exchange Act of 1934 is focused on the secondary market, when issued securities are bought and sold away from the issuing firm. Direct Participation Programs are not as liquid as listed stocks and bonds, which were regulated by the 1934 Act, though sometimes a buyer can be found. Choice *C* is incorrect because the Investment Company Act of 1940 focused on the regulation of investment companies, also known as mutual funds. Choice *D* is incorrect because the Investment Advisers Act of 1940 regulated persons who charge for their advice regarding buying and selling investments.

42. B: Choice *B* is correct because Subchapter S corporations and similar investments are included in the definition of direct participation program (DPP), no matter what industry is involved. Choices *A, C,* and *D* are incorrect because they are specifically excluded by the text of FINRA Rule 2310, which defines a direct participation program, as mentioned in the Securities Act of 1933.

43. B: Choice *B* is correct because the owners do not materially participate in the operation of the DPP, the DPP is not taxed, and the owner is taxed on passive income reported on the federal return. Passive losses can generally only be applied against passive income for the same year. Passive losses in excess of the passive income for the year, in some cases, may be carried over to the following year. Choice *A* is incorrect because the DPP is not taxed. Choice *C* is incorrect because the owners do not materially participate in the operation of the DPP. Choice *D* is incorrect because the DPP is not taxed and the owner receives taxable income or taxable loss, according to the financial results of the DPP.

44. A: Choice *A* is correct because subchapter corporations are taxed, and stockholders pay income tax on dividends. Choices *B, C,* and *D* are incorrect because they could all be a DPP.

45. D: Choice *D* is correct because some broker-dealers stay aware of the market for real estate limited partnerships. Choice *A* is incorrect because a limited partnership's operations are not designed to allow for daily trading. Choice *B* is incorrect because a limited partner may trade the partner's ownership interest with the general partner. While some partnership agreements may provide other partners the right of first refusal, this is not universal requirement. Choice *C* is incorrect because its market value is difficult to measure at any given time because of its illiquidity.

Understanding Trading, Customer Accounts, and Prohibited Activities

46. D: Choice *D* is correct because a security is purchased with the expectation of an increase in the price, at which time it would be sold at a profit. Choices *A, B,* and *C* are each done with the expectation of a positive return if the price decreases, because each involves the opportunity to purchase the security at a lower price than the current price, having either already having sold the borrowed security or purchased the security at a favorable price or purchased the prerogative to purchase the security at a favorable price, when compared with the anticipated future lower price.

47. C: Choice *C* is correct because a long position is the typical term for owning a security. Choices *A*, *B*, and *D* are incorrect.

48. C: Choice *C* is correct because the broker-dealer was a participant in the transaction. Choices *A*, *B*, and *D* are incorrect because they do not involve the broker-dealer as a participant in the transaction. In those cases, the broker-dealer is said to be acting in an agency capacity.

49. C: Choice *C* is correct because the broker-dealer is receiving compensation for facilitating a trade, though not involved in buying the security from, nor selling the security to, the customer. Choices *A*, *B*, and *D* are incorrect because they do not involve the broker-dealer receiving compensation for assisting in the completion of a trade.

50. B: Choice *B* is correct because markup/markdown is the difference between the price at which the broker-dealer buys a security and the price at which the broker-dealer sells the security, with one transaction being with a customer. Choice *A* is incorrect as that would involve no markup. Choice *C* is incorrect because compensation when acting in an agency capacity is commission. Choice *D* is incorrect, as compensation as a Registered Investment Adviser (RIA) may involve markup, commission, or one of various adviser fees.

51. A: Choice *A* is correct because the customer's occupation is not included in Rule 2121 as a relevant factor in determining compensation received from the customer. Choices *B*, *C*, and *D* are incorrect because they are included in Rule 2121 as relevant factors in determining compensation.

52. C: Choice *C* is correct because the purchase of the security at one price and selling to the customer at a different price is known as a net transaction. Choices *A*, *B*, and *D* are incorrect because those rules do not deal with compensation for net transactions with customers.

53. C: Choice *C* is correct because 5 percent is suggested as a guideline, allowing various listed factors to be taken into account. Choices *A*, *B*, and *D* are incorrect.

54. B: Choice *B* is correct because both refer to the conservative position of buying a security before selling it. A long or covered position refers to owning the security. Choices *A* and *C* are incorrect because "open" is not a commonly-used term for a position relative to a security. Choice *D* is incorrect because long indicates owning a security, whereas naked (or short) refers to selling a borrowed security one does not own. This is an aggressive strategy, with an unknown maximum possible loss. The cost to buy the security to replace the one that was borrowed could be much more than the proceeds of the short sale.

55. B: Choice *B* is correct because both rules have to do with published orders. Choice *A* is incorrect because this is covered in FINRA 6438 – Displaying Priced Quotations in Multiple Quotation Mediums. Choice *C* is incorrect because this is covered in FINRA 5220 – Offers at Stated Prices. Choice *D* is incorrect because this is covered in FINRA 5290 – Order Entry and Execution Practices.

56. B: Choice *B* is correct, as this is part of the rules for servicing a penny-stock customer. Choices *A*, *C*, and *D* are incorrect.

57. D: Choice *D* is correct because broker-dealers and municipal securities dealers have the obligation to arrange for the trade to be processed in the best way possible. Choice *A* is incorrect because this is covered in the rule MSRB G-14 – Reports of Sales or Purchases. Choice *B* and C are incorrect because they relate to mutual funds trading securities with portfolio affiliates or a category of affiliated persons.

58. D: Choice *D* is correct because these components are all considered in the calculation of the investment return. Choices *A* and *B* are incorrect as they are only some of the components of investment return. Choice *C* is incorrect as it is suggesting how to compare the return with some other benchmark.

59. D: Choice *D* is correct, as it includes the actual income tax, which may not be calculated until the investment is sold and all revenues and costs are known. Choices *A* and *B* are incorrect, as these have only some of the factors considered in the calculation. Choice *C* is incorrect, as it is using a contingent income tax calculation, which may be the best tax calculation that is reasonably available prior to all transactions being complete.

60. D: Choice *D* is correct because the exchange's rules determine when the stock begins to trade without a right to the dividend. Choices *A*, *B*, and *C* are incorrect because these dates determined by the board of directors of the company that issued the stock.

61. C: Choice *C* is correct because the nominal yield or coupon rate is stated as a percentage of the face amount when the bonds are issued. Choices *A*, *B*, and *D* compare the nominal yield with the price paid, averaged over the period of time to maturity or time to call, or merely the price paid.

62. D: Choice *D* is correct because taxable capital gains are the sales proceeds minus the cost basis. Choice *A* is incorrect because basis points report the interest rate, with one hundred basis points representing one percent. Choices *B* and C are incorrect because these are prices offered by a market maker or a broker-dealer to potential buyers and sellers.

63. C: Choice *C* is correct because sales proceeds are not received at the time of purchase, for which cost basis is calculated. Choices *A*, *B*, and *D* are incorrect because they are costs included in the purchase.

64. A: Choice *A* is correct because cost basis is used to determine taxable income, whose calculation is determined by the Internal Revenue Code. Choices *B*, *C*, and *D* are not used to determine taxable income.

65. A: Choice *A* is correct because changing the name of the issuing firm would have no financial effect. Choices *B*, *C*, and *D* are incorrect because each may add to the complexity of the cost basis calculation.

66. A: Choice *A* is correct because benchmarks and indices are commonly used to measure effectiveness of an investment manager. Choices *B*, *C*, and *D* are incorrect because they are each true.

67. A: Choice *A* is correct because this measures the time necessary to complete an agreed transaction. Trade settlement schedules are specified by some rules. Choices *B*, *C*, and *D* are incorrect.

68. A: Choice *A* is correct because each issuing firm keeps records of owners of its securities, so each change in ownership must be reflected in those records. Choices *B* and *C* are incorrect because publication is not used to change ownership of a security. Choice *D* is incorrect because this only occurs after the ownership change has been made on the books of the issuing firm.

Overview of the Regulatory Framework

69. B: Choice *B* is correct because this section lists, in addition to registration requirements, the members' and associated persons' actions in the industry and how they are expected to conduct themselves. Choice *A* is incorrect because this explains the meaning of words and phrases that are used through the By-Laws. Choice *C* is incorrect because this describes the application for membership and agreements for members to make. Choice *D* is incorrect because this explains which persons can perform securities or investment banking business.

70. C: Choice *C* is correct because this section describes the application for membership and the members' agreement to abide by all these sets of codes. Choice *A* is incorrect because this explains the meaning of words and phrases that are used through the By-Laws. Choice *B* is incorrect because this section lists, in addition to registration requirements, the members' and associated persons' actions in the industry and how they are expected to conduct themselves. Choice *D* is incorrect because this explains which persons can perform securities or investment banking business.

71. A: Choice *A* is correct because receiving a written complaint regarding a trade of municipal securities necessitates the provision of a copy of the investor brochure to the customer. Choice *B* is incorrect because the annual requirement is that the customer must be provided with a statement in writing that the investor brochure is available on the MSRB website. Choices *C* and *D* are incorrect because the requirement is to state that the firm is registered with the MSRB and the SEC.

72. B: Choice *B* is correct because a non-registered person may inquire as to a person's interest in meeting with a registered person from the firm to review investments. Choices *A* and *C* are incorrect because only a registered person is allowed to discuss these topics with a member of the public. Choice *D* is incorrect because a person who has passed a FINRA registration exam would be a registered person.

73. D: Choice *D* is correct because the information is the property of the issuer, and the member firm should only use it for the stated service the member is providing, unless the issuer directs otherwise. Choices *A*, *B*, and *C* are incorrect because FINRA Rule 2060 – Use of Information Obtained in Fiduciary Capacity does not prohibit a firm assisting an issuing corporation from fulfilling normal duties assigned by the issuer, which could include sending marketing information about the issuer's public offer, or other business correspondence, to the customers, and correcting customer records.

74. A: Choice *A* is correct because a person signing a U4 must be informed that, by signing the U4, the person is giving up certain rights to take disputes to court. Choices *B*, *C*, and *D* are incorrect because FINRA Rule 2263 – Arbitration Disclosure to Associated Persons Signing or Acknowledging Form U4 requires that the person signing a U4 filing must be informed that arbitration will be the only method used for resolving any disputes that might, in other circumstances, be settled in a court.

75. C: Choice *C* is correct because the rule requires written authorization to lend a customer's securities. Choices *A*, *B*, and *D* are incorrect because FINRA Rule 4330 – Customer Protection – Permissible Use of Customers' Securities is focused on obtaining written permission to lend the customer's securities, and does not address changing the format of the customer's account records, publishing the customer's assets, or providing the customer's information to government agencies.

Practice Test #3

Knowledge of Capital Markets

1. Where are the investments of an introducing broker's customers kept?
   a. At the SEC.
   b. At the introducing broker's headquarters office.
   c. At the clearing broker's business.
   d. At the introducing broker's bank.

2. Which of the following in NOT true regarding the definition of investment advisers?
   a. The Congress passed the act defining them as the result of a concern from the SEC about persons advising investors about what to buy and sell.
   b. They are defined in the Securities Exchange Act of 1934.
   c. An investment adviser is a person who provides guidance, receives a fee for providing guidance, and receives a significant proportion of the adviser's income from providing guidance to investors.
   d. If a person provides any guidance to an individual about buying or selling investments as only a small part of their work, that person is not defined as an investment adviser.

3. MSRB Rule G-32 – Disclosures in Connection with Primary Offerings requires reporting if the municipality issuing bonds has chosen to give priority to which of the following investors?
   a. Ordinary
   b. Retail
   c. Accredited
   d. Institutional

4. Which of the following statements is true regarding CUSIP numbers issued by the Committee on Uniform Securities Identification Procedures?
   a. They are used only on United States stocks and government and municipal bonds.
   b. They are used only on United States and Canadian registered stocks.
   c. They are used on all United States government and municipal bonds.
   d. They are used on all United States and Canadian registered stocks, and on United States government and municipal bonds

5. Which of the following statements is true regarding a mini-maxi underwriting agreement?
   a. This form of best efforts underwriting has a target sales volume for the agreement to be effective, after which additional sales may be made, up to a limit.
   b. This is an underwriting agreement in which the lead underwriter will receive no compensation unless the maximum available units are sold.
   c. This is an underwriting agreement in which the lead underwriter will receive no compensation unless a minimum number of available units is sold.
   d. This is an underwriting agreement in which the lead underwriter buys all securities issued.

163

6. Which of the following types of underwriting agreements requires the lead underwriter to take responsibility for a certain number of securities in the issue?
   a. Mini-maxi
   b. All or none
   c. Part or none
   d. Firm commitment

7. Which of the following stand ready to continuously buy at a "bid" price or sell at a "sell" price?
   a. Market maker
   b. Dealer
   c. Trader
   d. Custodian

8. Which of the following statements is true regarding a custodian for a trust?
   a. A custodian may be a natural person.
   b. The trustee is chosen by the custodian.
   c. The custodian maintains possession of the investments in the trust.
   d. The custodian has a fiduciary responsibility to make choices for the benefit of the beneficiary.

9. Which of the following statements is true regarding a Uniform Gift to Minors Act (UGMA) account?
   a. An attorney is required.
   b. Only a person other than a parent may give investments to the beneficiary.
   c. Only a parent may give investments to the beneficiary.
   d. The trustee may be a natural person or a business or an organization.

10. Which of the following statements is true regarding a transfer agent?
    a. Guidance regarding a transaction must be given orally and in written form.
    b. Guidance regarding a transaction must be in written form.
    c. Information is maintained regarding all the investments held by officers of the firm.
    d. FINRA sets rules regarding how and when the records are changed.

11. Which of the following statements is true regarding a depository?
    a. It is a firm that confirms securities transactions.
    b. It is a natural person that settles securities transactions.
    c. It is a firm that keeps electronic records of who owns investments.
    d. It is a stock exchange.

12. Which of the following is necessary in a registration statement?
    a. Description of the products and services to be provided by the issuing firm
    b. Names of members of the families of the founding officers
    c. Names and geographic location of subcontractors to be used in the work of the firm
    d. Names of competitors

Understanding Products and Their Risks

13. Which of the following has fiduciary responsibility in a direct participation program that is a real estate limited partnership?
    a. Board of Directors
    b. Limited partners having more than ten percent of ownership
    c. All limited partners
    d. General partner

14. Which of the following is correct regarding the general partner in a direct participation program that is a real estate limited partnership?
    a. The GP may have no ownership interest.
    b. The GP may have no ownership interest until the entity has a profitable return for two consecutive years.
    c. The GP must invest at least one percent of the entity's capital.
    d. The GP must invest at least ten percent of the entity's capital.

15. What is the general partner's decision-making role in a limited partnership?
    a. The GP decides how much capital each limited partner will contribute.
    b. The GP submits the annual budget to a board of directors for approval.
    c. The GP operates the program with a fiduciary relationship to limited partners.
    d. The GP makes all decisions regarding the partnership.

16. Which of the following is correct regarding assets and liabilities of a direct participation program that is a real estate limited partnership?
    a. The limited partnership owns all assets.
    b. The general partner would not guarantee a loan.
    c. The general partner would not receive compensation for services, other than profit distributions, as the limited partners receive.
    d. Limited partners may guarantee a loan.

17. Which of the following is correct regarding a limited partner in a direct participation program that is a real estate limited partnership?
    a. The limited partnership may have no limited partner.
    b. A limited partner generally participates in management decisions.
    c. A limited partner may have its ownership interest reduced if it fails to meet a capital call.
    d. An action of a limited partner may result in it taking on up to ten percent additional risk.

18. Which of the following is correct regarding a Section 1031 Tenant in Common (TIC) transaction?
    a. One intention is to delay payment of realized capital gains tax.
    b. Section 1031 requires the identification of candidate replacement properties within thirty days of the sale.
    c. Section 1031 requires the purchase of the replacement property within one year of the sale.
    d. Section 1031 exchanges are not valuable, when compared with the activity involved in complying.

19. Which of the following is correct regarding a Section 1031 Tenant in Common (TIC) mortgage?
    a. It will be a full-recourse mortgage for all participants who sign.
    b. Only participants with ten percent or more participation will sign.
    c. All participants sign the mortgage.
    d. The mortgage is a standard form, with no deviation for individual circumstances.

20. Which of the following is true of real estate limited partnerships and Tenant in Common transactions?
    a. Both file a Certificate of Limited Partnership with the state.
    b. Both allow ownership interest transfer with permission of the general partner.
    c. Both involve no personal liability.
    d. Both provide the pass-through tax advantage.

21. Which of the following is true of real estate direct participation programs?
    a. In a real estate limited partnership, each limited partner must contribute at least one percent of the total capital.
    b. In both a limited partnership and a Tenant in Common arrangement, all participants provide a guarantee on every loan.
    c. For limited partnerships, the IRS code limits the pass-through tax effects to fifty percent of the total financial results.
    d. For a TIC, the transaction must be completed in no more than 180 days.

22. Which of the following statements is true regarding Real Estate Investment Trust (REITs)?
    a. REITs are covered by the FINRA Rule 2310 definition of Direct Participation Programs.
    b. The Securities Act of 1933 defines REITs.
    c. The Investment Company Act of 1940 defines REITs.
    d. Under the Internal Revenue Code, REITs' earnings are taxed twice.

23. Which of the following type(s) of REITs resemble banks in how they earn a profit?
    a. Hybrid REITs
    b. Equity REITs
    c. Mortgage REITs
    d. Hybrid and Equity REITs

24. Which of the following statements is true regarding the Real Estate Investment Association?
    a. It was formed in 1987, after the 1986 tax act had reduced real estate opportunities.
    b. It was formed in 2008, after the 2007 real estate bubble burst.
    c. It was formed in 2018, as the economy was beginning to expand.
    d. It was formed in 2021, after the COVID pandemic reduced real estate activity.

25. Which of the following statements is true regarding the Institute for Portfolio Alternatives (IPA)?
    a. The IPA is devoted to the real estate industry.
    b. The IPA promotes Portfolio Diversifying Investments (PDI).
    c. The IPA promotes maintaining a stable business environment with limited change in regulation.
    d. The IPA works in the private sector, without significant communication outside its membership.

26. What is an essential characteristic of hedge funds?
    a. All hedge funds are very similar.
    b. Hedge funds generally avoid borrowing to purchase assets.
    c. Hedge fund is another name for a mutual fund.
    d. Hedge funds generally have a goal of "absolute return."

27. Which of the following statements is true regarding hedge funds' expenses?
    a. Hedge fund expense ratios are identical to that of the average mutual fund.
    b. Hedge funds spend proportionately less to research investment opportunities than the average mutual fund.
    c. Hedge funds may incur more cost by purchasing derivatives that a typical mutual fund manager does not purchase.
    d. Hedge funds pay the investment managers less compensation than a typical mutual fund does.

28. Which of the following statements is true regarding "offshore" and "onshore" hedge funds?
    a. A hedge fund may not set up both an "offshore" and an "onshore" fund.
    b. An "offshore" fund is generally set up as a Limited Liability Corporation (LLCs) or a limited partnership.
    c. An "onshore" fund is usually established as a corporation with Articles of Incorporation in the United States.
    d. U.S. investors in hedge funds pay U.S. taxes on earnings from hedge funds.

29. Which investment generally requires the investor to sign a Subscription Agreement?
    a. Mutual fund
    b. Tenant in Common (TIC) transaction
    c. Hedge fund
    d. Unit Investment Trust (UIT)

30. How does a subscription agreement help an investor who is considering purchases shares in a hedge fund?
    a. It explains why the investment is registered with the SEC.
    b. It explains why the investment is not registered with the Department of the Treasury.
    c. It evaluates the risk of the investment.
    d. It explains why an investor may only purchase no more than $25,000 worth of ownership.

31. Which of the following statements is true regarding mutual funds but not of hedge funds?
    a. The fund manager must notify the investors prior to changing the investment strategy.
    b. The fund owes a fiduciary responsibility to the investors.
    c. The fund may have dozens of investors.
    d. The fund's risks and operations are described in a document.

32. Which of the following is typically NOT included in an "Offering Document"?
    a. Plan for operations
    b. Minimum guaranteed return on investment over a three-year period
    c. Fund manager's approach to investing
    d. Fees

33. Which of the following statements is true regarding types of investors investing in a hedge fund?
    a. A hedge fund that plans to charge performance-based fees may have "qualified" investors.
    b. An "accredited" investor must have a higher net worth than a "qualified" investor.
    c. An accredited investor is an individual with annual income greater than $200,000 or a couple with annual income greater than $400,000.
    d. A "qualified" investor is also a "super-accredited" investor.

34. Which of the following is most similar to a typical mutual fund?
    a. Hedge fund
    b. Exchange-traded Note (ETN)
    c. Exchange-traded Fund (ETF)
    d. Limited partnership

35. Which of the following does Exchange-Traded Funds (ETFs) provide that mutual funds do not?
    a. Diversification
    b. Liquidity during the trading day
    c. Professional Management
    d. Conventional investment strategies

36. Which of the following are Registered Investment Advisers (RIAs)?
    a. Mutual funds
    b. Hedge funds
    c. Tenant in Common (TIC) transactions
    d. REITs

37. ETFs operate with a pricing exemption from which of the following acts?
    a. Securities Act of 1933
    b. Securities Exchange Act of 1934
    c. Investment Company Act of 1940
    d. Commodity Futures Modernization Act of 2000

38. Which of the following assists the investor in obtaining a return that is opposite of that of a target index?
    a. Inverse hedge fund
    b. Inverse mutual fund
    c. Inverse Real Estate Investment Trust (REIT)
    d. Inverse Exchange-Traded Fund (ETF)

39. Which of the following provides a return that uses borrowing to potentially improve returns above that of the target index?
    a. Mutual fund
    b. Inverse ETF
    c. ETF
    d. Leveraged ETF

40. The S&P 500 is an example of which of the following?
    a. Market ETF
    b. Inverse ETF
    c. Leveraged ETF
    d. Monolithic ETF

41. Which of the following has the most members?
    a. Market ETF
    b. Inverse ETF
    c. Leveraged ETF
    d. Inverse leveraged ETF

42. Which of the following indexes tracks the small company segment of the U.S. market?
    a. S&P 500
    b. Russell 2000
    c. Dow Jones Industrial Average (DJIA)
    d. NASDAQ

43. Which of the following indexes tracks the return of 98 percent of publicly-traded U.S. stocks?
    a. Dow Jones Industrial Average (DJIA)
    b. S&P 500
    c. Russell 3000
    d. NASDAQ 100

44. Which of the following market indexes is a component of the Composite Index of Leading Indicators, also known as the Leading Economic Index (LEI)?
    a. Dow Jones Industrial Average (DJIA)
    b. S&P 500
    c. Russell 3000
    d. NASDAQ 100

45. Which of the following is the most well-known, oldest, and largest ETF?
    a. SPDR Dow Jones Industrial Average ETF (DIA)
    b. Invesco QQQ Trust (QQQ)
    c. iShares Russell 2000 ETF (IWM)
    d. SPDR® S&P 500® ETF Trust" (SPY)

Understanding Trading, Customer Accounts, and Prohibited Activities

46. On which date does ownership change when a security is sold?
    a. Settlement date
    b. Declaration date
    c. Record date
    d. Ex-dividend date

47. Which of the following resulted in corporate stock and corporate bonds settling more quickly?
    a. SEC rule in 2017 called "T+2"
    b. SEC Regulation T
    c. Consumer Credit Protection Act of 1968 (CCPA)
    d. Sarbanes-Oxley (SOX) Act of 2002

48. Which of the following is NOT true regarding settlement?
    a. Settlement may occur one trade day prior to the trade date (T-1).
    b. If the buyer or seller prefers to settle during other than regular-way, this special settlement is agreed to before the trade takes place.
    c. If the buyer and seller agree a cash trade, it may settle on the trade date (T).
    d. If the seller is not able to provide ownership by the time expected, the seller may request additional time to settle.

49. Which of the following is the oldest method of ownership settlement?
    a. Book entry settlement
    b. Stock certificate delivery settlement
    c. Electronic settlement
    d. Paperless settlement

50. Which of the following is NOT a corporate action?
    a. Tender offer
    b. Stock reverse split
    c. Stock buyback
    d. Change in market price of its securities

51. Which of the following is typically approved by a board of directors when the trading price is so high that it inhibits trading?
    a. Rights offer
    b. Reverse stock split
    c. Tender offer
    d. Stock split

52. Which of the following results in an increase in treasury stock?
    a. Merger
    b. Buyback
    c. Tender offer
    d. Rights offer

53. Which of the following does NOT occur when a reverse stock split is approved by the board of directors?
    a. The new shares may have twice the par value of the old shares.
    b. The firm buys shares from shareholders to reduce the quantity of shares outstanding.
    c. One new share is exchanged for two old shares.
    d. The new shares will begin trading at twice the price of the old shares.

54. Which of the following is a reason for the board of directors to approve a rights offer?
   a. To provide another security's shares in exchange for the desired shares
   b. To publicly announce an offer to purchase shares for a certain price if a minimum quantity of shares are provided in response to the offer
   c. To replace old shares with new shares with twice the par value
   d. To raise additional capital by offering current shareholders the opportunity to purchase the number of shares to maintain proportional ownership

55. Which of the following prevents persons involved with a securities offering from artificially influencing the price?
   a. IRS Code
   b. Regulation M
   c. Investment Company Act of 1940
   d. FINRA Rules

56. Which of the following is true regarding a reverse stock split?
   a. The market price for a share of stock is reduced.
   b. The cost basis for a share of stock is adjusted.
   c. The quantity of treasury stock is increased.
   d. This is required in the event of a merger.

57. How is notice of a corporate action given?
   a. For over-the-counter shares, the SEC provides notices.
   b. For over-the-counter shares, the NYSE provides notices.
   c. For exchange-traded shares, the exchange provides notices.
   d. For exchange-traded shares, FINRA communicates the actions.

58. Which of the following statements is true regarding proxies?
   a. FINRA Rule 2251 governs proxies for owners of stocks, corporate bonds, and municipal bonds.
   b. A FINRA member must provide proxy materials to the beneficial owner of stock whether or not the issuer provides enough copies of proxy materials.
   c. A FINRA member must provide proxy materials to the beneficial owner of stock whether or not the issuer requests this service.
   d. A shareholder may authorize another party to cast the votes which the shareholder is entitled to cast.

59. 1934 Act Section 14 – Proxies provides guidance to which of the following?
   a. FINRA members
   b. Boards of directors
   c. Over-the-counter market makers
   d. Qualified Investors

60. Which of the following directs FINRA member firms to keep record of the supervisor approving establishment of the account?
   a. 1934 Act 15c2-12 – Municipal Securities Disclosure
   b. FINRA 2231 – Customer Account Statements
   c. FINRA 4512 – Customer Account Information
   d. FINRA 4514 – Authorization Records for Negotiable Instruments Drawn

61. Under FINRA 4512, what information must a member firm maintain for a customer who is a natural person who is only purchasing mutual funds of the customer's choice?
    a. Social Security number or tax identification
    b. Occupation and employer's name and address
    c. Whether the customer is a representative for another member firm
    d. An alternative contact

62. What is the minimum frequency for customer account statements named in FINRA 2231?
    a. Within five business days after requested by the customer
    b. Every calendar year
    c. Every calendar quarter
    d. Every calendar month

63. Which of the following directs that municipal securities dealers and broker-dealers who assist a municipality to offer municipal securities to the general public do their reasonable best to make certain the municipality submits to the MSRB expected information that would aid a potential investor in making a decision whether to buy the offered security?
    a. 1934 Act 15c2-12 – Municipal Securities Disclosure
    b. FINRA 2231 – Customer Account Statements
    c. MSRB G-47 – Time of Trade Disclosure
    d. MSRB G-13 – Quotations

64. Which of the following statements is true regarding FINRA 4514 – Authorization Records for Negotiable Instruments Drawn from a Customer's Account?
    a. A customer must give oral or written permission for a representative to withdraw money from the customer's account.
    b. A customer must give written permission for a representative to withdraw money or money-like assets from the customer's account.
    c. A customer must give permission before a representative removes bearer bonds from the member firm's premises.
    d. A customer must give oral or written permission for the representative to keep blank checks signed by the customer in the representative's file.

65. Which of the following statements is true regarding a cash account?
    a. Only cash may be held in the account.
    b. All transactions must be paid for in full.
    c. Purchases may be made on margin, but no short selling is allowed
    d. Short selling is allowed, but the cash must not be used to purchase any other investments.

66. Which of the following statements is true regarding the Federal Reserve Board Regulation T?
    a. Short sales must be made in a cash account.
    b. Margin purchases must be made in a cash account.
    c. Payments are made promptly, not later than T+2, for securities purchased from a margin account.
    d. Repayment of the borrowed part of a margin purchase from a cash account must be made promptly, not later than T+1.

67. What portion of the cost of a security purchased on margin must be paid by the customer?
   a.   At least 45 percent
   b.   At least 25 percent (or the amount over $1,000)
   c.   At least 30 percent
   d.   At least 50 percent (or the amount over $500)

68. For which of the following are members of a national exchange allowed to trade without a general prohibition?
   a.   The member's own account
   b.   A registered representative's account
   c.   An account for which a registered representative may act with discretion
   d.   Market makers

Overview of the Regulatory Framework

69. Which of the following events regarding a member firm results in the firm being subject to discontinuance of that membership, according to FINRA By-laws, Article III, Section 3 and legislation and regulation referenced in that section?
   a.   The member is disciplined by a local school board.
   b.   The member is cited by a police officer for a misdemeanor.
   c.   The member is disciplined by a state securities commission.
   d.   The member is fined by the Internal Revenue Service for a non-timely filing of a federal income tax return.

70. Which of the following is an obligation of each member firm under FINRA Rule 3110(e) – Responsibility of Member to Investigate Applicants for Registration?
   a.   Document the applicant's identity
   b.   Review the applicant's driver's license
   c.   Review the applicant's passport
   d.   Document contacting the applicant's employers for the last twenty years

71. Which of the following is NOT required to have each partner, director, officer, and employee fingerprinted under SEC Rule 17f-2 – Fingerprinting of Securities Industry Personnel, unless an exemption applies?
   a.   Every bank
   b.   Every broker
   c.   Every registered transfer agent
   d.   Every registered clearing agency

72. Which of the following may prevent a firm from hiring an individual, according to Securities Exchange Act of 1934 Section 3(a)(39) – Definitions and Application of Title (Statutory Disqualification)?
   a.   Disciplinary action by a Human Resources Department in a previous employment
   b.   Conviction of a felony within ten years prior to an application for membership or participation
   c.   Bankruptcy other than a business bankruptcy within seven years prior to an application for membership or participation
   d.   More than one divorce in the five years prior to an application for membership or participation

73. Which of the following is NOT included in the definition of Associated Person under FINRA 1011 Definitions (b) "Associated Person"?
    a. Any person who is only in senior management
    b. Any person who is a sole proprietor
    c. Any person who is in investment banking controlled indirectly by the applicant
    d. Any person who does only clerical work

74. Which of the following is NOT mentioned in FINRA Rule 8310 Sanctions for Violation of the Rules?
    a. FINRA rules
    b. Direction based upon the FINRA rules
    c. Rules of the Municipal Securities Rulemaking Board
    d. Internal Revenue Code

75. Which of the following may FINRA impose as a penalty named in Rule 8310 Sanctions for Violation of the Rules?
    a. Prison sentence in a state facility
    b. Prison sentence in a federal facility
    c. Loss of the right to vote in a national election
    d. Censure

Answer Explanations #3

Knowledge of Capital Markets

1. C: Choice C is correct because an introducing broker may take an order for a clearing broker to complete. Funds and investments of an introducing broker's customer are kept at the clearing broker's business. Choice *A* is incorrect the SEC provides oversight to the securities markets and their SROs, but does not act as a participant in the market. Choices *B* is incorrect because the introducing broker does not have adequate capital to qualify to hold its customers' investments. Choice D is incorrect because an introducing broker arranges for its customers' investments to be held at a clearing broker's business.

2. B: Choice *B* is correct because investment advisers are not defined in the Securities Exchange Act of 1934, which regulates the secondary market. The 1934 Act built on the Securities Act of 1933, which regulates the primary market. After the stock market crash of 1929, and even after the Securities Act of 1933 and the Securities Exchange Act of 1934 provided some responses to the market crash, the SEC was concerned about persons providing advice to those who purchase or sell securities.

So, Congress passed the Investment Advisers Act of 1940 to define and regulate investment advisers. Choice A is incorrect because Congress did pass the Investment Advisers Act of 1940 in response to a concern from the SEC about the behavior of persons providing guidance to investors about buying and selling securities. Choice *C* is incorrect because an investment adviser is a person who does all three of the following: provides specific kinds of guidance to investors, receives a fee for providing guidance, and receives a significant proportion of the adviser's income from providing guidance. Choice *D* is incorrect because the definition may not apply to a person who provides investment guidance as a very small part of their work.

3. B: Choice *B* is correct because MSRB Rule G-32 requires reporting if retail investors are given priority by the municipality issuing the bonds. Choice *A* is incorrect because ordinary is not a regulatory category of investors. Choices *C* and *D* are incorrect because the rule does not require reporting if the municipality gives priority to accredited or institutional investors.

4. D: Choice *D* is correct because CUSIP numbers are used on all United States and Canadian registered stocks, and on United States government and municipal bonds. Choices *A*, *B*, and *C* are incorrect because these choices each list only some of the categories of investments used with CUSIP numbers.

5. A: Choice *A* is correct because a mini-maxi underwriting agreement requires the lead underwriter to sell a determined quantity of securities, or else the agreement will not effective. However, if that quantity is sold, the lead underwriter may sell additional units or shares up to the limit available. Choice *B* is incorrect because it describes an all or none agreement. Choice *C* is incorrect because it describes a part or none agreement. Choice *D* is incorrect because it describes a firm commitment agreement.

6. D: Choice D is correct because in a firm commitment undertaking, the lead underwriter takes responsibility for all securities in the issue, by buying all shares in the issue, and then re-sells them at a profit to earn compensation. Choices *A*, *B*, and *C* are incorrect because they each specify a sales target, but, while the targets provide incentive, the lead underwriter is not obligated to reach a target.

7. A: Choice *A* is correct because a market maker provides a ready market for a security by continuously offering to "make a market" in the security by offering to purchase the security at a "bid" price or sell at a "sell" price. The difference in the two prices provide compensation to the market maker. Choice *B* is incorrect because dealers purchase investments for their own purposes. Choice *C* is incorrect because traders are dealers who buy and sell investments for their own purposes, intending to make short-term profits. Choice *D* is incorrect because a custodian maintains possession of assets for the benefit of the beneficiary named in the document that describes the agreement.

8. C: Choice *C* is correct because the custodian is named in the document that establishes the trust, and holds the items owned by the trust. Choice *A* is incorrect because a custodian is a company, such as a financial institution. Choice *B* is incorrect because the trustee chooses the custodian. Choice *D* is incorrect, unless the trustee is the custodian, because the trustee has the fiduciary responsibility.

9. D: Choice *D* is correct because the UGMA trustee can be one of a wide range of possible individuals or organizations. Choice *A* is incorrect because, while an attorney may be involved, a UGMA account at a bank for investment firm may be opened with the trust named in the registration, and the beneficiary stated as the minor, with no attorney involved. Choice *B* is incorrect because a parent may gift items to the minor child. Choice *C* is incorrect because the donor need not be a parent of the beneficiary.

10. B: Choice *B* is correct because instructions must be provided in written form. Choice *A* is incorrect because instructions need not be provided orally. Choice *C* is incorrect because only the records of ownership of securities issued by the firm are maintained by the transfer agent. Choice *D* is incorrect because the SEC determines standards of processing, including amount of time allowed for recording changes of ownership.

11. C: Choice *C* is correct because a depository holds information that demonstrates investment ownership. Choice *A* is incorrect because a clearing corporation confirms investment transactions. Choice *B* is incorrect because a clearing firm settles purchases and sales of investments. Choice *D* is incorrect because a stock exchange is a venue where buy orders are matched with sales orders. The results of those matches are communicated to a depository, who processes the change in ownership.

12. A: Choice *A* is correct because the S-1 registration statement of a public offering must include a prospectus and statement of additional information. The prospectus provides information necessary for a prospective investor to make a prudent decision regarding the risk involved in the security. This includes the persons who manage the company, how the business will operate, its assets, liabilities, revenue and expenses, and the items or services provided. The additional information may include other relevant information, such as whether the company has sold securities that are not registered. Choices *B, C,* and *D* are incorrect, as these are not considered part of the essential items of information that a potential investor would need to know to make a prudent decision.

Understanding Products and Their Risks

13. D: Choice *D* is correct because the general partner receives the invested funds from limited partners, manages operations, and keeps financial records. Choice *A* is incorrect because a direct participation program that is a real estate limited partnership has no board of directors. Choices *B* and *C* are incorrect because no limited partner has any other participant's invested funds and therefore no fiduciary responsibility.

14. C: Choice *C* is correct because the general partner must contribute at least one percent of the DPP's capital. Choices *A, B,* and *D* are incorrect.

15. C: Choice *C is* correct because the general partner operates the program, with the responsibility to do so to benefit the limited partners. Choice A is incorrect because each limited partner decides how much to

176

invest, perhaps subject to a minimum and/or a maximum. If provided in the partnership agreement, the general partner may request additional capital from the limited partners, with possibly adverse effects, if a limited partner is not able to fulfill the request or chooses not to do so. Choice *B* is incorrect because a limited partnership has no board of directors. Choice *D* is incorrect because some major decisions may be made by limited partners holding a majority ownership interest.

16. A: Choice *A* is correct because all assets are held in the name of the limited partnership. Choice *B* is incorrect because the general partner could guarantee a loan. Choice *C* is incorrect because the general partner does receive compensation for managing the limited partnership, in addition to receiving a proportionate part of distributed profits. Choice *D* is incorrect because limited partners would not guarantee a loan.

17. C: Choice *C* is correct because a limited partner's failure to provide funds in response to a capital call as provided in the capital call agreement could result in the loss of reduction in that partner's ownership stake. Choice *A* is incorrect because a limited partnership must have at least one limited partner. Choices *B* and D are incorrect because a limited partner does not participate in management decisions. Otherwise, its status could change to general partner, resulting in its assuming unlimited risk.

18. A: Choice *A* is correct because Section 1031 of the Internal Revenue Code allows funds from a real estate sale to be used to purchase another property and not pay capital gains tax on the realized gain in that tax year. Choice *B* is incorrect because Section 1031 allows forty-five days to find possible purchases. Choice *C* is incorrect because Section 1031 allows the purchase to be completed by the earliest of the following: one hundred eighty days from the date of sale, or the last income tax filing date for that year. Choice *D* is incorrect because a Section 1031 exchange can be very profitable by allowing the funds that would otherwise be paid as tax on a large realized capital gain, to be re-invested in another real estate property.

19. C: Choice *C* is correct because all participants are borrowers and therefore the financial institution will have them all sign the mortgage. Choice *A* is incorrect because the participants would generally have risk limited to their investment in the transaction with no risk to their personal assets. Choice *B* is incorrect because all TIC participants sign the mortgage. Choice *D* is incorrect because no standard mortgage form is used, as a situation may have extenuating circumstances, whereby the lender may require recourse for such things as criminal activities by the borrowers.

20. D: Choice *D* is correct because both allow real estate owners to coordinate with other similar owners to qualify for the "pass-through" tax treatment of financial results. Both are considered securities. Choice *A* is incorrect because limited partnerships file a Certificate of Limited Partnership with the state. In contrast, a Tenant in Common (TIC) relationship is of limited duration, and no such filing is made, even though for tax reasons, it may be a limited liability company or partnership. A TIC participant receives a deed as documentation of possession. Choice *B* is incorrect because only the limited partnership allows transfer of ownership with permission of the general partner. In a TIC transaction, the lender reviews each possible mortgage participant for approval. Choice *C* is incorrect because TIC participants are each required to provide needed funds, according to their percentage of participation. Limited partners may have no personal risk unless they participate in management decisions.

21. D: Choice *D* is correct because the IRS code requires that the TIC transaction be completed by the earlier of the following 180 days after the initial sale, or by the last date for filing an income tax return for the year in which the transaction occurred. Choice *A* is incorrect because a limited partner's ownership is not required to be a certain amount. However, the general partner must provide at least one percent of the capital. Choice *B* is incorrect because in a limited partnership, only the general partner assumes obligation for a loan. In a TIC transaction, each participant signs every mortgage. Each TIC transaction is unique, and in some cases a mortgage company could require a personal obligation in case specific types of actions are taken, such as illegal behavior by the participants. Choice *C* is incorrect because the IRS code allows the entire financial results to flow through to the participants.

22. B: Choice *B* is true because the Securities Act of 1933 determines that REITs are securities, and so a prospectus must be provided to any person who buys ownership when first issued in the primary market. Choice A is incorrect because the following are specifically excluded from FINRA Rule 2310: REITs, Section 401 plans, Section 403(a) plans, Section 403(b) plans, and Section 408 IRA plans. Choice C is incorrect because REITs were not covered in the 1940 act that regulates mutual funds. Choice D is incorrect because a primary advantage of REITs is that, if certain Internal Revenue Code conditions are met, the tax efficiency of REITs may be considered superior to mutual funds, whose ordinary dividends and interest payments and capital gains are taxed at the individual level, as well as at the corporate level.

23. C: Choice *C* is correct because a mortgage REITs' profits come from the difference between the mortgage loans made to real estate owners and the amounts borrowed from investors. Generally, the mortgages purchased are guaranteed by a federal agency or the federal government itself. Banks earn a profit on the difference between the interest paid on deposits and the rates on loans made to borrowers. Choice *A* is incorrect because, while some profit is made on the interest differential, profits also come from rents and gains from buying and selling of business properties. Choice *B* is incorrect because Equity REITs, the most common type of REITs, do not make their profit from interest differential, but from rents and business real estate purchases and sales. Choice *D* is incorrect because hybrid and equity REITs do not make their profit only from interest rate differences.

24. A: Choice *A* is the correct answer because, after the 1986 tax act, some real estate professions joined to research new opportunities in the real estate industry, and encourage communication by its members to share helpful information. Choices *B, C,* and *D* are incorrect.

25. B: Choice *B* is true because the Institute for Portfolio Alternatives actively encourages development of opportunities to purchase assets whose business patterns are not likely to match that of traditional investments, such as stocks and bonds. Choice *A* is untrue, because the IPA relates not only to real estate markets such as non-listed REITs, but also interval funds, opportunity zone funds, business development companies (BDCs) and other private placements whose investments may not be devoted exclusively to real estate. Choice *C* is untrue because the IPA is an advocate of changes which are expected to result in better future results. Choice *D* is incorrect because IPA communicates with securities regulators and maintains public relations activity to educate people about non-traditional investments.

26. D: Choice *D* is correct because hedge funds generally have a goal of attaining a positive return, whether the broad market is having positive or negative returns. This is called an "absolute return." The word "hedge" generally refers to methods of purchasing assets whose returns do not correlate. That is, if one asset is decreasing in value, the other is expected to increase in value. Choice *A* is incorrect because hedge funds encompass many various types of funds, with different approaches to managing investments. Choice *B* is incorrect because several hedge funds borrow to purchase investments, so the return on capital can be greater when the values increase than if the fund only purchased assets equal to its liquid funds. Choice *C* is incorrect because hedge funds include a broad category of characteristics, many that are not common characteristics with mutual funds. Unlike many hedge funds, mutual funds are generally highly liquid.

27. C: Choice *C* is correct because hedge funds may regularly incur more transaction costs, purchasing derivatives such as options to buy or sell investments that most mutual fund managers would not. Options that are not exercised would result in costs that could increase the expense ratio above that of mutual funds. Choice A is incorrect because research costs and managers' fees are generally higher for hedge funds than for the typical mutual fund. Choice B is incorrect because hedge funds typically research non-traditional investments for which data is not so readily available as those investments analyzed by typical mutual fund investment managers. Choice *D* is incorrect because the expectation of higher than market returns generally results in hedge fund managers receiving higher fees than the average mutual fund investment manager.

28. D: Choice *D* is correct because all income earned by a U.S. person is subject to the Internal Revenue code. Choice *A* is incorrect because a hedge fund may set up both an "offshore" fund for non-U.S. investors and an "onshore" fund for U.S. investors. Choice *B* is incorrect because an "offshore" hedge fund is typically set up as a corporation. Choice *C* is incorrect because an "onshore" hedge fund is generally established as a Limited Liability Corporation (LLC) or a limited partnership.

29. C: Choice *C* is correct because a subscription agreement outlines for investors the process of purchasing ownership in a limited partnership and assures the fund managers that the investor is eligible to participate in the hedge fund. Choices *A* and *D* are incorrect because a mutual fund and a Unit Investment Trust (UIT) are registered with the SEC and each provide a prospectus to the investor. Choice *B* is incorrect because a TIC transaction involves signing a mortgage rather than purchasing ownership in an entity.

30. C: Choice *C* is correct because the hedge fund may use focused investments in a specific firm or industry rather than diversification, arbitrage (buying and selling an asset in two markets or two assets at the same time), short selling (borrowing an asset and selling it), trading in currency or commodities, or margin (borrowing funds to purchase assets). Choice *A* is incorrect because the investment is not registered with the SEC, or else the subscription agreement would not be necessary, as a prospectus would describe the investment's risks and characteristics. Choice *B* is incorrect because the subscription agreement explains why the investment is not registered with the SEC. Choice *D* is incorrect because the minimum investment may be $100,000 or as much as $1,000,000.

31. A: Choice *A* is correct because, while a mutual fund states its investment strategy and is bound to it, unless notice is given or the shareholders vote to approve, a hedge fund may typically change investment strategy without giving notice to investors. Choice *B* is incorrect because both owe a fiduciary responsibility to the investors. Choice *C* is incorrect because a mutual fund may have an unlimited number of shareholders. A hedge fund meeting the description of Section 3(c)(1) of the Investment Company Act of 1940 is limited to less than one hundred investors, and a hedge fund meeting the description of Section 3(c)(7) of the Investment Company Act of 1940 is limited to less than five hundred investors. Choice *D* is incorrect because a mutual fund provides a prospectus to an investor, an "offshore" hedge fund provides a document known as an "Offering Document" or a "Private Placement Memorandum (PPM)", and an "onshore" hedge fund typically organizes as a Limited Liability Corporation (LLC) or as a limited partnership and provides a "Partnership Agreement."

32. B: Choice *B* is correct because hedge funds generally provide no guaranteed return over any period. Choices *A, C,* and *D* are incorrect because these are topics that are included in an offshore hedge fund's "Offering Document" or "Private Placement Memorandum (PPM)."

33. A: Choice *A* is correct because a hedge fund that charges performance fees must restrict investors to "qualified" investors, that is, those with assets in excess of liabilities by $2.1 million or more. Choice *B* is incorrect because a "qualified" investor must have net assets of $2.1 million, whereas an "accredited" investor must have net assets of $1 million, excluding the primary residence. Choice *C* is incorrect because a couple need only have annual income of $300,000 or more. Choice *D* is incorrect because a "super-accredited" investor is either a natural person with investments of at least $5 million, a trust that was set up primarily to purchase ownership in this particular fund, or a firm managing invested assets of at least $25 million.

34. C: Choice *C* is correct because ETFs are registered investment companies and provide diversification, professional management, and liquidity, as mutual funds do. Choice *A* is incorrect because of uncertain diversification and illiquidity. Choice *B* is incorrect because ETNs do not necessarily provide diversification or professional management. Choice *D* is incorrect because limited partnerships do not necessarily provide diversification or liquidity.

35. B: Choice *B* is correct because ETFs are traded on an exchange. Choices *A*, *C*, and *D* are typically characteristics of both ETFs and mutual funds.

36. A: Choice *A* is correct because the Investment Company Act of 1940 requires mutual funds to be registered investment advisers. Choice *B* is incorrect because, though some hedge funds may be investment advisers, not all are. Choice C is incorrect because TIC transactions do not involve establishing an entity, but rather involve investors signing a mortgage. Choice *D* is incorrect because REITs are not registered investment advisers and are not covered by the Investment Company Act of 1940.

37. C: Choice *C* is correct because it establishes the rule that investment companies value their portfolios at the next calculated net asset value (NAV), which happens when the markets close. ETFs need a pricing exemption because their shares trade on an exchange, so the market value is not necessarily the same as the NAV at any given time. Choices *A*, *B*, and *D* are incorrect.

38. D: Choice *D* is correct, as inverse ETFs assist in providing a positive return when the target index has a negative return. Choices *A*, *B*, and *C* are incorrect as they are entities, and therefore are not subject to inverse arrangements, except by holding inverse ETFs, inverse options, or other inverse investments in their portfolios.

39. D: Choice *D* is correct because a leveraged ETF intends to obtain a return in excess of that of the target index by borrowing to buy investments and/or buying appropriate investments such as options, swaps or futures that provide a reasonable possibility of attaining a return above that of the target index. Choice *A* is incorrect because, though some mutual funds may use some leverage or purchase derivative instruments for a similar purpose, must mutual funds limit the use of such strategies. Choice *B* is incorrect because its goal is to obtain a return that is the opposite of the target index, not to exceed its return. Choice *C* is incorrect because a typical ETF does not use borrowing to a large extent, or it would be classified as a leveraged ETF.

40. A: Choice *A* is correct because the S&P 500 is an ETF that tracks an index that is considered to represent the market as a whole. Choice *B* is incorrect because the S&P 500 is not an example of an ETF seeking the opposite return of a target index. Choice *C* is incorrect because the S&P 500 is not an example of an ETF using borrowing to obtain a return in excess of the target index. Choice *D* is incorrect because it is not a typical term for any popular type of ETF.

180

41. A: Choice *A* is correct because by far the most ETFs are market ETFs, whose intention is to gain a return over the long term which generally matches the expected favorable return of the broad market. Choices *B, C,* and *D* are incorrect because they are specialized, and there are not as many members in any of these categories.

42. B: Choice *B* is correct because the Russell 2000 reflects the return of 2000 of the smallest companies among the 3000 largest companies publicly trading in the U.S. Choice *A* is incorrect because it reflects the broad market. Choice *C* is incorrect because it reflects the experience of thirty large companies, who are considered to reflect the broad market. Choice *D* is incorrect because the NASDAQ reflects the experience of over 100 stocks of the largest American and foreign companies whose stocks trade on the NASDAQ exchange.

43. C: Choice *C* tracks publicly-traded stocks of 3,000 of the largest American companies, which is about 98% of all of them. Choice *A* is incorrect because it only tracks thirty companies' stocks. Choice *B* is incorrect because it only tracks about 500 stocks, even though it is considered a measure of the broad market. Choice *D* is incorrect because it tracks stocks of about 100 companies trading on the NASDAQ

44. B: Choice *C* is correct because it is broadly considered an accurate reflection of the broad market, which is seen as a significant leading economic indicator for the economy as a whole. Choices *A, C,* and *D* are also considered important reflections of the broad market but are not used in the development of the monthly LEI report.

45. D: Choice *D* is correct. The SPDR® S&P 500® ETF Trust" (SPY) tracks the S&P 500 Index, and it is quite liquid, having reached a trading volume of 250 million shares in a day, which makes it attractive to many investors. Choices *A, B,* and *C* are incorrect because they are not the most well-known, oldest, and largest ETFs, even though they each track well-respected indexes.

Understanding Trading, Customer Accounts, and Prohibited Activities

46. A: Choice *A* is correct because this is the date on which the ownership change is recorded on the books of the issuing corporation. Choices *B, C,* and *D* are incorrect because these have to do with dividends declared and paid, and the effect of the market price of the stock, not on change of ownership.

47. A: Choice A is correct because the SEC changed the standard trading schedule, called "regular way" settlement, from "trade plus three [days]" (T+3) to "trade plus two [days]" (T+2). This was in recognition that technology advances made the shorter time frame attainable, and the exchanges and investors would benefit from the shorter settlement time. Choice B is incorrect because Regulation T governs details around cash accounts and how much investors may borrow from a broker or dealer in order to purchase securities. The limit is fifty percent (50%). The remainder must be paid from the investor's own funds. Choice C is incorrect because the Consumer Credit Protection Act of 1968 (CCPA) initiated protection for consumers from improper loan practices by such lenders as banks and credit card companies by providing better disclosure. Choice D is incorrect because the purpose of the Sarbanes-Oxley (SOX) Act of 2002 was to require accurate corporate financial reporting.

48. A: Choice *A* is correct because trades do not settle prior to the date the sale is agreed to. Choices *B, C,* and *D* are incorrect because these are all true statements.

49. B: Choice *B* is correct because paper stock certificates were printed and needed to be delivered. Choices *A, C,* and *D* are incorrect because they refer to the current method of transferring ownership at settlement.

50. D: Choice *D* is correct because corporate actions typically only occur when approved by the shareholders, when required shareholders' responses are submitted, or when approved by the board of directors. Change in market price does not require any of those actions. Choices *A*, *B*, and *C* are incorrect because they are corporate actions.

51. D: Choice *D* is correct because a stock split reduces the market price and is intended to encourage investors to purchase shares. Choice *A* is incorrect because a rights offer is generally connected to a new stock offering. Choice *B* is incorrect because a reverse stock split usually occurs when the market price is extremely low. Choice *C* is incorrect because a tender offer is made by an outside firm who wishes to purchase shares of the company.

52. B: Choice *B* is correct because when the board of directors approves the buyback of stock, treasury stock is the name for the shares acquired on the open market. Choices *A*, *C*, and *D* are incorrect because they do not result in the increase of treasury stock.

53. B: Choice *B* is correct because the firm does not buy shares from shareholders to accomplish a reverse stock split. Choices *A*, *C*, and *D* are incorrect because they do occur when a reverse stock split is approved by the board of directors.

54. D: Choice *D* is correct because this allows shareholders with significant percentage ownership to maintain their same level of influence in stockholder elections. Choice *A* is incorrect because a rights offer does not involve another security's shares. Choice *B* is incorrect because this is a tender offer, typically made by an outside firm. Choice *C* is incorrect because old shares will not be replaced.

55. B: Choice *B* is correct because Regulation M helps ensure the market price of a public offering is based on supply and demand, rather than persons involved in promoting the issue unfairly manipulating the market price artificially. Choices *A*, C, and *D* are incorrect because these do not prohibit persons involved with a public offering from manipulating the market price.

56. B: Choice *B* is correct because the par value for the stock is increased, so the cost basis is spread among a smaller number of shares. Choice *A* is incorrect because the market price will be increased. Choice C is incorrect because the quantity of treasury shares would decrease. Choice *D* is incorrect because a merger would not typically require a reverse stock split.

57. C: Choice *C* is correct because exchanges ensure notice deadlines are met by providing notification for shares traded on that exchange. Choices *A* and *B* are incorrect because FINRA provides notices for over-the-counter shares. Choice *D* is incorrect because the exchange provides notification for shares traded on that exchange.

58. D: Choice *D* is correct because proxy voting is a common practice for shareholder voting. Choice *A* is incorrect because the MSRB governs proxy activities for municipal bonds. Choices *B* and *C* are incorrect because FINRA must provide proxy materials to the beneficial owner only if enough copies are provided, and the service is requested.

59. B: Choice *B* is correct because 1934 Act Section 14 – Proxies directs board of directors as to the importance of giving information to shareholders, the information to be provided, the text of the proxy document, and how proxies may be requested. Choices *A*, C, and *D* are incorrect because this section is not directed at them.

60. C: Choice *C* is correct because this rule requires the member firm to maintain various items of information, including contact information, whether minor or of legal age, registered representative assigned to service the account, signature of supervisor approving establishing the account, and if an organization, legal names of authorized persons. Choices *A*, *B*, and *D* are incorrect because they do not deal with the recording of the supervisor's name or signature.

61. D: Choice *D* is correct because FINRA 4512 does require an alternate contact for every customer who is a natural person. Choices *A*, *B*, and *C* are incorrect because these items are only expected if the customer is placing orders for investments besides their own selected mutual funds, and these items can be obtained by reasonable effort.

62. C: Choice *C* is correct because the rule provides guidance to provide investments in the account, trades since last report, and any liquid funds on hand. Choices *A*, *B*, and *D* do not represent the correct frequency for statements.

63. A: Choice *A* is correct because such information as changes in the financial strength of the municipality offering the security would be helpful to a potential investor making a decision whether to purchase the security. Choice *B* is incorrect because this rule has to do with the content and frequency of customer account statements sent by FINRA member firms to their customer. Choice *C* is incorrect because this rule specifies that the dealer informs the customer, at least by the trade date, any relevant aspects of the investment and trade. Choice *D* is incorrect because this rule deals with quotes made reflecting prices and quantities of municipal securities actually available by the firm making the quotes.

64. B: Choice *B* is correct because the rule is intended to protect customer from a representative removing funds or similar items from the customer's account without the customer's intending that to be done. Choice *A* is incorrect because the permission must be given in writing. Choice *C* is incorrect because the rule prohibits removal of cash or cash-like items from the customer's account. If bearer bonds were removed from the member firm's premises but were still recorded in the customer's account, the rule would likely not apply. Choice *D* is incorrect because the rule deals specifically with the withdrawal of cash or similar assets.

65. B: Choice *B* is correct because a cash account may not be used to purchase investments by borrowing part of the purchase price. Choice *A* is incorrect because investments other than cash may be held in a cash account. Choice *C* is incorrect because no purchases on margin may be made in a cash account. Choice *D* is incorrect because the short sales may not be made in a cash account.

66. C: Choice *C* is correct because Regulation T assures that payments will be made on a timely basis. Choices *A*, *B*, and *D* are incorrect because short sales and margin purchases must be made from a margin account.

67. D: Choice *D* is correct because at least half of the purchase price, or the part of the purchase price in excess of $500, must be paid by the customer. Choices *A*, *B*, and *C* are incorrect because the Federal Reserve Board of Governors is allowed to set the proportion of the purchase price of a security that must be paid in cash. This has been as low as 40% and as high as 100%. Since 1974, the requirement has been fifty percent.

68. D: Choice *D* is correct because an exception was made for market makers. Choices *A*, *B*, and *C* are incorrect because a national exchange specialist or member is generally prohibited from trading for those accounts.

Overview of the Regulatory Framework

69. C: Choice *C* is correct because the FINRA By-laws require member firms to be in good standing with all state securities commission with jurisdiction over the member firm. Choices *A*, *B*, and *D* are incorrect because FINRA By-laws, Article III, Section 3 and legislation and regulation referenced in that section do not address discipline by a local school board, being cited by a police officer for a misdemeanor, or being fined by the IRA.

70. A: Choice *A* is correct because the member firm is obligated to document the applicant's identity. Choices *B* and *C* are incorrect because neither the driver's license nor the passport are required as the documentation. Choice *D* is incorrect because the member is required to document contacting employers of only the last three years.

71. A: Choice *A* is correct because banks are not required to have their personnel fingerprinted under this rule. Choices *B*, *C*, and *D* are incorrect because all of these are included in the rule.

72. B: Choice *B* is correct because conviction of a felony less than ten years before the application may be cause for statutory disqualification. Choices *A*, *C*, or *D* are incorrect because the Securities Exchange Act of 1934 Section 3(a)(39) – Definitions and Application of Title (Statutory Disqualification) does not refer to action by a Human Resources Department in a previous employment, bankruptcy, or divorce as cause for disqualification.

73. D: Choice a *D* is correct because a person who is only doing clerical work is not considered an "associated person." Choices *A*, *B*, and *C* are incorrect because a person in senior management, a person who is a sole proprietor, and a person who is in investment banking controlled indirectly by the applicant are included in the definition of Associated Person under FINRA 1011 Definitions (b) "Associated Person."

74. D: Choice *D* is correct because FINRA Rule 8310 does not mention FINRA imposing penalties for violating the Internal Revenue Code. Choices *A*, *B*, and *C* are incorrect because FINRA Rule 8310 mentions FINRA may impose penalties for violations of all of these.

75. D: Choice *D* is correct because FINRA Rule 8310 allows any other appropriate penalty to be imposed. Choices *A*, *B*, and *C* are incorrect because they are not named in FINRA Rule 8310.

Index

Greetings!

First, we would like to give a huge "thank you" for choosing us and this study guide for your Series SIE exam. We hope that it will lead you to success on this exam and for your years to come.

Our team has tried to make your preparations as thorough as possible by covering all of the topics you should be expected to know. In addition, our writers attempted to create practice questions identical to what you will see on the day of your actual test. We have also included many test-taking strategies to help you learn the material, maintain the knowledge, and take the test with confidence.

We strive for excellence in our products, and if you have any comments or concerns over the quality of something in this study guide, please send us an email so that we may improve.

We are continually producing and updating study guides in several different subjects. If you are looking for something in particular, all of our products are available on Amazon. You may also send us an email!

Sincerely,
APEX Test Prep
info@apexprep.com

FREE

Free Study Tips Videos/DVD

In addition to this guide, we have created a FREE set of videos with helpful study tips. **These FREE videos provide you with top-notch tips to conquer your exam and reach your goals.**

Our simple request is that you give us feedback about the book in exchange for these strategy-packed videos. We would love to hear what you thought about the book, whether positive, negative, or neutral. It is our #1 goal to provide you with quality products and customer service.

To receive your **FREE Study Tips Videos**, scan the QR code or email freevideos@apexprep.com. Please put "FREE Videos" in the subject line and include the following in the email:

    a. The title of the book

    b. Your rating of the book on a scale of 1-5, with 5 being the highest score

    c. Any thoughts or feedback about the book

Thank you!